Ian Chappell is widely regarded as one of the most successful captains of the Australian Test team, with the team never losing a series during his captaincy. Since retiring from competitive cricket, the 1976 Wisden Cricketer of the Year has been a regular commentator with the Nine Network and several overseas broadcasters, and has written for such publications as *The Age*, *The Indian Express*, and *The Daily Telegraph* in the UK.

A GOLDEN AGE

AUSTRALIAN CRICKET'S TWO DECADES AT THE TOP

IAN CHAPPELL

MACMILLAN

Pan Macmillan Australia

First published 2006 in Macmillan by Pan Macmillan Australia Pty Limited
1 Market Street, Sydney

National Library of Australia
Cataloguing-in-Publication data:

Chappell, Ian, 1943– .
A golden age: Australian cricket's two decades at the top.

ISBN-13: 978 1 4050 3750 1

ISBN-10: 1 4050 3750 4

1. Cricket – Australia – Anecdotes. 2. Cricket players – Australia –
Anecdotes. 3. Cricket captains – Australia – Anecdotes. I. Title.

796.358650994

Typeset in 11.5/16.5 pt Sabon by Midland Typesetters, Australia
Printed in Australia by McPherson's Printing Group

This book is dedicated to Bill 'Tiger' O'Reilly, whose name doesn't appear in any of the Golden Era teams but who was nominated by Sir Donald Bradman as the greatest bowler he ever saw.

Tiger was a great inspiration to me as a cricket writer. In my early days in the press box he told me, 'Son, you are in a privileged position. If you see something about the game you don't agree with, write about it. If they don't take any notice then write about it again and if they still don't take any notice, write about it again.'

I have done my best to live up to Tiger's challenge.

INTRODUCTION

The fifth Test at The Oval in 1972 was one of the best games of cricket I played in: the match fluctuated through six tension-filled days, until midway through the penultimate session, when Australia finally got the upper hand and went on to defeat a tough England side by five wickets.

It was a victory inspired by Doug Walters' hilarious speech at the pre-match dinner when he imitated our manager, Ray Steele, in exhorting the team: 'Aussies take it lying down. Pig's bloody arse they do.'

Out on the field it was Dennis Lillee's turn to boost his teammates when, at the fall of the ninth wicket in England's second innings, he declared, 'We can't let these bastards score any more runs.' He then made sure of it by clean bowling the obstinate Alan Knott to contain our victory target to 242. That thrilling win over the best side around became a watershed match for an emerging Australian side: it was the one that convinced us we were good enough to challenge any team and win.

From then until we crushed a talented but naïve West Indies side in 1975–76 the Australian team was unbeaten in a series. We dominated with a balanced attack headed by the indomitable Lillee and a lethal Jeff Thomson. In addition it was a strong batting line-up underpinned by the class of Greg Chappell and the match-winning stroke play of Walters. Fielding also played its part as an exceptional group of catchers inspired by the acrobatic and skilful wicket-keeping of Rod Marsh let very little pass without interception.

It was an entertaining team that aggressively sought victory and enjoyed each other's company. A lot of fun was derived from a period where many strong bonds were formed between the players, and nowadays when we are reunited it is the celebratory victory parties that are recalled rather than the runs scored and wickets taken. The team was blissfully ignorant of the reputation being built on the field, but in time the period was classed as the fourth Golden Era of Australian cricket.

Having played in one I was then fortunate to witness Australia's next Golden Era from the commentary box.

Just like the 1972 side, the highly successful team of the mid-Nineties had a watershed match: the first Test at Headingley in 1989. Unlike in 1972, it took six years for that crucial victory to materialise into world domination, but there is no doubt the Headingley win provided the spark of confidence that spawned a steely attitude and eventually led Australia to the top.

On this occasion it was the captain Allan Border who inspired the 1989 side with an uncharacteristically aggressive knock at a crucial time in the first innings. Border's more belligerent attitude towards the opposition reversed a trend which had seen Australia hit the bottom in 1984–85 and then slowly climb off the floor. In 1989 Border suddenly decided he wanted to be the leader of the team. Whilst his career didn't extend long enough to see Australia reach the top, his change of heart proved to be an inspiration for three young players, Steve Waugh, Ian Healy and Mark Taylor, who all played an important role in the team, eventually becoming world champions.

Waugh, Healy and Taylor had all been drafted into the team following the mid-Eighties debacle, not just because of their skill but also their attitude: they were competitors. Whereas Border had witnessed mainly despair before the 1989 tour (apart from the World Cup win in 1987), he suddenly saw a light at the end of the tunnel. The young players provided a spark; enthusiasm and confidence replaced despair and pessimism, and gradually the side built to a crescendo like a well-tuned orchestra.

Waugh, Healy and Taylor were eventually joined by other skilful, aggressive players in Mark Waugh and Michael Slater and, later on, Ricky Ponting. However, it was the addition of two young bowlers who would go on to become world-beaters that ensured the team would eventually crush all opposition. Shane Warne and Glenn McGrath were the detonators that blew the opposition apart after they'd been stunned by Australia's quick-scoring batsmen.

The combination of top-class bowling and aggressive stroke play was a sure-fire recipe for success, one that has stood Australian teams in good stead throughout more than a century of Test cricket. During Australia's amazing world-record run of sixteen victories it was said that Steve Waugh's team took the game to another level by consistently scoring quickly in Test cricket.

Whilst it's true that Waugh's team scored extremely quickly, with Matthew Hayden and Justin Langer leading the charge and Adam Gilchrist's blistering attacks from the middle order, I'd remind the modern fan of the following. Didn't Victor Trumper score a century before lunch at Old Trafford in 1902? Wasn't it Don Bradman in 1930 who became the first (and only) man to amass three hundred runs in a day of Test cricket, scoring centuries in the first and second sessions? In 1935–36 at the Wanderers ground, Stan 'Napper' McCabe hit the ball with such ferocity during an extraordinary innings of 189 not out (165 minutes) that the South African captain Herbert 'Billy' Wade appealed against the light because he felt his fieldsmen were in danger. And three times in the Seventies Walters completed a Test century in a session, the most famous being at the WACA, where, to achieve the feat, he clubbed a six off the final ball of the day. Australian teams have always scored quickly whenever the opportunity presented itself, and that is why the country has far and away the best overall record in Test cricket.

If any one person was responsible for initiating Australia's most recent outbreak of quick scoring in Test cricket it was Mark Taylor. He inherited a very good side from Border but he did what a captain should do: he looked to make the team better.

Taylor decided the aggressive batting line-up he inherited was an asset that wasn't being fully exploited. Under the optimistic Taylor the team shed the slightly pessimistic outlook that remained from Border's reign, and from then on the Australian team continued to send a strong message to their opponents from the opening ball of every Test: we have come to WIN this match.

This more aggressive Australian approach led the team to the 1994–95 series victory in the Caribbean, the first such win since 1972–73 and the one that signalled its rise to world-champion status. Then followed a series win over South Africa in the Republic in 1996–97 and the first victory in Pakistan (1998–99) since Richie Benaud led his side there in 1959–60. These were all feats that hadn't occurred under the leadership of Border and that's why I rate Taylor as the best of the four captains in this period.

The one achievement that eluded Taylor was a series win in India. Steve Waugh was also denied this accomplishment when V. V. S. Laxman played a remarkable innings in Kolkata to snatch victory from the all-conquering Australians and reverse the direction of a series that appeared to be headed safely into the clutches of the touring side.

Ponting will be listed as the captain of the Australian side

(2004–05) that achieved a series win in India for the first time since Bill Lawry's team did it in 1969–70. In reality it was Adam Gilchrist who captained the side in the two victories (when Ponting was injured), whilst the skipper led the team in their sole defeat at Mumbai.

Unfortunately, Ponting will be remembered as the Australian captain who lost the Ashes in 2005 following an unbroken successful run since Border's team triumphantly regained them in England in 1989. It was a glorious run whilst it lasted and undoubtedly a memorable part of the fifth Golden Era of Australian cricket.

By early 1989 Allan Border was maturing as a leader. His main success at Test level had come via the spinners and it appeared as though the selectors were looking to provide him with extra help in that area. Steve Whitfield was a thirty-eight year old left-arm orthodox spinner who had successfully partnered off spinner Peter Taylor in the Northern Districts club side and he'd just been chosen to make his debut in the New South Wales (NSW) side. He didn't make it to the Australian team but represented NSW on three occasions.

[*The Sun-Herald*, 5 February 1989]

With the Test series between Australia and the West Indies fast coming to a close, it's interesting to evaluate the jobs done by the respective skippers. Allan Border and Viv Richards are both great players and statistically have a lot in common, but their personalities are as distant as their styles of play.

If I wanted someone to save a Test with a back-to-the-wall innings I'd choose Border. If I wanted an innings of brilliance to win a Test I'd call on Richards. Between them they're the saviour and the savage.

As captains their approach is as different as the two teams they lead.

After the Test at the SCG it's easy to see why the West Indies' preference is to play four fast bowlers – Viv Richards isn't at all comfortable as a skipper handling spinners. Whilst he was burdened with an out-of-form off spinner in Roger Harper and as support only had two part-time offies in Carl Hooper and himself, he not once enhanced the efforts of the tweakers in the SCG Test. In fact on most occasions he was a hindrance to their bowling. No spin bowler can operate with only two men in one half of the field and seven cluttering up the side to which the ball is spinning. Ironically, Viv didn't set those fields for his own off spin bowling.

The other thing that caught my eye was in the twenty-minute period on the third day when Viv was off the field having treatment for a bruised shin. Gordon Greenidge took over the captaincy and immediately Hooper came around the wicket to the left-handed batsman. This increased his chances of taking Allan Border's wicket about five-fold. Yet as soon as Richards came back on the field, Hooper reverted to coming from over the wicket and bowling to seven on the off with only a deep backward square and a mid-on protecting the leg side.

Despite winning three Tests in a row to wrap up the Frank Worrell Trophy, there have been glaring deficiencies in Viv's captaincy this series. The outstanding example was in Perth, when Curtly Ambrose, the best bowler in the series, only bowled a handful of balls to Graeme Wood during his century. Then there has also been the lack of individualised field placings for the Australian batsmen during the series.

This has only meant that the West Indies' victories have taken longer than they should have. Nevertheless, it also leads you to the conclusion that it wouldn't have mattered who captained the Windies in this series – they would still have won the first three Tests. I thought Viv's best captaincy in the series was on the final day in Melbourne, where he really stamped his personality on the play.

In the one Test where the captain really could have had some influence on the result, at the SCG, Viv was found wanting. He made two correct moves: he won the toss and batted, and at the end of the game he was gracious in defeat.

At times in this match the West Indies players appeared flummoxed as the game was allowed to just roll along, and no one was more frustrated than fast bowler Malcolm Marshall. His absence from the attack for so long on the second day and then his brilliant bowling on the third day probably only added to his frustration. Used correctly, Marshall could easily have restricted the Australian lead or even ensured that they didn't gain a first-innings advantage.

Allan Border, on the other hand, made all the right moves after being disadvantaged by losing the toss and then watching as Greenidge, Desmond Haynes and Richie Richardson proceeded to pile up the runs. He remained patient and resourceful, as he always does at the SCG, and eventually he was rewarded with not only a great victory, but also a great personal triumph.

Allan has often said, 'A captain is only as good as his team.' However, he found out at the SCG that there's a big difference between captaincy and strong leadership. With an important tour of England coming up, Allan now needs to re-evaluate his captaincy.

I get the feeling Allan has been waiting desperately for the day when Australia comes up with an attack of four fast bowlers. Then I assume he's going to rub his hands with glee and try to blow the opposition away.

Well, before he dies of old age waiting, he should look at what he's achieved so far and with what type of armoury.

He's currently completed thirty-seven Tests as captain of Australia and seven of them have resulted in victories. Four of those wins have been recorded at the SCG, with a spinner taking ten or more wickets in the match three times. On the remaining occasion Peter Sleep, the leg spinner, took five wickets in the second innings against England, as did Bob Holland at Lord's in Border's sole Test victory on the 1985 tour.

Only two of his Test wins have been achieved by excellent fast bowling: one over New Zealand at the SCG in 1985–86, and last season's win over Sri Lanka in Perth. Two wins out of seven doesn't suggest he's playing the percentages by waiting around for the heavy artillery to arrive. Much better to get the best out of the light infantry that's already on hand.

To add to that argument, the tie achieved at Madras in 1986–87 (the only other Test under Border's guidance where Australia has come close to winning) was the result of a fine bowling performance by off spinner Greg Matthews, in which he took ten wickets for the match.

The moral of all that? When Allan is forced, by the nature of the pitch and the make-up of his attack, into being resourceful, he's a damn good captain. But given an attack based on pace with a little spin, his train of thought is usually derailed and the result is often an almighty crash. As soon as you see Allan put two men back for the lofted hook shot and then the Australian bowlers start busily banging in bouncers, you know there's trouble ahead.

There are signs that the Australian selectors are taking matters into their own hands. The squad they selected for the Adelaide Test contains only two pace bowlers, whilst there are three spinners, plus the more than useful left-arm orthodox tweakers of the skipper himself. If at the end of the Adelaide Test Border has handled this type of attack well, it will be a sign that he's maturing as a Test skipper and that he's putting to good use at other grounds the lessons he's learnt at the SCG.

This could lead to a surprise selection in the Ashes squad. Surely it can't be just coincidence that thirty-eight-year-old Steve

Whitfield has been selected in the NSW side. Australia badly needs a front-line left-arm orthodox spinner for the tour of England and the best around is young Paul Jackson from Victoria. Unfortunately this talented youngster isn't taking wickets in Shield cricket at present and is fast running out of time to press his claim.

However, if he's successful, Whitfield will have three games at the SCG to impress the national selectors. He also has the added advantage of having played many club matches with Peter Taylor (who successfully made the transition to International cricket) and his Northern Districts record compares more than favourably with that of the competitive off spinner.

All that adds up to Steve Whitfield's chance to come from oblivion to a tour of England. If he achieves this lofty transition, the man he could replace is ex-team-mate Peter Taylor. That would be a strange twist to the saga of 'Peter who?'

It's also a strange twist of fate that Border has at least been the equal of Viv Richards as a captain in this series and yet he will finish well and truly on the losing side. Nevertheless, he should have learnt a lot, and if he puts those lessons into practice during the Ashes series he could easily get his revenge against Graham Gooch or whomever the English selectors choose as captain.

By the end of the series in 1988–89 Allan Border must have been heartily sick of the sight of the West Indies. He'd played them in three five-Test series in the Eighties and lost nine times for only two wins. In 1988–89 he'd just captained Australia to a 3–1 series loss against the Windies, which suggested Border's team wasn't making any progress. However, they were about to prove that theory wrong in England.

Oh, by the way, Michael Spinks didn't recover to go the distance against Mike Tyson in 1988. He was knocked out in the first round and promptly retired from boxing.

––––

[*The Sun-Herald*, 12 February 1989]

The Australian team has become a hardened bunch of cricketers after surviving a tough series in the sun against the West Indies. All the same, they need to guard against any softening up in the cold English climate.

In the past two series against England (one away and one home) the Australian team has tended to be a bit too friendly to the opposition on the field. The English players have thrived on this, winning both series comfortably. I'd like to see the Australians develop a bit of hate for their opposition during playing hours.

Now would be a good time to start the process.

The Englishmen have had a tendency in recent years to buckle in tough series. Their record in their last three encounters with the West Indies is appalling. They've lost two series five–nil and the one in England last season four–nil. One draw and fourteen losses in their last fifteen Tests against the West Indies is a disgraceful record, a point that shouldn't be lost on the Australian team.

On the other hand, the Australians have managed to draw four and even win two whilst losing nine of their last fifteen Tests against the Windies. In the last two series they've even managed to win two and draw two after losing the first three Tests both times. This suggests there's a resilience in the Australian team that's missing in the English line-up.

However, both of the wins over the West Indies have come after the series has been decided, as did the win over England at the SCG in 1986–87. Whilst the Australians have shown they have resilience, they've also displayed shortcomings when the loot is on the line. They seem to lack the confidence or required aggression to take the initiative early in the series, when the opportunity is there to establish a psychological advantage. There were a number of examples in this just-completed series.

On the first day at the Gabba the Australians had a great chance to establish superiority over the West Indies on a good pitch and up against a depleted pace attack. They fluffed it and that was their most costly mistake of the series.

In Perth they battled on level terms with the West Indies for the first four days. Then they undid all the good work with a poor batting display on the final day. Leaving Perth one–nil down with a Test to be played in Sydney would have put a little more pressure on the West Indies in Melbourne.

And finally, the Test in Adelaide. I would have thought that having been pushed around for the first three Tests and then having inflicted a loss on the Windies at the SCG, the Australians would have been keen to go for the jugular once more. Allan Border had the ideal opportunity to do just that with a declaration on the fourth evening if there'd been more urgency about their second-innings batting. Border must learn to bait the hook with his declarations and not copy Viv Richards' example of using exploding dynamite to ensure the fish don't have a chance.

I get the feeling Viv doesn't want to get in a contest where the odds are nearly even. This could be because he has a stereotype (all pace) attack, and if they're collared (as they were in the World Series Cricket third final) then it's difficult to stem the flow of runs. It's a pity the Australians missed a number of opportunities to put some pressure on the West Indies because when they did put the onus on them at the SCG they were often found wanting. Still, it was encouraging to see the resilience shown after the first three losses. Coming back for a win and the better of a draw was equivalent to Michael Spinks staggering to his feet after taking a pounding from Mike Tyson in the first round and going the distance for a loss on points.

All in all it was a series that meant a lot but lacked a little. The biggest black marks were the umpiring and the poor treatment handed out to the arbiters by the players. No one likes to receive a poor decision, but they are part and parcel of the game. To accept the umpire's decision is sometimes a painful thing to do, but I haven't yet seen a player who belts his bat against his pads or stares in disbelief when he's on the right end of a poor decision. You can't have it both ways.

For their part the umpires were only average. Whilst I understand the need to blood new umpires in International cricket, I think it should be done with commonsense. It was ludicrous to have two guys standing at the SCG who only had the experience of one Test between them.

So many snicks were missed in Adelaide that I can only think there was an epidemic of industrial deafness or that the men in charge had taken a leaf out of the book of umpire Greg Waugh from the Caribbean island of Dominica. When he turned down an appeal for caught behind, the disbelieving bowler, off spinner Lance Gibbs, asked, 'Why?'

'Because he only barely touched it,' replied umpire Waugh.

One area where the umpires did improve during the series was calling no-balls. There were 371 in total, an average of about sixteen a day. To keep the law as it is would be nothing short of cricketing suicide and perhaps, as Clive Lloyd suggests, the front-foot law is also contributing to the umpires' problems in picking up the ball quickly enough to give correct decisions. Heaven knows, the persistent call of no-ball is becoming more boring than slow over rates.

Despite those little hiccups it was a memorable series in many ways, with a number of fine individual performances. Two of those that stand out are the bowling feats of Merv Hughes in Perth and Michael Whitney in Adelaide. Both men are strong of heart and produced inspirational spells. At times they look like they spend their spare time haunting houses as they snarl and glare at batsmen when they don't like the way things are proceeding. Off the field Mike is affable and entertaining, and Merv is a likeable gentle giant who can keep David Boon's young baby quiet for long spells by playing aeroplane games with a dummy.

But if those two are on the Ashes tour then I don't think there's much to worry about regarding the Australians being too friendly on the field.

In 1987–88 Ian Botham played for Queensland (captained by Allan Border) in the Sheffield Shield competition. He was signed to a three-year contract but this was terminated after one season because of some off-field indiscretions. These included a disagreement with a passenger on a plane flying to Perth for the Shield final and a heated argument with Border in Launceston.

———

[*The Sun-Herald*, 7 May 1989]

Can Ian Botham bounce back from serious injury to once again be a force in International cricket?

The man who could play a big part in ensuring the answer to that question is no, at least for this season, is his closest pal in the opposition, Australian captain Allan Border.

It's a strange relationship between Border and Botham. After all the heartache the Englishman caused the Queensland side during the calamitous summer of 1987–88, Border still speaks about their reunion this summer in England with almost an air of reverence. That's a sign of either a priest-like ability to forgive or a naïvety which occasionally clouds the judging of character. Whatever the reason, Botham has used the relationship to his great benefit on the field since Border took over the Australian captaincy.

There's nothing wrong with developing a friendship with an

opposition player, but it must be put on hold during each day's play. Botham is able to switch his charm on and off according to the situation in the game, which is exactly the way it should be. As a cricketer Botham has always been at his best when he's being written off by the media. Galvanised into action by those sorts of barbs, there's nothing in his bowling approach that remotely suggests friendship. Usually it's the English media that is doing the writing off and consequently in recent times he's performed best on his home turf.

Whilst Botham isn't exactly being written off at present, no commentator seems willing to predict that he'll return to his most dangerous best. Present circumstances then suggest local fans would be correct in rushing off to invest some of their pay packet on England, figuring that Botham will be needled into something like his devastating old self. However, an Australian wishing to get involved in any such transaction needs to weigh up the difference between Botham playing purely as a batsman, as distinct from in the past when he was a genuine all-rounder.

Botham has said that if he can't bowl satisfactorily in International cricket he's confident he can play as a number-four batsman. New Chairman of Selectors Ted Dexter has pointedly stated that Botham has compiled a batsman-like fourteen Test centuries so far in his career. As Botham has been something of an ogre to recent Australian sides, it's in Dexter's best interests to remind the opposition of his potential presence and danger at every opportunity.

But just a note of warning to Ted. There's a lot less pressure batting as an all-rounder than there is when your place in the team depends solely on the output of runs. This fact becomes even more important when you consider Botham's batting style. He plays his best when he's free of responsibility and allowed to play his natural hitting game.

An overly aggressive misdemeanour as an all-rounder can be forgiven on the basis of mental weariness owing to a long stint with the ball. But lash out unsuccessfully as a top-order batsman and you receive a few rather meaningful glares from your team-mates. Do it twice and the selectors show you the door and thank you for attending. Your disappearance into the dark night is usually followed with, 'And don't call us, we'll call you.'

Botham has scored four Test centuries against Australia. The most recent was at the Gabba in 1986–87, when he dominated the Australian bowling, not because of a confidence bred from being a successful all-rounder, but by courtesy of some frightfully timid captaincy by Allan Border. The beefy all-rounder's first fifty runs were virtually gift-wrapped and handed to him by Border's insistence on placing most of the fieldsmen in the deep and waiting for Botham to commit an indiscretion. Botham saved all his indiscretions for the next summer when he was playing under Border's captaincy in Queensland.

One Australian who has seen through Botham's Jekyll and Hyde impersonations is talented all-rounder Steve Waugh. He goes right after Botham, matching aggression with equal aggression – just as he did last summer against Viv Richards. That's the sort of attitude the Australians need to develop, and indeed it's exactly what Richards (a much closer friend of Botham's than Border) has done when confronted by the England all-rounder. If you need any proof of the validity of that approach, then compare Botham's record against the Windies with his overall Test record. There's a huge discrepancy.

Should Botham be selected at some stage during the season (either as an all-rounder or a batsman) the Australians could short-circuit his attempts to dominate a third successive series against a Border-led outfit by following the Waugh path.

Since the retirement of the 'big three' (Dennis Lillee, Greg Chappell and Rod Marsh) at the end of the 1983–84 season, Australia had had a rough time. Two lowly home series wins over New Zealand and Sri Lanka was all they had to show in forty-six Tests. There were only seven wins to go with an embarrassing eighteen losses in that period but it was all about to change with the victory that set Australia on the path to the glory years of the Nineties.

———

[Melbourne *Herald Sun*, 15 June 1989]

Australia produced its best Test match performance since they won back the Ashes in 1982–83, when they crushed England at Headingley.

It was an emphatic victory coming at the start of the series and gained on overseas soil. But, most importantly, the match was won in true Australian style. The team was right behind skipper Allan Border as he employed aggressive tactics from the outset.

About six months ago Allan said he wanted to remain Australian captain at least until the team was on the road to recovery. He took the right turn to find the path to success at Headingley.

Border has had a chequered career as Australian captain, with many limited-overs wins, but the Test victories have been about as evenly spaced as visits from Halley's Comet. However, his captaincy was so positive at Headingley and the team responded so well that we could be on the verge of an Australian cricket renaissance. From the moment Allan strode to the crease with Australia in a spot of bother at 2 for 57, every move he made had the stamp of authority all over it. The fact that he'd moved himself back to his favourite number-four spot was a sign that Border was intent on making the running. Sprint he did, gradually running away from David Gower, who had a horror match.

Anyone who says captains can't do much to influence their side would have changed their mind if they'd been at Headingley. The actions of the two skippers were mirror images of their teams' fortunes.

Border was aggressive and attacked at every opportunity, eventually winning the game. Gower was defensive right from the moment he gave Australia first use of the pitch and he continued to back-pedal his way to a humiliating defeat. England has a lot of work to do if they are going to recover from that setback.

For more than a century Australia has remained the most successful team in Test-match cricket because of their aggressive style of play. This has been missing in recent years, but it reappeared with a vengeance at Headingley. It was a pleasure to watch. The Australian team is now a confident unit, well led and capably manned in most positions. It only requires the right balance in the bowling attack and there's no reason why they shouldn't reclaim the Ashes.

There's a lot that's wrong with English cricket and it would have been a pity if they had wriggled off the hook in the first Test. The Australians exposed the weaknesses both in batting and bowling and it's now up to Border to keep his men firmly on track to make sure England don't pick themselves off the floor.

The victory at Headingley will also place enormous pressure on David Gower's captaincy, and that won't hurt Australia's cause. This is where Border needs to be ruthlessly aggressive and maintain the same policies, with perhaps a slight change of personnel, at Lord's. Another setback for Gower would provide England with a real headache as there are plenty of challengers for his middle-order batting spot, and yet he's been named captain for the six Tests.

Having successfully dealt the Headingley hoodoo a killer blow, Border needs to begin planning now for Lord's. That means getting at least one of his spinners into form and ensuring Geoff Marsh and David Boon have every opportunity to play a long innings before the Test.

Australia's batting has a look of real solidarity now, with Steve Waugh adding the touch of stroke-playing genius that can make it a real threat in Test-match cricket. The bowling hasn't quite reached that level, but it's adequate with Terry Alderman fit. Alderman was predictably Australia's spearhead; however, Merv Hughes surprised the English batsmen. Whilst he will always be a little expensive, this can be tolerated if Merv continues to unsettle the top-order players with his aggression.

Merv's bowling (not to mention his batting) has been a real bonus for Australia, but the most important ingredients in the victory at Headingley were Allan Border's willingness to attack and the way the team responded to his aggressive approach. In the past, Australia has had some good victories, but too often these have come after the series was decided in their opponent's favour. In most series the Australians have failed to take the early initiative, usually because the importance of doing so has escaped Border's attention. A mate of mine has a saying for the problem: 'The fish stinks from the head.'

But, equally, the rose's sweet smell comes from the petals.

Border's change of approach has been appreciated by the team and they look so much better when playing in the accepted Australian style.

The victory at Headingley was well-engineered, emphatic and enjoyable. Allan Border, I dips me lid.

Allan Border did the unthinkable when he said he would quit the captaincy if things didn't improve after the team had lost in New Zealand on the 1985–86 tour. However, by 1989 he had taken responsibility for the leadership of the team and he was a revitalised skipper.

[*The Sun-Herald*, 16 July 1989]

When Allan Border walked out to bat at number four in the first Test, I sensed a change had come over the Australian captain. After a couple of sighters he despatched a bouncer through mid-wicket with a vicious pull shot. There shouldn't have been anything unusual about that as it's his favourite shot and one he plays with great certainty. But somehow it was different.

I've seen Allan play that same shot many times with similar results, but it's never before carried a message of such authority. Unfortunately on most previous occasions it was played during another backs-to-the-wall knock to save his country. In those situations the odd shot in anger was usually to let the opposition know that they may have subdued his team, but they would never totally dominate Allan Border.

What was different about that pull shot at Headingley was the timing of it. Not the fact that it hit the middle of the bat: Border could do that with his eyes closed. The timing in the context of the series was the thing that mattered. For the first time in the opening Test of a series, he appeared to be accepting full responsibility for leading his team into a winning position. That's why it was a different Allan Border.

What followed was an example of his most aggressive captaincy, as he plotted the downfall of the English batsmen. From that moment on he's never looked back, unless it's been to watch another of his hook shots disappear across the fine-leg boundary rope.

Border has been the man in total charge of the Australian team ever since that pull shot and he's never looked so good as a Test captain. Border was notifying the opposition that they could no longer continue to push his team around. Here was a captain who had climbed out from underneath the wreckage of a car crash and promptly gone to the aid of the injured. Border's sudden ascendancy to the rank of fearless leader has been nothing short of heroic. Mind you, it shouldn't have been totally unexpected as Border is a very determined character who goes about his business with a lot of pride.

Such has been the team's response to Border's aggressive approach that he's hardly had to raise a bat in anger since, and yet the team is marching steadfastly towards victory over England.

Previously, burdened by the weight of captaincy as well as being the leading batsman, Border seemed destined to finish his career with a question mark against his Test captaincy. However, in the space of five weeks his captaincy reputation has rocketed to new levels.

It hasn't even been a gradual change. One minute he was a conservative Test captain who shied away from responsibility. The next minute he was an aggressive, show-'em-the-way leader who was bulldozing everything in his path. The transformation's been as dramatic as the kid who cops a continual beating in the schoolyard and suddenly turns around and floors the biggest bully with a perfect right cross. Border's leadership has really made an impact.

Australian cricket is lucky to have a bloke like Allan Border. A lesser man would have had his spirit broken.

Border did actually threaten to quit as captain on one occasion. But it's a measure of the respect the team has for him that they immediately became a more closely knit bunch in an attempt to lighten the skipper's load.

In hindsight, Border's outburst probably did more good than harm. As much as I don't like to hear an Australian captain talk about deserting his post, it at least had the effect of making the players look in the mirror and admit that they should be doing a lot better with their talent.

Finally, his honest approach is paying off. The players have been needled and nudged into performing at their peak. All those dark days of the past must seem like a distant nightmare as Border now controls a team which is overwhelming its hapless opposition.

Whilst Border is enjoying that situation, he hasn't once resorted to gloating. He's more relaxed now, confident in the knowledge that his team can do the job even if he fails with the bat. That's allowed him to concentrate more on his leadership. I remember thinking when he walked into the press conference on the Saturday night at Lord's how Allan looked years younger. Gone was the furrowed brow and in its place was a beaming face. His eyes were dancing in the spotlight rather than – as they were so often in the past – concealed in the darkness of the wings.

Allan Border's past reluctance to lead from the front has meant it wasn't possible to say, 'He's a champion in every regard.' A champion batsman, yes. A champion bloke, most certainly. But never a champion Test captain.

However, a man of such immense pride was never going to be satisfied with only two out of three.

I was in England as a journalist and commentator in 1977, and played in an invitation XI against the Australian Youth team that contained Geoff Marsh and Wayne Phillips as well as a sixteen-year-old David Boon. On that occasion Boon swept Tony Greig to the boundary to claim victory for the young Australians, and twelve years later he played a similar shot at Old Trafford to regain the Ashes.

During the 1989 Old Trafford Test it was announced a number of English players – some of whom had competed in the Ashes series – had signed for a rebel tour of South Africa.

[Melbourne *Herald Sun*, 3 August 1989]

When David Boon swept Nick Cook to the mid-wicket boundary to regain the Ashes for Australia, my mind went back to 1977: I saw him play a similar shot to win a match for the Australian Youth team which was then touring England. At that time the opposition contained a young Australian named Allan Border, who was playing for Gloucester seconds. Those two shots were almost identical. The first will hardly rate a second thought in Allan's memory bank of matches, but Boon's latest match-winning blow will always remain deeply etched in Allan's cricket memories.

Border has earned every proud moment. He's sweated for every run and he's worked hard for every victory as a skipper.

Nothing has ever been easy for Allan Border, and when something good has come his way he's accepted it graciously. Typical of the man, five minutes after the greatest moment of his cricket career he was quietly chatting with the vanquished skipper, David Gower, and commiserating with him on his losses and defections. Border recalled the moment when he'd heard a number of Australians had opted for a tour of South Africa. And he talked of how it affected him as he prepared for the disastrous tour of 1985. It was as if he was trying to help Gower through what was probably his lowest moment in cricket before he would allow himself the luxury of enjoying his greatest achievement. It may have been the first hint of compassion shown by Allan to his opposite number in the whole summer, but I'm sure it will be appreciated as David faces up to the troubled days that follow.

The only sour note for Border, as the sprayed champagne washed over him and the truth sank in, was the thought of the South African announcement spoiling what should have been a day of Australian headlines.

Still, all that really mattered was that HIS team, the side that Allan had led so capably from the time he first set foot on the Headingley ground, had won the coveted Ashes back. From the noise that was bursting forth from the Australian dressing room I don't think his loyal team-mates were going to allow much else to infiltrate his thoughts for many hours.

They deserved the chance to let their hair down, the whole seventeen. The planning for the campaign had been spot on, the sacrifices had been many, the sweat had been expended; now it was time to follow a grand old Australian tradition: when you achieve something that's dear to you, go out and get well and truly sozzled.

As I watched the beginnings of bulk hangovers, I cast my mind back to 1974–75. Rod Marsh had raced over to me at the SCG when we beat England, grabbed me by the hand and said, 'We've got the bastards back.'

Winning the mythical Ashes does funny things to guys who are not normally hidebound by tradition.

But this isn't the time to dwell on Ashes series of the past. This is a victory that has been deservedly won by the brilliance of a modern side that hasn't overlooked the qualities of a bit of old-fashioned commonsense.

They won by superior batting, bowling and fielding. However, this position of strength was gained by applying the pressure until the opposition blew apart, like Nigel Mansell's tyre in the 1985 Adelaide Formula One Grand Prix. It was a side led by a captain who has discovered the art of aggressive leadership on the tour and then has the courage to keep on attacking to stretch his advantage.

Border had many allies in his work. The batting of Steve Waugh, Mark Taylor and Dean Jones was both exhilarating and solid. It provided a sound base for a lot of the pressure that was applied by the bowlers. This was perfectly capitalised on by the consistent Terry Alderman and the hard-working Geoff Lawson, whilst Merv Hughes and Trevor Hohns both contributed in their co-starring roles.

It's been a pleasure to watch Border's team play. Unlike some teams who have grafted their way to an Ashes win, this side has chased victory with as much dash and daring as any. If the opposition has put up too little resistance, then, as Allan Border claims, this can mostly be put down to not being allowed to play any better. Some of England's disarray can be attributed to the South African situation now that the truth is out, but Gower had a victory over Border in a similar situation just four years ago.

Whatever the side issues, you can't be any more conclusive than beating the opposition three times out of four.

As I again recalled David Boon's two match-winning sweep shots, I thought how he'd grown from a boy to a man. Dust to dust, ashes to ashes. Allan Border and his team may feel like death when the celebration winds down, but they'll remember that moment as long as they live.

After the announcement of the rebel tour to South Africa, the Chairman of Selectors, former England captain Ted Dexter, decided to take some punitive action before the next Test.

[Melbourne *Herald Sun*, 10 August 1989]

I have always thought that conservative-thinking English cricket selectors assist Australia. Nothing that Ted Dexter and company have done this summer has changed that opinion. If what the selection committee have come up with for Trent Bridge is rebuilding, I don't want them working on my renovations.

They made a token effort to discover some Test-class talent by choosing newcomers Mike Atherton and Devon Malcolm. But why they didn't go the whole way and also select the promising Nasser Hussain, and an all-rounder and a spinner with long-term prospects, is beyond me.

There seems to be a time-honoured tradition among English selectors. If there's any sort of crisis they always fall back on an 'experienced' player, rather than take a punt on a youngster with potential. This policy is pursued fervently, even though the players selected have proved on a number of occasions that they're short of Test class, even when playing at their peak.

If Allan Border and his team are anything like their predecessors, they'll be chuckling quietly and drinking a toast to the England selectors. 'Long may they reign.'

What the England team desperately needs is new blood. The areas that need improving are the work rate, enthusiasm and team spirit. All three of those qualities have, to a large extent, been missing this summer, and it's time the England selectors found a group of players who are interested in restoring not only lost pride but a lot of other things that are missing from English cricket.

The South African tourists (Mike Gatting apart) have tipped their hand. They weren't really interested in English cricket; they were only looking after number one.

With the Ashes lost the time was right for a proper clean-out, but the selectors weren't game to take the plunge. They weren't prepared to totally eradicate the 'old boys' club' atmosphere and bring in a bunch of youngsters who would get down to the business of dragging English cricket out of the chasm it's fallen into.

Here are two perfect examples of the thinking which is eroding English cricket:

Graham Gooch claims that he doesn't want to be selected for England until he finds form in the county matches. That's nonsensical. Gooch should be thinking that his next Test innings could be the one that brings him out of the doldrums; a slump which, incidentally, he isn't experiencing in county cricket. Gooch's name should be crossed off all future lists. It's time that pride in playing for England was restored as the most important thing on a player's mind. The selectors have the perfect opportunity to do this by making an example of Gooch.

Then there's the Devon Malcolm affair. When asked why Malcolm was missing from the Derbyshire line-up after being selected for his England debut, his coach replied, 'We thought it would be unfair to expect him to bowl thirty overs or so in the Hampshire game and then have nets before the Test match.'

Pardon? In the words of John McEnroe: 'You cannot be serious?' Especially when Malcolm himself says, 'I feel that I'm a better bowler now I'm getting into the side [Derbyshire] more regularly.' His county have a policy of rotating their fast bowlers and it just so happened that the Hampshire match was Malcolm's turn to sit it out. Who is more important, Derbyshire or England?

It's a pity Derbyshire's policy doesn't extend to rotating the administration. A rest might do some of them the world of good.

Allan Border's aggressive tactics and the excellent form of his team have exposed many weaknesses in the opposition. Time and time again, the England batting techniques have been laid bare for everyone to see and the point has been continually driven home as Border meticulously places individual field settings to trap each batsman.

Amazingly, I've not witnessed one England top-order batsman working assiduously in the nets to overcome any of the problems the Australians have exposed. However, one player who has worked to overcome a deficiency is keeper Jack Russell. Surprise, surprise, he's been consistently defying the Australian bowlers.

Dexter should have read the riot act to Gower. Then, encouraged by the success of newcomers Russell and Angus Fraser, he should have announced at least three more new caps and explained exactly what was required to drag England out of the mire. To complete the purge, he should have made his position clear by telling the world that Gooch would never again be considered for selection in an England side.

Sometimes you have to be cruel to be kind. Allan, there's nothing else for it, pal, you'll just have to beat them again to drive home the point.

What a difference a few victories make. From the first Test in June to the fifth at Trent Bridge in mid-August Allan Border had gone from being an ultra-conservative captain to ultra-aggressive bordering on arrogant. That dramatic change is depicted in the next two columns.

[Melbourne *Herald Sun*, 30 August 1989]

In a summer where Allan Border has made David Gower's life a misery he tried to inflict the ultimate humiliation by bowling England out in less than sixty-seven overs to finish with a five–nil victory margin. He was only denied by bad light and Robin Smith. It was a show of strength bordering on arrogance, which confirmed that Allan really has developed a ruthless streak in his summer of revenge.

Alderman has been the Australian spearhead and Border based his declaration on the swing bowler's personal strike rate in the 1989 series. But, whilst Terry continued to strike at better than a wicket every forty balls, it was asking a bit too much to hope for an overall demolition rate of about twenty balls fewer than the Test match norm.

Whilst Border's declaration could be explained by over-confidence, arrogance or mental tiredness at the end of a long series, it did have some factual backing. Twice before in the series the Australians had bowled out the hapless Englishmen in under sixty overs to clinch victory. Two out of three ain't bad.

It certainly provided excitement right to the end of an astonishing one-sided series and a large number of memorable highlights.

Not surprisingly, Alderman won the Australian award for the Man of the Series. This earned him a touch over fifteen hundred dollars and a magnum of champagne; just what you need when you're about to set off on a Greek island holiday.

My lasting memory of Alderman will be his off-cutter thudding into the pads of another leaden-footed Englishman. The most important of these was Graham Gooch in the first Test at Headingley, and it added to the enjoyment that Bill Lawry leapt out of his seat and screamed (not for the first time in the series) 'Gooch is gone.'

Gooch really was gone by the end of the series, and Alderman admitted to a lot of satisfaction from his own favourite dismissal, when he claimed the England opener caught and bowled in the final innings of the series. Eighty-three wickets in two series in England is a phenomenal haul and the Australian Cricket Board (ACB) should think seriously of paying for Terry's holiday.

There were many batting highlights but the most entertaining innings was Steve Waugh's scintillating stroke-filled knock at Headingley. His back-foot drives on that occasion were thrilling, and I haven't seen an Australian batsman make it look so easy since the days of Doug Walters.

Dean Jones proved himself to be the most versatile player in a strong Australian line-up. He played the support role at Headingley and yet he was equally at home in full cry during centuries at Edgbaston and The Oval.

Fittingly, the captain played the most decisive knock of the series. Border's sixty-six in the first innings at Headingley set the pattern for Australia, and his players followed him like the kids skipping along behind the Pied Piper. The six he hooked off

Phil DeFreitas early in his innings was a warning to England not to mess with him; they couldn't have been any more embarrassed if they'd capitulated there and then.

However, for pure consistency, technique and freedom of stroke play, Mark Taylor would have to get the nod as Australia's batsman of the series. Over eight hundred Test runs is a magnificent return in any Ashes contest, let alone your first one. It's quite incredible that the only three men who have passed that lofty mark in Ashes series all did it in their opening foray: Sir Donald Bradman, Englishman Wally Hammond and Taylor. Mark keeps good company. He also keeps his bat very straight and knows how to use it to attack. Some of his flowing cover-drives were a joy to watch, but it was one back-foot on-drive which I enjoyed the most. This was the area where his batting developed considerably on the tour, and that shot just summed up the improvement.

However, there was one crumb of comfort for England in a summer of sadness. Robin Smith gets the award for the hardest hitter. He hit two pull shots off Trevor Hohns that David Boon will remember for the rest of his life; one of them could've ended it. But, for sheer joy and perfection of sound off the bat, one square cut off Merv Hughes at Trent Bridge gets the gold medal. It was a joy to behold, but that's where the joy ended for England.

Fittingly, Allan Border finally got his hands on a replica of the urn on the 107th anniversary of the beginning of the Ashes magic. The mock obituary written by a young journalist of the London *Sporting Times* said that 'English cricket died at The Oval, 29 August 1882.' He went on to add that it, 'would be deeply lamented by a large circle of sorrowing friends and acquaintants. RIP.'

Allan Border and his boys have just hammered another nail in the coffin.

[*Cricket Life* magazine, September 1989]

The Australians outplayed England as a team to regain the Ashes, but the key to the victory was the work of one man, Allan Border. Border's authoritative leadership set the pattern of play for the team. Australian teams have always been at their best when they're attacking, and once Border set the example, the team responded brilliantly.

Border's policy of boldness required a distinct change of style in his captaincy. It's one thing to decide to make a change, but it takes immense courage to then actually go out on the field and put it into practice. With typical determination Border achieved his aim and did so with style.

He announced his intentions early in the first Test when he played the most decisive innings of the series. He strode to the wicket at Headingley with Australia in trouble at 2 for 57 and proceeded to attack the England bowling. He not only got Australia out of a tight corner, he sent a sharp message to the Englishmen that they were dealing with a different Allan Border. Not a different player – he was still the same world-class accumulator of runs – but an aggressive captain who was prepared to attack with the bat and in the field.

That was the example the Australians needed and having been shown the way they rewarded Border with the Ashes.

I have always believed that the amount of work a captain does off the field in planning and building team spirit will be reflected in the team's performance. Border's team was full of fighting spirit and the specialised field placings which were produced for each English batsman were telling factors in the Ashes win. Probably the most important of those was the on-side trap set for Graham Gooch. This reduced his effectiveness and contributed greatly to England's mediocre performances.

There was no magic formula to Australia's success; they just played good team cricket. They batted well and aggressively. They bowled at the stumps and probed for weaknesses with a little bit of movement. And they backed all this with a keen and competent fielding side. That's been a common formula for success throughout more than a century of Test cricket.

Australia is a well-balanced side. In batting they have a nice blend of right- and left-handed stroke-makers and grafters. Their bowling attack is persistent and varied and they were accurate enough to allow Border's well-laid traps to work. The Australian selectors deserve credit for assembling this excellent combination as it was a vital ingredient in regaining the Ashes.

The team has achieved a level of excellence by following the skipper's example and working hard in the nets. The Australians had the good sense and courage to keep practising their skills, even when the results weren't forthcoming. Though they've tasted victory they're such a dedicated bunch that there's been no let-up on the field or in the nets.

Apart from Border's captaincy and his vital innings at Headingley, the next most important contributions came from Terry Alderman and Mark Taylor.

Alderman constantly harassed the English batsmen with his accurate off-cutters and occasional outswing. His consistent good form throughout the series was important, but it was his dominance of the English top order in the first Test that was crucial. Before the series the big question mark about this Australian side was its ability to bowl England out twice. Alderman showed his team-mates it could be done and they never looked back.

Taylor's century at Headingley ranks only just behind Border's dig in importance to Australia. He hardly made a mistake in his first Test innings on English soil and frustrated the opposition. That innings, in conditions that were favourable to the bowlers, helped establish a mental advantage over England that lasted throughout the series.

The next most important innings was the boundary-studded effort by Steve Waugh at Headingley. This was one of the finest exhibitions of stroke play I've seen in a Test match. His undefeated 177, scored at a scorching pace, gave the bowlers time to take the wickets needed for victory, and it also afforded them the luxury of having runs to play with, which helped to exert pressure on the English batsmen.

Geoff Marsh also deserves some credit for his work as Border's lieutenant. He's been a strong ally and has helped Allan through some rough times.

There were many other good contributions from Australian players during the series, but because dominance was established in the first Test I give priority to those performances. That position of ascendancy was first gained by Allan Border's batting, and he maintained it throughout the series with his authoritative captaincy. He was the man most responsible for Australia regaining the Ashes.

In the 2006 New Year honours Michael Vaughan was awarded an OBE for his imaginative leadership, which saw England finally regain the Ashes. However, there was a long period where job security and England captaincy weren't mentioned in the same sentence.

[*The Sun-Herald*, 10 September 1989]

Any dad who wants his son to captain England might think a surname starting with G is a good place to begin. In recent times Gower, Gatting and Gooch have all led England.

However, there's a catch. All three of them have also been sacked from the job, with David Gower currently leading the league with two sackings. Judging from the childish manner which Gower displayed on occasions during the summer in England and the strange way he tried to make light of losing the captaincy, I'd say the job had become a bit too much for him. Not surprising after Ted Dexter had trumpeted him as the man to lead a brave new era.

However, that was nothing compared with Dexter's latest bombshell. He's apparently become so disillusioned with his former golden-haired boy that he doesn't consider Gower good enough to hold his place as a player. I find that a staggering turn-about, as I believe Gower is still one of the best batsmen in England. I can only assume the selectors believe having the former captain on the tour will make life too difficult for the new captain, Graham Gooch.

Gooch has been chosen to lead England on the West Indies tour and a short trip to India. Yes, the man that Ted Dexter said only months ago didn't impress him as a captain. It's true: 'A drowning man will clutch at straws.'

Graham Gooch is the latest model on the England captaincy merry-go-round. A new coat of paint and she's ready to go again, but what happens when you scratch the surface?

I first saw Gooch at Edgbaston in 1975, when he bagged a pair on his Test debut. What amazed me about Gooch's second nought was the haste with which he departed the scene. He didn't even wait for the umpire to raise his finger after he got a feather touch to a good delivery from Jeff Thomson. First black mark.

Then I saw Gooch in an International batting competition at The Oval in 1979. A dispute arose over the rules during his contest with Clive Lloyd, and his wife started laying down the law, telling Graham what he should be doing. Second black mark: what's his wife doing at the cricket?

Gooch became captain of Essex in 1986, but after two seasons he resigned because he felt it was affecting his batting. Third black mark. You never quit the captaincy; you either retire or make 'em rip the stripes off your blazer.

Then, finally, in the middle of a disastrous 1989 series against Australia, Gooch opted out of the Trent Bridge Test to find form in county cricket. An established Test batsman should consider his next innings as the one that'll bring him out of the trot. Fourth black mark.

On the positive side, Gooch has gone back to leading Essex and they're a successful team. He's now more at ease in the job, and having witnessed the vast change that came over Allan Border's captaincy during the recent Ashes series it would be unwise to underestimate any cricketer's ability to catch on to the intricacies of leadership.

The other plus mark is Gooch's record against the West Indies. He's done well against their four-pronged pace attacks, although his last tour of the Caribbean (1986) was nowhere near as successful as the first one, in 1981. It was on his second tour that he discussed coming home early as the demonstrators hounded him because of his South African rebel escapade. Even though the Caribbean cricket chiefs have said they have no problem with Gooch leading this tour, they're not speaking for the many anti-apartheid supporters in the Caribbean.

If Gooch allows the demonstrators to get to him on this tour it will have a profound effect on team morale. Gooch tends to be introspective and mopes a little when his own form is down. This is the last thing you want from the skipper, especially when he's likely to be in charge of a few young players looking for guidance in the Caribbean. Gooch has obviously matured a lot since the Seventies, but I still don't see him as the tough type of character England need as they try to rebuild their crumbling cricket team.

Apart from Mike Gatting, the G's haven't inspired much confidence as leaders. Perhaps the England selectors should start searching for a captain who is the G for Gutsy type. Then maybe the results will be G for Good.

There was a stage in the late Eighties, when the West Indies was dominating world cricket with fast bowling, that the Australian Cricket Board chairman Fred Bennett was lobbying to virtually eliminate the bouncer from the game. He didn't get far but the 'one bouncer per batsman per over' law, which was introduced for a period, was nearly as senseless.

[*The Sun-Herald*, 7 January 1990]

Believe everything that is written and spoken about short-pitched bowling and it would be up there with Terrorism and Religious Wars as an enemy of world peace.

Don't believe it. Short-pitched bowling in the right doses keeps cricket healthy. It sorts the men from the boys, and without it the game would be mighty dull.

Two unrelated events in the last few days brought the much discussed subject to a head yet again. First, there was a delivery by Sri Lanka's Graeme Labrooy to Geoff Marsh in the International played in Perth. It was a nasty delivery which climbed off a good length on the bouncy WACA pitch, but because it struck the batsman on the glove above shoulder height it's a no-ball.

This is a nonsensical playing condition. It not only restricts the faster bowlers, but it also limits the number of horizontal bat shots the spectators are going to see. There are many who enjoy seeing a good cut, pull or hook shot.

The playing condition used in limited-overs cricket in England, which allows a bowler to get the ball up to head height, is a much fairer one.

The next short-pitched comedy routine was acted out at the Gabba on the final day of the Shield match between New South Wales and Queensland. In the late overs Mark Waugh and Brad McNamara bowled a number of bouncers to Robbie Kerr and Steve Storey in an attempt to stop their charge to victory. One commentator expressed the opinion that the umpire should speak to the bowlers about overdoing the short stuff.

Speak to the bowlers my foot! Any first-class batsman worth his salt should be able to dismiss a bouncer attack from medium pacers like Mark Waugh and McNamara in the time it takes to say 'bouncer'.

Storey did exactly that when he deposited two of McNamara's deliveries onto the dog track for six. That ended McNamara's spell and any further discussion on the umpires stepping in.

If batsmen are mollycoddled then despatching a bouncer will become a lost art. If that happens, cricket administrators will be called upon to make more stringent rulings on short-pitched bowling. Heaven help the game if that occurs.

At the moment the limitations in one-day games are one-sided. If the bowlers continue to have restrictions heaped on them, the game will become a farcical batting exhibition, appealing only to those who attend night cricket purely as a variation on going to the pub to get sloshed. If similar restrictions are introduced to first-class and Test cricket the game will become a high-scoring bore.

To keep both short-pitched bowling in check and a good game on the continuing path to prosperity, administrators only need to concentrate on four points:

1) Ensure that wherever possible curators produce pitches with

predictable but good bounce and a bit of pace. That will give any self-respecting batsman the chance to defend himself by either hooking or avoiding the short-pitched ball. At the same time it will mercifully rid the game of gentle, medium-pace trundlers. Instead, selectors and captains will have to turn to big-hearted spinners with the skill to bamboozle batsmen with flight and spin.

2) Issue an edict that all batting coaches teach their pupils the correct footwork for back-foot play. Then the players can make up their own minds in a match whether they deal with bouncers by hooking, cutting or taking evasive measures. The good coaches will screw up the memo and throw it away, because that's what they'll already be teaching.

3) Make all teams bowl a reasonable number of balls in a day's play (nothing less than one hundred per hour) so that the delicate balance between bat and ball is maintained. This will mean the genuine quicks will be difficult to hook early in the day, but later on, when they tire, a batsman who's quick on his feet and has the skill and nerve to fight fire with fire will force them to rethink any planned intimidation. That way, fast bowlers will only intimidate those who display an inclination to be somewhere else, for example, the ice-cream shop or the pin-ball parlour.

4) Instruct umpires to be stricter on calling wides any time a bouncer is ill-directed. If it's more than just over the batsman's head or out of reach on either side of the wicket, then it's a wide. The law should include the wording used in the playing condition for limited-overs cricket in Australia: 'A ball which deprives a batsman of playing a genuine cricket shot'. It's amazing that in Australia administrators go to great lengths to stop fast bowlers bouncing one over shoulder height in a limited-overs match, but in Test or first-class matches quickies are allowed to land a cricket ball almost on the Moon without any penalty.

Put that four-point plan into effect and there won't be any need for a peace-keeping corps in cricket. Batsmen and bowlers will reach their own agreement on short-pitched bowling.

During their successful 1991–92 World Cup campaign under Imran Khan I described the Pakistan side as a skilled rabble. As you will see they were building the foundations of that reputation in Australia in 1990 as Imran sent home leg spinner Abdul Qadir before a ball was bowled in the Test series.

[*The Sun-Herald*, 14 January 1990]

Rather than ordered chaos, you get the feeling captain Imran Khan orders chaos before Pakistan plays each Test series.

Whilst most members of the Australian cricket public were writing off Pakistan before the first Test at the MCG, Imran was busy explaining how they were in an even worse state of disarray in the Caribbean in 1988 and on their 1987 tour of England.

It's hard to imagine a more chaotic build-up to a Test series than Pakistan's performance on this tour, but Imran was adamant the previous two were worse. In England they went on to win the series and despite having their confidence shattered by a five–nil loss in the limited-overs matches, they bounced back to level at one all against the West Indies. Imran describes that as the best series he's ever played in.

With that sort of record Imran is entitled to be called Captain Chaos. Any captain who sends home the best leg spinner in the world on the eve of the first Test has to be able to live with disorder being the order of the day. However, his job was made easier by having at his disposal one of the finest fast bowlers in the game.

Wasim Akram has developed into a magnificent pace bowler since the day he routed Australia at the MCG in 1985 to send them crashing to defeat in a World Championship of Cricket match. Wasim has pace, strength and the ability to swing the ball both ways and move it off the seam. Added to all that skill, he's also got the courage to enable him to push through the pain barrier. He's the type of bowler captains dream about.

But even Wasim likes a bit of disorder in his build-up to the game. He had a precautionary x-ray on his troublesome groin the day before the Melbourne Test. I happened to walk past the manager's (Intikhab Alam) room at the precise time they were getting ready to leave for the doctor. Well, precise isn't precisely the word. When Intikhab looked bemused to see his fast bowler standing at the door, Wasim said, 'Come on, skip, we arranged to meet at ten past two.'

'Son,' replied the genial Intikhab, looking at his timepiece, 'you need a new watch. I'll see you downstairs in ten minutes.'

I'll bet most of the Australian batsmen would be prepared to buy Wasim a new watch – one that doesn't have the hours eleven to six on the face.

Akram bowled beautifully, without luck, to destroy the top half of the Australian batting order. If he'd had the Gulargambone third XI fielding for him that destruction would have been completed much earlier in the day. The Pakistan fielding is a disgrace.

There are far too many Pakistani players who don't want to be out there fielding. They don't want the ball to come to them, and worst of all they *fear* the ball coming at them.

As a kid, my father told me if I wanted to be a cricketer I'd better enjoy fielding. He reasoned that if you enjoyed it you'd be better at the task. Then he took me out in the backyard and had me practise with a cricket ball so I'd never have a fear of the ball. Pakistani junior cricket could use a coach like my father.

Unfortunately, their standards have been set by players like their magnificent batsman Hanif Mohammad, father of present opener Shoaib. When he wasn't churning out runs, Hanif spent most of his time sitting in the pavilion with his feet up watching the game. There was only one way to ensure Hanif stayed on the ground when it came time to field. It happened in the only Test I ever played against him. The wicket-keeper for Pakistan, Abdul Kadir, was dismissed third ball of the match when he had his thumb broken by a lifting delivery from Graham McKenzie. That meant Hanif had to keep wickets. Have you ever seen a kid forced to mow the lawn? That was Hanif keeping at the MCG.

Ever since Hanif's time there's been a reluctance among Pakistan's players, apart from the true scrappers like Imran, Javed and Wasim Akram, to stay on the field. If you don't want to be out there, the concentration wanders and hence the catches go down. Not only were the catches going down in Australia's first innings; most of the attempts to catch the ball were feeble. In most cases the catches never looked like being held.

It was a bowler's nightmare, but even that level of incompetence couldn't spoil what was a marvellous performance by Wasim. He gave credence to Imran's statement that he's leading the most varied attack in the world. He also made Imran's claim that Pakistan are the second-best team in the world sound a lot more plausible than it had in the lead-up to the Test.

If Pakistan do go on to win the series it will be a triumph for the captain. If they lose to Australia it'll be because of their deplorable fielding, which looks like ordered chaos.

In 1987–88 a long-term off-field quarrel between England and Pakistan officials finally boiled over into an ugly on-field finger-wagging slanging match between captain Mike Gatting and umpire Shakoor Rana. By 1990 another row was brewing between Pakistan and Australia.

[*The Sun-Herald*, 4 February 1990]

I was certain I learnt at school that this is the way you spelt TROUBLE. However, the more I hear, the more I wonder if I got it wrong, if it should be spelt P-A-K-I-S-T-A-N.

Wherever Imran Khan and his team have gone in Australia this summer, PAKISTAN seems to have followed them. But mostly Melbourne seems to have been the capital of controversy. After Australia benefited from six lbw's in the second innings of the MCG Test, Imran and manager Intikhab Alam had the hide to say they would only divulge their thoughts on the decisions in the umpires' report.

This seemed to offend some critics, who thought it would've been much better if Imran and Intikhab had taken a leaf out of the book of Australian coach, Bob Simpson, and manager, Colin Egar. In 1988–89 the Australian pair were highly critical of the umpires in Karachi in the middle of the Test match. According to the critics' line of thinking, 'Do the right thing' applied only to rubbish you toss in a bin.

Intikhab then ran foul of umpire Robin Bailhache in the match against Victoria. When run-'em-out-of-town Robin pulled out a red card to dismiss young leg spinner Mushtaq Ahmed from the attack for running on the pitch, Intikhab ordered his team into the dressing room. After some hurried discussions and an agreement not to ban Mushtaq from bowling in that innings, the game continued.

Taking the team off the field was a drastic action, but maybe Intikhab, recalling the Australian outburst in Karachi, had expected that the umpiring in this country would be perfect.

Then Imran went to Canberra and PAKISTAN followed. Firstly he didn't play in the Prime Minister's match, thereby refusing to bow to the wishes of Mr Hawke. Then the team copped plenty of flack for not entering into the spirit of a limited-overs game and sacrificing their wickets in an attempt to entertain the crowd after the match was well and truly lost.

Once again, Imran and his men were billed as the culprits. But they probably don't believe they've snubbed their hosts any more than Allan Border's team did in Karachi when they threatened to quit the tour in the middle of the first Test.

What we have building up here is a classic Mike Gatting–Shakoor Rana affair: another International controversy looming on the field. Why does it continue to happen? Because the administrators do nothing to diffuse the bomb.

It's hypocritical for the Australians to say that controversy always follows Pakistan and blame them lock, stock and barrel. Part of Imran and Intikhab's problem seems to arise from them being at the forefront of the fight for an International umpiring panel. It's a widely held view that every time they 'create' an umpiring incident it helps their cause.

Sure, Pakistan is fighting for an umpiring panel, but it's the players of all countries who've made it almost impossible for the old system to work. The refusal by players to accept the umpires' judgement has become universal and Pakistan is no better and no worse than any other country.

In the recent Adelaide Test, when Wasim Akram was refused an appeal for caught behind, the bowler remained at his follow-through position with arms outstretched in dismay, and the keeper moved into a position where he was ready to support any protest by the bowler. An ugly situation was brewing. But Imran Khan, with a swift motion of his hand and a few words, quickly had the players back in their places ready to continue the game. There was no trouble.

When a similar situation occurred in the Pakistan innings and the Australian bowler and wicket-keeper were 'gathering themselves', I didn't see any reaction from Allan Border. The protest was allowed to continue for a while, and in doing so indicated the umpire had made an obvious mistake.

No one country is to blame. No one country is blameless.

If Pakistan loses the series, then back home it'll be widely claimed it was all due to biased Australian umpiring in general and the Melbourne lbw's in particular. Exactly as was the case when the Australians returned home from their last tour of Pakistan. That loss was put down to biased umpiring and a diabolical plot by the groundsman in Karachi.

The phrase 'we wuzz robbed' has been heard at sporting contests for a long time and it's in no danger of becoming extinct. If the administrators don't do something about the situation, something like appointing a strong bunch of officials with the power and the credibility to control the game on a global basis, there'll be more ugly incidents on the field. That'll mean trouble. Not spelt P-A-K-I-S-T-A-N, but with a capital T.

In August 1984 at the Eagle Farm racecourse in Brisbane, a ring-in scandal erupted when the horse Fine Cotton was replaced by the better credentialled Bold Personality.

By 1990 Allan Border's captaincy had improved so dramatically you could've been forgiven for suspecting that Richie Benaud had been surreptitiously substituted as Australian captain.

———

[*The Sun-Herald*, 11 February 1990]

For Allan Border the captaincy of Australia has meant the worst of times and the best of times.

In the early part of his leadership career he didn't experience the thrill of victory for eleven consecutive Tests. From the third Test against New Zealand in 1985–86 until the fourth Test against England in 1986–87 the Australian team was either defeated or drew with the opposition. However, in the last fourteen Tests the boot has been on the other foot. From the fourth Test against the West Indies in 1989–90 up to the present, it's the opposition who have found themselves either defeated or drawn with Allan Border's team.

It's a remarkable turnaround. A form reversal like that in cricket is a fine thing. In racing circles it's more likely to be a Fine Cotton.

Almost as remarkable as the form reversal has been the change in approach to captaincy by Allan Border. In those early times,

Allan, admittedly handicapped by an attack that didn't bowl line and length, was tentative as a skipper. He tended to wait for the opposition to make the first move. It was rare that he went on the offensive and usually happened only when he was in charge of a good spin attack. Hence his remarkable record of victories at the SCG.

However, at Headingley in 1989 a change came over Allan. He finally had one bowler (Terry Alderman) who was prepared to bowl line and length. Encouraged by this he went on the attack. He set traps for the English batsmen, hounded them into submission and in the end had renowned stroke-makers like Graham Gooch and David Gower batting like Kanga cricketers. The captain changed his thinking and transformed the team into an unbeatable combination.

The two most important players in this transformation have been Alderman and Mark Taylor, Alderman not just because he bowled accurately and with penetration, but because of the example he set the other bowlers. With his encouragement, Geoff Lawson (who had been wayward in 1985) became a more accurate swing and seam bowler; and Merv Hughes, guided by Terry, now bowls a lot more deliveries in the danger zone.

Taylor's arrival on the Test scene was originally heralded because it gave Australia a left- and right-hand opening combination. After just fourteen Tests (his career has coincided with Border's undefeated streak) he's being talked about in glowing terms as one of Australia's best opening batsmen.

Terry Alderman was the middle piece in the jigsaw puzzle; the piece that gave a clue to the overall picture. With Mark Taylor in place the picture was identifiable.

Border has had the patience to piece all these bits together. There were times when it looked like he'd thrown the board in the air and walked away from the scattered mess. But drawing on that extra resolve that has characterised his batting, he only got up, went for a walk, took a deep breath and then went back to the unfinished puzzle.

Allan is a man who has a lot of pride in his own performance. His standards have become those for the Australian team. One of the most impressive things about his team was the way they went about the build-up to the two Test matches after they'd regained the Ashes at Old Trafford. The team's work rate never dropped for a second. The desire to crush the opposition was so great that Taylor and Geoff Marsh staged their own private party during the Test following the Ashes celebration, by batting right through the opening day and amassing 319 runs.

Border at times gets peeved that his team doesn't receive enough credit for the job they've done. He complains that too much emphasis is placed on the opposition folding.

There are precedents aplenty to suggest his team is no different from many of the great Australian combinations of the past. The 1920–21 side under Warwick Armstrong strung together eight successive victories over England. That's a demoralised opposition. Sir Donald Bradman led Australia to seven victories over England without a loss from late 1946 until 1948. England didn't recover until the 1954–55 series. In 1958–59 Richie Benaud's fine combination pulverised the English opposition, winning four and drawing one. Then through 1974–75, in nine Tests, the Australian team won five, lost one and drew the rest against England – a team shattered by the fine bowling of Dennis Lillee and Jeff Thomson.

Border's team has done exactly the same as those great sides. Firstly, they beat the opposition, and then they demoralised them.

Allan shouldn't get too upset about his team not receiving due credit for their performances. The denigration of the opposition mainly comes from the English media, and that's a sure sign Australia is enjoying the best of times.

Mark Taylor's first game as captain of NSW was in the Shield final of 1989–90, which the Blues won by 345 runs with the skipper making a century in each innings.

[*The Sun-Herald*, 25 March 1990]

New South Wales has one Taylor who is struggling to sow, whilst another is starting to reap.

Peter Taylor, off spinner and handy bat, has fluctuated between Peter who and Peter hero during his four-year career. Currently he's in the former category as he languishes as twelfth man for NSW, just a few days after top-scoring in both innings of a Test for Australia.

Mark first came to prominence when he was mistaken for Peter on the Test selectors' list. But once he made the Australian side in his own right, he really made his presence felt. His start against the West Indies wasn't memorable, but it did reveal a good temperament. Then he proceeded to tear apart the English attack to show that he possessed a technique to match his temperament.

On Friday at the SCG, the NSW selectors relegated Peter to twelfth man and appointed Mark skipper in place of the injured Geoff Lawson. Mark received the news of his elevation just thirty minutes before play started. He promptly lost his first toss, but neither of these shocks appeared to make any difference to the unflappable left-hander. He just strapped on the pads and batted all day to compile a remarkable century. Business as usual for the run-hungry opener.

However, it may not have been quite his usual business. Apart from maintaining his extraordinary appetite for run-making, this Mark Taylor century could well have set him on a path to becoming captain of Australia.

The first thing a captain requires is the skill to hold his place in the team. In this regard, Taylor receives a credit mark. The next thing you need to know is his skill won't be impaired by the onus of leadership. For his first Test Taylor receives ten out of ten.

In one remarkable day Mark Taylor has taken a significant advantage over one of his main captaincy rivals, Steve Waugh. For some time now the senior player in the Waugh office has been touted as Australian captaincy material. When an opportunity came out of the blue to put forward a claim, Steve was in the worst form of his career. Mark Taylor was at his best. Hence Taylor reaped the reward for being in the runs.

To gain the number-one job in Australian cricket sometime in the future, Taylor will have to develop his captaincy skills and display an aptitude for leadership. As a large part of captaincy revolves around commonsense, you must assume Mark Taylor will excel. He has maintained a level-headed approach to Test cricket, and importantly he's proved himself a fast learner.

He has two other attributes which appeal. Firstly, a correct but simple batting technique. I like a cricketer who doesn't complicate matters. And secondly he's an excellent slip catcher. That's a good spot from which to oversee proceedings, and he can also set a good example to his team.

If you look through the list of candidates for future Australian captain, Mark Taylor's performance in the Shield final has seen him make a significant move up the list. There's also current vice-captain, Geoff Marsh, who will get the opportunity next season to pop out from under the shadows of both Allan Border and Graeme Wood, as he'll probably get the WA captaincy.

Next would be David Boon. He's had a lot of experience as an International player and his tough approach to the game has been of invaluable assistance to Border. However, he's been deposed as Tasmanian captain and at best he would be looked upon as an interim Australian skipper.

Dean Jones was Victorian captain for a while, but he didn't enjoy much success and eventually relinquished the job. His brilliantly individual style is not really suited to moulding a side.

Of the bowlers, only Lawson could come under serious consideration. He's been far and away the best of the Shield captains this season and has played a significant role in NSW participating in a home final. He's a good captain, but he's getting on as a fast bowler and he's unlikely to outlast Border.

In fact, Border is showing no signs of wear and tear. And whilst Australia continues to perform so well, I don't see him rushing into retirement. Unless something untoward happens, I envisage Border defending Australia's World Cup crown in early 1992. That leaves ample time for some candidates to self-destruct and others to emerge. Judging from what we've seen in the last fifteen months, I can imagine Mark Taylor being one of the latter.

It's a remarkable turnabout for a man who first came to prominence purely because he was mistakenly thought to be the Taylor called in to stitch up the Englishmen in 1986–87.

Technology has improved immensely in the last decade, but nothing I've seen makes me think we should be referring more decisions to the third umpire. Much of what is used on television should be regarded as information and entertainment for the viewer rather than a definitive answer to a batsman's immediate future. For instance, a shot taken from a camera placed one hundred metres away in an elevated position in the stands cannot provide superior evidence for an lbw decision than a human being standing just twenty metres from the batsman.

———

[*Cricket Life* magazine, August 1990]

The group Fairground Attraction sang, 'It's got to be, perr-fect', and when it comes to video replays to aid cricket umpires, I agree. I don't believe umpires should call on video assistance from off the field until replays can provide correct answers to all decisions, without interrupting the flow of the game.

At the moment a video replay can give you a near one hundred per cent correct answer on run-outs and stumpings, and nothing else. Television replays have shown that good umpires average about ninety-five per cent success rate on those two decisions. So why do they need outside assistance?

This is one case where the use of technology would create more problems than it would solve.

A batsman adjudged run out on the evidence of a video replay is going to feel aggrieved if he doesn't have the same right of appeal when an opposition player is given not out following a concerted plea for caught behind. This could lead to on-field tension and arguments between players.

At present most batsmen accept the odd bad decision because they believe things even out over a long career. However, if changes are made that create an imbalance in the evening-out process, then look out for trouble.

Players would lose confidence in an umpire who relied on video replays. The competent arbiter gives his decision quickly and firmly leaving the impression that he has absolutely no doubt his decision is correct. Players prefer this style of umpire, and if he does make what is considered to be an odd mistake it's generally accepted as part of cricket life.

On the other hand, the ditherer makes players nervous. This usually results in a lot of unnecessary appealing, which compounds the umpire's problems and creates tension in the middle.

Another thing that counts against the video replay is the interruption to the flow of the game. It could take a couple of minutes for the answer to be relayed to the centre, and not only does that hold up a game that already has too few overs bowled in a day, but also helps to create a controversy. It gives the media another person to query. At the moment, if a television replay shows an umpire has made a mistake on a run-out, the adjudicator involved only has to reply to the media, 'From all the evidence available to me from my position I gave the correct decision.' If he says that, the matter is closed, except to those journalists with a thick hide or some other part of their anatomy.

However, if an umpire calls for assistance from a mate sitting in front of a video screen, he might as well give the order 'controversy, front and centre', because it's immediately out in the centre and it'll soon be on the front page.

What happens if the third umpire has to renege on giving a ruling because his video is out of action, or the television company providing the service can't give a replay? Then the man in the middle, who has shown himself to be unsure, has to make the decision anyhow. The questions arising from that situation are limitless for a good journalist.

There are inherent problems with having an adjudicator off the field. If the third umpire isn't ensconced in a room on his own, surely his decisions are then subject to outside influence? And let's say there's been interference during a run-out. The third umpire might be able to see the end result on his screen, but is he aware of what occurred before the wicket was broken?

There's no way a third umpire can apply the same level of concentration to his task as the men out in the middle.

Then there's the standard of television replay from country to country. This can vary enormously depending on equipment and the skill of the operators. So do we have justice for some and not for others? Or does someone 'fork out' a huge amount to supplement the less efficient networks' coverage?

The magic eye provides tennis with a similar anomaly. It's used at Wimbledon, but not on the back courts, whilst at the French Open (also a Grand Slam tournament), it's not used at all. It's also not infallible. If a serve is long but doesn't break the circuit and set off the beeper, a linesman who is relying on the magic eye may assume the serve is good. This often leads to an argument.

In my book Illie Nastase effectively reduced the magic eye to its correct standing. When it produced a ludicrous call at Wimbledon, Illie got down on hands and knees and eye-balled the machine. Then he turned to the umpire and said, 'I see the problem. It's made in Russia.'

Instead of looking for artificial aids, more thought should be given to improving the standard of umpiring around the world and the relationship between players and adjudicators. Administrators should give the captains involved a list and tell them to choose the umpires for each Test. This would quickly reduce the number of complaints. It would also bring the captains together off the field a little more often and perhaps lead to a better relationship between the two teams.

The glorious uncertainty in cricket relies heavily on the human input – the fallibility of the players, umpires and curators. I think Test cricket should bring in perfect umpires (robots) and perfect wickets (artificial), the same day the players achieve perfection.

As long as the W's (wins) and L's (losses) go against the captain's name I believe he should always be the one to run a cricket team. As a captain I wouldn't delegate anything that would impinge on winning or losing the game. Also, why limit yourself to one source of knowledge? If a batsman is having trouble, call in an ex-player who knows a lot about coaching batsmen, and similarly for any other type of player who may be struggling. Having full-time batting and bowling coaches who are with the team all the time will only result in them trying to justify their wage. That is likely to lead to unnecessary tinkering and, really, not much goes wrong with a good international cricketer's technique. When something is slightly amiss the player should be the first to know.

———

[*The Age*, 24 October 1990]

My idea of an Australian cricket coach is something you ride around in on a tour of England.

The role of International cricket coach came into vogue in the 1980s. Rather than modernising cricket, I think it's put the cart before the horse. If Test teams are so desperately in need of coaching, then young players aren't being properly prepared for the climb up the ladder.

Apart from the fact that I'm a firm believer that only the captain can run an International cricket team, I also think top-class coaches are wasted working with the best players. The best twelve cricketers in the country should be well qualified to do the occasional bit of fine tuning that's required at that level. It's all part of the training.

A first-class cricketer is constantly noting the way his team-mates practise, so it becomes second nature when he's out in the middle. In addition, Australian players are continually playing against each other in Shield cricket, so they should notice any changes that occur in a team-mate's game. And anyway, most of the problems that occur result from a loss of confidence. That's a job for the captain – it's all part of the process of building team spirit.

There aren't that many good cricket coaches around. The best of them should be working with the elite players from age thirteen or fourteen, honing techniques and forming attitudes that will allow them to survive and then flourish at first-class level. They should have a complete cricket education by the time they're seventeen. The only thing missing will be the best advice a coach can give: 'Son, no matter how good my coaching's been, you're on your own out in the middle. Best you start working things out for yourself.' So armed, a cricketer worthy of an Australian cap can overcome any problem that's likely to arise during his career. He may occasionally need a bit of fine tuning, but not constant coaching.

The original reason for Bob Simpson's appointment as Australian team coach was an Australian Cricket Board (ACB) attempt to bolster Allan Border's captaincy. There was no sign of change in Border's Test leadership for three years, then came that remarkable transformation in 1989. Allan suddenly decided in England that he was the right man for the job and he began running the team. It's the only way it can work.

If the coach's role is upgraded it undermines the captain's

authority. I believe a continuation of this policy in Australian first-class cricket will have a detrimental effect on captaincy. *Prospective* captains are the leaders who need the advice and assistance of our best coaches. Captains need to be groomed.

The same applies to spin bowlers. We've just realised the need to produce spinners rather than wait for them to walk in off the street. Spin bowling schools are now being organised in each state by former Test players Ashley Mallett and Peter Philpott. While these classes are mainly catering for the up-and-coming spin bowlers, Greg Matthews wasn't too proud to plonk his thirty-five bucks on the table to see what he could learn. Since those sessions he's been the best spin bowler in Australia.

Properly utilised, our best coaches can help the stars of the future, whilst their knowledge isn't lost to the present players. Producing good cricketers requires specialised coaching. With proper planning, Craig McDermott might not have been transformed from a promising young bowler of genuine pace into an inaccurate medium pacer. Tragically for Australian cricket, he's never recovered. And God forbid that Steve Waugh's footwork, which has been in disarray for twelve months with no visible signs of any repair work, will see him lose his way.

I often hear the excuse that captains have too much of a workload. If that's the case, why relieve them of the vital duties and leave only the less important tasks? That's not the way to become the clever cricket country.

As a youngster I had the good fortune to receive a thorough cricket education. Consequently, I was horrified every time I read former great Australian leggie Bill 'Tiger' O'Reilly advocate that: 'Any kid who sees a coach coming should run a mile.' However, a closer inspection of the list of great Australian players from the bush who had no coaching has changed my thinking. The list includes Sir Donald Bradman, Stan McCabe, Doug Walters and

O'Reilly himself. They learnt about the game and themselves by continually playing and practising cricket.

I now believe that if you can't get good coaching, then you're better off having none. With no coaching you have to learn the hard way. That's a valuable grounding for the tough world of Test cricket, where you really are 'on you're own out in the middle'.

Australia's dominance over England had only commenced in 1989, but once Border's side put them on the slippery dip there was no stopping the downhill slide. It made it easier to predict the results of Ashes series in those days.

———

[*The Sun-Herald*, 28 October 1990]

I believe Australia will win the forthcoming Ashes series. I also think Allan Border's team will achieve dominance over Graham Gooch's side with a bit in hand.

Australia has a distinct advantage. They're superior to England in batting and bowling. As Test matches are won either by so many runs or so many wickets, that's a hell of a start.

'Wanna bet?' I hear Englishmen cry. Well, if you do, here's a form guide.

Australia's top six batsmen are the best unit among the Test-playing countries. England may dismiss them cheaply once in a match, but I don't expect lightning or Devon Malcolm to strike twice in the same place.

Australia also has an experienced and potent strike force. It includes Terry Alderman and Geoff Lawson, who've taken in excess of 150 Test wickets, whilst Merv Hughes is just a dozen short of the century mark. Then there's Carl Rackemann and Bruce Reid, both of whom can be lethal in Australia with the extra bounce. They've all experienced success at home.

England, on the other hand, don't have a bowler who has taken fifty Test wickets. In addition, Gladstone Small is their only bowler to have taken five wickets in an innings in a Test in Australia and the only England paceman who has played a Test in this country. The English selectors are gambling on the success of an on-the-job training scheme.

Still not convinced Australia is a good bet? Well, what about captaincy?

Allan Border has been to hell and made it all the way back when he regained the Ashes in 1989. Since that victory he's been confident and competent and his team has responded well to his leadership.

Graham Gooch has been to the hell where all England captains seem to find themselves – on the scrap heap. He's made it back, but only to claim victory over New Zealand and India, and both of those wins were at home. That doesn't rank with Border's win over the arch-enemy on their own soil.

Still not ready to part with your hard-earned? Well, let's get a bit more personal, or, to be precise, talk personnel.

Australia is capable of making 350 under most conditions when batting first. That means they're not going to lose unless they bowl like the Kingoonya third XI. Their batting might fail occasionally on a pitch that's receptive to spin, but that's not a problem they're likely to confront, as England don't have two top-class spinners.

Australia's strength with the bat is built on the solid foundation of Mark Taylor's simple and mightily effective technique. For England to win the Ashes, they'll have to find a way to restrict Mark's machine-like mashing of their attack. If they don't, they're going to be chasing a lot of leather with David Boon, Border, Dean Jones and Steve Waugh capable of building on the starts Taylor and Geoff Marsh provide.

That makes the Taylor–Malcolm confrontation a vital one at the start of the innings. Sharing top billing will be the Gooch–Alderman encounter. If Gooch fails to overcome the mental block he had when facing Alderman in England, then it will make his job as captain twice as difficult. In that case the English media could well hound him, and in so doing become one of Border's greatest allies.

As an opening combination, Gooch and Mike Atherton did well in England last season. However, Atherton is not a natural opener, and if he has problems adjusting to Australian conditions and loses confidence Alderman and company will be circling like vultures. The sight of Atherton having his furniture rearranged for nought in the tour opener must've had Terry licking his lips and flapping his arms.

England desperately need Gooch and Atherton to be successful as it'll make Allan Lamb and Robin Smith, the two South African–born aggressors, a more potent force.

Also eagerly awaiting the outcome of the new-ball battle will be the brilliant but erratic David Gower. He's an ideal second-drop batsman, but he'll probably start the Test series at number three. Gower's career in recent times has been like a trip over an outback road – rough and hazy. If he approaches this series as an opportunity to re-establish himself as a leading batsman, he'll be a big help to Gooch. If, however, he looks upon the tour as a last chance to renew old acquaintances and compare wine vintages, then he'd be better off touring the Hunter Valley.

Despite the disparity, England could well close the gap if the young players mellow quickly. In the end it could be the maturity and quality of Taylor and Alderman that win Australia the prize.

However, none of that means much because, as we hear so

often, 'it's all on paper and they play Test matches on turf'. Sure, but the folding stuff's made out of paper and that's what attracts the punter.

An exciting draw is an integral part of Test cricket. Thankfully, a lot of boring high-scoring draws have been eliminated from the game since the 1990s with the introduction of laws that help make up time lost to bad weather. Aggressive batting fostered by a surfeit of one-day games has also helped lessen the incidence of draws, which is a good thing because results are important in attracting fans to the game. However, the ability of batsmen to survive against the odds, as Ricky Ponting did at Old Trafford in 2005, should never become a lost art. If it wasn't lost it was at least 'whereabouts unknown' as far as England was concerned in the Eighties and Nineties.

[*The Age*, 5 December 1990]

Whatever happened to the real art of English batsmanship – dependability? Is it dead? Or is it just missing, whereabouts unknown?

There's no doubt that these days English batting has a soft underbelly. Meek and mild capitulation has become the norm and England's legendary ability to wriggle out of tight situations to claim an honourable draw has diminished to the point of being on the verge of extinction.

During the Eighties there were unmistakable signs that something was dreadfully wrong with English batting. An undistinguished period of fourteen losses in fifteen Tests against the West

Indies was ample evidence that the art of defending their wicket was dying among English batsmen. To complete the grisly picture, England's batsmen capitulated in 1989 against a rampaging Australian side. The unthinkable had happened to English cricket: Australian batting techniques were far superior to those being produced by the country that invented the game.

'This has to change,' cried Englishmen throughout the land. But judging from what I saw at the Gabba between 23 and 25 November, nothing has changed.

Even when England held the whip-hand with a lead of forty-two on the first innings, the batting still crumbled like a soggy biscuit. They handed Australia a Test victory which should have been much more hard fought than it eventually was. Australia won the match with one decent partnership. By producing normal Test batting for a little over three hours, Mark Taylor and Geoff Marsh enabled Australia to waltz away with the game. That doesn't say a lot for England's batting. And why, when England were crying out for some attacking batting at the Adelaide Oval in the limited-overs match against New Zealand, did Mike Atherton decide the time had come to display a bit of good old English stickability?

Atherton is an enigma. He's young, he has tons of ability, but he's playing like a county cricketer who has been in the game for twenty seasons. He needs a kick up the backside. When he's batting, Mike isn't always on the lookout for runs, or hustling between wickets. He doesn't exude an intent which keeps bowlers on the defensive; instead, he's batting as though he's having a hit in the nets, where runs aren't counted. He makes David Gower look hyperactive on the cricket field and his malaise is symptomatic of what's wrong with English batsmanship. They have too many players who don't display the urgency and desperation required when you're in a fight to the death for your country.

71

What's needed is an infusion of the spirit that used to be inbuilt and came with a fifteen-year warranty in the times of Ken Barrington and John Edrich.

Not only does batting look like a chore to some of the England players, it also looks like a task they don't understand. They don't appear to have any plan in mind when they're at the crease.

The British bulldog spirit does still exist in the England side. Angus Fraser is imbued with it. Jack Russell is a good example of how cross-breeding can be successful. And despite not being, as Fleet Street journalists describe it, 'English through and through', Allan Lamb, Robin Smith and Chris Lewis could show some of their home-grown colleagues a thing or two about fighting for the Union Jack.

How can a system that developed such great attacking batsmen as Denis Compton, Peter May and Ted Dexter and such technically fine players as Barrington, Edrich, Geoff Boycott and Colin Cowdrey suddenly dry up? Any system that hasn't produced a top-class batsman since Gooch, Gatting and Gower needs a major overhaul. The G-men all made their debuts in the 1970s.

For some reason the English county system is churning out technically deficient batsmen. Even worse, it seems to be dulling the spirit of adventure that ignites a flame in a batsman, sending him striding to the crease with every intention to entertain and, on the odd occasion when trouble demands it, endure.

In recent times, England has produced players who have the desire to stay in, but not the technique to accomplish the task. They've also selected players with the adventurous spirit to tear the opposition apart, but without the wherewithal to achieve the feat.

In my playing days, many English county cricketers were of the opinion that Australian batsmanship was of a lesser quality than theirs because we weren't 'tight enough'. That used to get up my nose like an overdose of English mustard.

I can laugh about it now, because there's absolutely no doubt that English batsmanship is the inferior product. In the last seven Ashes Tests they've meekly caved in on at least one occasion in each encounter. Long may their inferiority reign.

When you consider that he finished with an average in excess of fifty it's hard to believe that Steve Waugh's career was ever in decline. However, that was definitely the case when Australia toured the Caribbean and Desert Storm was brewing, in early 1991.

[*The Age*, 9 January 1991]

Whilst the winds of war are blowing across the desert sands in the Middle East, there's also a rustling in the trees at the Waugh household. Steve Waugh has problems with his batting and it could be time for brother Mark to take his Test place.

One of Steve's failings was highlighted by Devon Malcolm at the SCG. Waugh looked very uncomfortable when Malcolm made the ball lift towards his rib-cage. Steve has developed a bad habit of turning his head slightly when the ball is dug in short by a fast bowler, and once his eye is off the ball he's at risk. He's likely to be hit or dismissed. Either way it's painful.

Waugh finishes in an ungainly pose, where he jumps backwards, taking his eyes off the ball, and plays with his gloves and bat thrust forward in front of his body. The Australian selectors must have been disturbed by what they saw at the SCG, especially with a tour of the Caribbean imminent.

In most Tests the West Indies will play four fast bowlers and they'll be banging a few in short at Steve. Because Waugh doesn't hook or pull, he becomes a sitting shot for any quickie who bowls his bouncer straight. To compound his problems, Steve doesn't really cut either – he plays an angled bat, back-foot drive. This shot can bring a few boundaries, some of which go racing across the turf in front of point and look spectacular. But more often than not they result in the ball flying over the slips to the fence. They excite the fans, but they wouldn't instil a lot of confidence in the captain, or suggest a long stay at the crease.

Waugh's deficiencies were really exposed by Pakistan's fine left-armer Wasim Akram. Wasim combined the lifting delivery into the rib-cage area with a deadly in-swinging yorker to destroy the confidence of a player who had demolished the English bowling just a few months earlier.

When Waugh first encountered Wasim he was in blazing form with three undefeated centuries in the space of nine Tests. Since then, his ten Test innings have brought only a meagre return of 166 at the paltry average of a little under seventeen. His unconvincing forty-eight in the first innings at the SCG against England is his highest score in that period.

One of the most damning pieces of evidence against Steve was his innings in the second Test at the MCG. He came into that game straight from a record-breaking double century against Western Australia and should have been in peak form. Instead, he played like a man who was struggling, before he was bowled for nineteen.

The question is what to do with Steve. If the selectors feel he must go to the West Indies, do they leave him in a successful Australian side and hope he'll restore confidence with a big score in the last two Tests against England? Or do they drop him for his brother Mark and hope he'll regain touch in the two Shield matches that remain before the touring party leaves?

Mark is a similar type of player – a dashing stroke-maker who can bowl some useful spells of medium pace. Both are brilliant in the field, with Mark a little better in the slips. As a batsman, Mark is technically more correct because his footwork is superior. However, Steve has a good temperament and is a renowned fighter, whilst Mark is untested at the top level.

I think the time has come to find out how well-equipped Mark is to handle Test-match bowling and, in particular, Malcolm's menacing short deliveries. I think he should play in Adelaide and Perth, whilst Steve returns to Shield cricket to plunder the bowling and build up confidence for the Caribbean.

If Mark succeeds, then it gives Allan Border an option for the number-six spot in the Caribbean. He has Steve, who has already played against the West Indies with some success, or there's Mark, who will at least have had a taste of Test cricket before he takes on a tough tour.

If Mark fails, then the selectors have a decision to make. Do they still take Mark on tour, or do they select Tom Moody, who has a Test century to his name but hasn't been in the best form this season?

And Simon O'Donnell could add to the dilemma by scoring a couple of Shield centuries in the remaining games before the touring side is selected. O'Donnell is a similar style of player to the Waugh brothers, without their accumulation of first-class runs. Nevertheless, Simon is a fierce competitor and an integral part of Australia's successful limited-overs side. I'm sure the selectors would love to have him in the sixteen, but I doubt there's a spot for him if the Waugh twins make the tour.

Whatever happens, it's going to be a nerve-racking time over the next month, with the likelihood of a call to arms in the Middle East and the sound of battle stations in the Waugh zone.

In the decade after Jimmy Higgs' retirement in February 1981 Australia only claimed eighty-two Test wickets with leg spin. Bob Holland (34), Peter Sleep (31) and Trevor Hohns (17) had all retired by February 1991 and the lack of a top-class leg spinner was a major problem in Australian cricket. Shane Warne soon rectified that situation.

[*The Age*, 23 January 1991]

Whilst Greg Matthews has always done things his way, I bet he'd prefer to ply his wares in tandem with another spinner.

In the first two Tests he provided good support for the pace bowlers, but in Sydney, where he needed help from a spinner, none was forthcoming.

Australia's lack of a top-class leg spinner cost them victory at the SCG, and it could well be the missing ingredient at Adelaide Oval. The secret to winning cricket matches in Adelaide is to select an attack with plenty of variety, including two top-class spinners, one of whom should be a leggie.

In recent years it has become fashionable to declare the Adelaide Oval pitch too good. It has become known (unfairly) as a non-result pitch. This situation has arisen because of Australia's lack of top-class spin bowling, especially the leg spin variety. We've been trying to win Tests in Adelaide with attacks relying heavily on pace bowling, and that's a near impossible task. However, it's no good turning up in Adelaide with two spinners, thinking victory is just a formality. The spinners must be able to flight the ball and use a lot of overspin to extract favourable bounce from the pitch.

I believe this has been the reason for the lack of success in Adelaide in the Eighties. Spinners arrive there expecting the ball to turn a lot, and when the pitch is not a replica of the SCG they immediately assume they've been unlucky enough to run into the only 'non turner' seen at the ground in the last decade. Not so.

Two of the most successful bowlers at Adelaide Oval in the last twenty years were the South Australian spin twins Ashley Mallett and Terry Jenner. Both got the ball to bounce quite a bit – Mallet by utilising his height and flight; Jenner with flight and overspin.

The difference between Mallett and Jenner and the spinners who have unsuccessfully tried their hand at Adelaide Oval is flexibility. Not in the fingers, but in the field placings. Ashley and Terry were not so wed to the close-in positions like bat pad and silly mid-off. They were also able to effectively employ catching positions about ten to fifteen metres from the bat in front of the wicket. This allows a bit of freedom to flight the ball and impart overspin, which causes extra bounce and conse- quently any mis-hit carries some distance in the air.

Matthews is one of the few spinners in recent years who is capable of pushing back his catching men and not looking totally innocuous. However, like every other successful spinner, he performs better when there is pressure being applied by another bowler. At the MCG he was a source of frustration for the batsmen, whilst Bruce Reid was attacking and applying the finishing touches at the other end. At the SCG, Matthews troubled the English batsmen with his off spin, but unfortunately for much of the time he wasn't the beneficiary of similar pressure being exerted by his partner. The sooner Australia can find a spin twin for Matthews, the more effective he'll become.

Once again, in Adelaide he is the spin attack. Once again the selectors have been forced, by lack of available talent, to base the attack on speed.

To bolster the pace attack, Craig McDermott has been preferred to Carl Rackemann. McDermott is a more attacking bowler than his Queensland team-mate and he has the added value of being an outswing bowler. If there's any doubt about Terry Alderman being fully fit, I think McDermott will play and Terry will be rested.

The other change to the side is the swapping of the Waugh twins – Mark for Steve. With the tour of the West Indies so close this could place them on a war footing. Steve's poor form along with his problems against pace bowling would have been the main reason for the selectors deciding it was time to look at Mark's Test temperament.

Mark deserves his chance, and if he wants to ensure a long career in the Australian Test side he could do a Greg Matthews. Before each of the last two seasons, Matthews attended the Ashley Mallett–Peter Philpott spin school. With Mark's all-round skill, I think he could be an effective change bowler, both as a medium pacer and as a leggie. With a bit of help and advice from leg spinners like Philpott and Jenner, he could add another string to his bow. Mark's not the answer to Australia's spin bowling problems, but he could at least lift a little of the burden from Greg Matthews' heavily laden shoulders.

It's supposed to be hell having an older brother, or so I'm told, and even worse if he has already made his mark in Test cricket. But no one told Mark Waugh about this in January 1991, at the auspicious beginning of his illustrious career.

[*The Sun-Herald*, 27 January 1991]

It can be hell having a talented younger brother: ask Steve Waugh.

Steve arrived in this world a few minutes ahead of his twin brother, Mark. But Steve had to wait twenty-seven Tests, play forty-two innings and agonise over two scores in the Nineties before he finally made his first century. Mark nonchalantly raced to a brilliant century on his first day in Test cricket, taking a mere 125 balls to reach the magical mark.

Until recently Mark's nickname was Afghanistan because he was the forgotten Waugh. That needs updating, as now he's very much on our minds. As I watched Mark glide gracefully into position and deal with anything on his pads with elegant ease, my mind went back twenty years to my younger brother Greg's Test debut century in Perth.

There are a lot of similarities between Greg and Mark. Both are strong drivers and, because of their upright style, they tend to be talked about as coming from the classical mould. In 1970 Greg came to the wicket with England on top at 5 for 107. Mark arrived at the crease with the Australian score a dismal 4 for 104. Both scored a high percentage of their runs through the on-side.

Coincidentally, Greg had two seasons of county cricket with Somerset before he played Test cricket. Mark has had two seasons with Essex. They both had the advantage of playing their first Test against bowlers they'd faced in county cricket. Both had the backing of a lot of first-class runs before they entered the Test arena, although Mark's 7,501 is inordinately high for an Australian.

The way he played, it actually looked like Mark had already made 7,000 Test runs. He was never in any trouble, and on a day when most of the Australian batsmen seemed unduly subdued, Mark was confidently aggressive at all times. His passage to the fifties was safe and sure but his journey from there to the century was scintillating.

Waugh went onto red alert when Phil Tufnell first took the ball. He sent five scorching shots to the boundary from the left-arm spinner as he skipped down the pitch to engage the enemy. In all, he hit fifteen beautifully timed boundaries as he rolled serenely to his century at a rate of just under a run a ball.

However, Mark Waugh's sense of timing is better than his knowledge of history. It's nearly ninety-five years since Ranjitsinhji scored a century in a session on his debut for England. His masterpiece at Old Trafford in 1896 was the last time that incredible feat was achieved in an Australia–England series.

Mark, hovering only five runs from what would have been an exceptional century between tea and stumps, casually walked off the Adelaide Oval with five overs remaining in the day's play.

Whilst that may be a regret in the years to come, Mark had none as he settled into a celebratory beer in the dressing room at the Adelaide Oval. It had been a completely satisfying first day in Test cricket.

If Mark had had any nerves on the most trying of all days for a Test cricketer, he'd managed to keep them under control. Having waited so long for the opportunity to be tested at the highest level, Mark didn't waste any time in graduating with honours.

Despite all the signs of outward calm and the smile of satisfaction, I guess deep down there had to be one tinge of sadness. As he swallowed his beer and drank in the congratulatory comments of his team-mates, Mark pondered the plight of Steve. 'It's tough,' he said, 'but better one of us in the team than none.' He bats in a similarly pragmatic manner.

I'd had the good fortune to enjoy my younger brother's debut century as a team-mate. It's hard to imagine how difficult it would've been for Steve to balance his emotions as he watched from afar. But once Steve has come to grips with the agony and the ecstasy of his dilemma, I can assure him there's really no better motivation than having a talented sibling. For someone as competitive as Steve it will act as the spur to ensure he does his best at all times. Any time he feels a little weary or disinterested, it will only take a moment to reflect on the embarrassment if he gets left behind by Mark and the adrenalin will start pumping.

Having originally lost his batting spot to Mark and watched as he made the most of his opportunity, Steve will be aware of what that means. The road to a quick return to the Test side has been closed off.

Nevertheless, Steve will be spurred on by the realisation that when he does make his return, he'll be doing it in the company of his younger brother. That would be a special thrill for the Waugh twins. It would also be a great relief to the two people who have the toughest job of the lot – their parents, Beverly and Rodger.

South Africa's return to the international cricket scene was welcome, but not half as much as the advances they have made in human rights.

[*The Age*, 6 February 1991]

The recent announcement by South Africa's President De Klerk that apartheid will be dismantled within the next few months is great news for humanity.

If Mr De Klerk's deeds can match his words it'll also be good news for the game of cricket.

The return of South Africa to International cricket would be a much-needed boost to the game. It would give the International Cricket Council (ICC) eight member countries, and I think a merit-selected side from South Africa would very quickly rank in the top half rather than the bottom half of the draw.

Obviously there is much to be done before South Africa returns to Test and International competition. Nevertheless, their re-entry would create tremendous interest and spark off some exciting rivalries. The first series of matches against the West Indies should be a lively contest.

South Africa's return to competition would also present administrators with a few ticklish problems. For instance, will South Africa regain the power of veto over ICC decisions as one of the founding members, along with Australia and England?

I think not. South Africa's return to the fold would be the perfect opportunity for the ICC to bury this obnoxious power.

What happens to the 'rebel' players who are currently serving bans for having toured South Africa?

I would hope commonsense would prevail and they would be available for selection for their country. It would be an anomaly if the South Africans who participated in those series were able to play International cricket whilst players from other countries had to sit and watch. England, as the most recent tourists to South Africa, would be the team that would benefit most from the lifting of the bans.

Should South Africa's return be marked with a series of matches against a predominately white or black team? A series against either England or Australia would be the most logical. This would require some neat juggling of the itinerary but a series of this nature would create fewer problems, especially if the first South African side selected on merit happened to be an all-white outfit.

Where should the first series with the West Indies be played? It would probably be best played in South Africa so that they would be extending the hand of friendship. This should pave the way for a much more peaceful first tour of the Caribbean by a South African side.

If (and it's a big IF) South Africa has convinced the world that their plans to shelve apartheid are irreversible by the time the 1992 World Cup comes around, it might be appropriate for them to play a couple of exhibition matches as a lead-up to the competition. This would give South Africa good exposure in a slightly more relaxed atmosphere, whilst not putting anybody's nose out of joint.

Their return to International cricket should result in the following World Cup being increased to ten teams, with two non-member nations getting the opportunity to qualify for competition.

Then there's the question of players like Allan Lamb, Robin Smith and Kepler Wessels. They have all played for countries other than their country of birth for reasons beyond their control. What happens to them when South Africa returns to competition?

Again, I hope commonsense would apply. They should be given the opportunity to choose who they play for, but having made their choice they should not be allowed to chop and change.

I should imagine Lamb and Smith would stay with England, but Wessels, who lives in South Africa, would play with them if selected.

And what about Graeme Hick? Should he be given the opportunity to choose to play for South Africa after representing England?

This is a ticklish one. The ideal thing would be to give Hick the choice now before he plays for England. But this is impossible given that the timing of South Africa's return is unknown. Having waited seven years to play for England, Hick would not want to spend a couple more years on the sidelines and risk never playing International cricket if South Africa's planned changes don't eventuate.

On the other hand, Hick may feel that as a native of South Africa he'd be better suited playing with a team of a similar nature.

So, there are many things to be done and many problems to be solved. But the obvious benefits to the game of cricket are the prospect of new faces, exciting talent and good grounds which will provide night cricket in a country other than Australia. All good reasons to eagerly await South Africa's return to International cricket. However, they pale into insignificance when compared with the knowledge that it's come about because a group of people has at last been accorded the most basic of human rights – equality.

The West Indies had dominated world cricket since 1977 and Australia plummeted to the depths in the mid-Eighties. By 1991 the West Indies were still strong but on the wane, and Australia was on the rise.

[*The Sun-Herald*, 10 February 1991]

The Australian team has its best chance for a long time to beat the West Indies and claim the unofficial title of Test match champions.

Two things will decide the fate of the Frank Worrell Trophy: whether the Australians can retain their resolve against a side that is their equal in skill and determination, and whether they can maintain a sense of humour.

The West Indies first test the opposition's courage and then their patience. If either is lost in battle then it's all over; the Windies will steamroll the Australians. If that happens it's time to strike up the steel band and sing, 'I'm glad to say I'm on my way, won't be back for many a day.'

This is where Allan Border will need to watch his coach, Bob Simpson. Bob is prone to adopting a siege mentality if things get rough (as they did in Pakistan in 1988), and if he does so in the Caribbean and the team follows suit it'll be a disaster.

That's when a dose of Merv Hughes' humour will come in handy. Merv will be a great favourite with the locals as they love fast bowlers and characters. If he can keep the crowds laughing and his team-mates loose, Merv will have done a great job for Border.

Not being sidetracked is important because there's no doubt the Australians have the playing skills to compete with the West Indies.

For starters, Border must exploit Australia's superiority in one-day games to build confidence for the Test series. The five-match, one-day International series is Australia's opportunity to gain a psychological advantage by winning convincingly. The one-day series is also a chance for the top section of the batting order (David Boon apart) to rebuild their confidence. They must be capable of blunting the steady stream of top-class pace bowling if Australia is to continually score around 300 an innings in the Tests and remain competitive.

To achieve this target regularly, you need a few good back-foot players. Boon is a fine player of the horizontal bat shots and he leaves for the Caribbean in excellent form. However, I think he would appreciate some help from Border in challenging the West Indies' pace bowlers. It's time for Border to dust off his excellent pull shot and draft it back into service.

How the Australians approach the many short-pitched deliveries they receive will give an insight to their thinking. If they attack when the opportunity presents itself, it will indicate they are confident of victory. If they try to duck and weave all the time, it will suggest that they are waiting for the West Indies to make mistakes. I don't believe Australia can win employing the second method.

The only way to overcome the West Indies' short-pitched attack is to get behind each delivery and score runs off the back foot. This way they are forced to try another approach. Once that is achieved it's a minor victory, and if Viv Richards is the West Indies captain it may turn out to be a major triumph.

Viv is limited in his vision as a captain. He doesn't see much beyond rotating the four fast bowlers and deciding on whether to have three slips and two gullies or four slips and one gully, plus the mandatory bat pad. So, changing the West Indies' mode of attack blunts Viv's effectiveness.

How the Australians bowl to the West Indies is also important. The outswinger troubles the Windies' batsmen because they love to be constantly hitting the ball rather than letting it go. This is where Terry Alderman and Bruce Reid could be a lethal combination.

One thing the Australians shouldn't engage in is a head-to-head short-pitched battle. That would be as smart as the Allied forces tackling Saddam Hussein's army in a ground war without the benefit of air cover. This is where Allan Border must be strong. He shouldn't encourage sporadic short-pitched attacks by placing two men out for the hook shot.

When the Windies' batsmen are on top it's a great temptation for the opposition captain to go on the defensive. However, they strike the ball so powerfully and the grounds in the Caribbean are so small that this ploy is doomed. The best method of defence in this situation would be for Border to go on attacking judiciously.

To beat the Windies you have to be prepared to soak up plenty of punishment. In the recent past the Australians have been a bit overawed by the West Indies. This goes back to Kim Hughes' time, when he complained about Clive Lloyd's team not showing any respect for the Australians.

Well, you have to earn respect. You don't ask for it and you don't beg for it. You win it, by the quality and courage of your play.

By playing that way and retaining a sense of humour, Allan Border's team will be giving themselves the best chance of becoming the Test match champions.

In February 1999 Jagmohan Dalmiya, then the president of the ICC, gathered together a large group of ex-players in Calcutta (now Kolkata) to discuss the means to starting a Test World Championship.

It became obvious that my idea of a qualifying system was not ideal because players who helped get a team to the final might not be playing by the time the match was actually contested. However, it was decided that a period of about sixty-five days was needed to complete a series of matches that would fairly decide which was the champion team. What a pity we still only have a meaningless computer ranking system and an ill-conceived Super Series Test match between Australia and a Rest of the World team (SCG, October 2005) rather than a ding-dong battle every four years to determine the best Test side in the world.

———

[*The Age*, 20 February 1991]

Does Test cricket lack qualifications? I'm not talking about the credentials of the players but a system which locks the teams in combat as they strive to qualify for a higher level of competition.

The series that's about to start in the Caribbean is the perfect example of what is missing. We keep hearing about this series between Australia and the West Indies being an unofficial battle to decide who is the Test match champion. Well, why not have a World Championship that produces an official winner? It would be simple to arrange and would be an exciting adjunct to Test competition. In the process it would also help to liven up regular Test series.

A World Championship of Test cricket could be programmed to fall two years after each World Cup. I'd plan for the first World Championship final to be held in 1994.

The format for qualification would be as follows: Select one match from each series and nominate it as the qualifying Test for the World Championship semi-finals. There are seven Test-playing nations, so this would mean twenty-one qualifying matches – each country playing six. They would be rotated on a home and away basis.

I would allot two points for a first-innings win and six points for an outright in each of these matches. These points would be totally irrelevant to the actual Test series and only relate to qualifying for the World Championship semi-finals.

If a qualifying Test was washed out, then there would be a back-up match as the designated championship qualifier. In the case of a one-off Test it would need to be played to at least a first-innings result to satisfy the qualification demands.

The top four teams on points after their six qualifying matches would play in the semi-finals.

Let us say that the top four in order were the West Indies, Australia, Pakistan and England. The West Indies and Australia would play at home with their opponents being drawn from a hat. If a semi-final wasn't won outright, the highest points-scorer in the qualifying matches would go through to the final.

Let us assume that the West Indies and Australia go through to meet in the final. That would be played to a conclusion (outright), at a ground nominated by the West Indies (as the team that finished with the highest number of points in the qualifying rounds).

The idea of a 'duel to the death' final would appeal to the spectators and would eliminate any thoughts of a draw in the players' minds. This should ensure both sides get stuck into it right from the start, adding a bit of urgency to the match.

The final (and the two semi-finals) should come under the total control of the International Cricket Council. This would be the ideal opportunity for them to use their authority to improve the current poor image of Test cricket.

Things like abysmal over rates and other equally menacing malpractices could be eradicated in these showpiece Tests. If the crowds were given a few exciting World Championship matches, I don't think it would be long before they were demanding something similar in regular Test matches.

The qualifying matches would need to be completed by the end of the 1993–94 season in case England hosted the final (don't laugh, a lot can happen in a couple of years). This would allow them to hold the match in the middle of their season.

That could mean utilising the results of matches that have already been played to determine the qualifiers for the first World Championship. This would be done by drawing from a hat to decide which Tests counted.

These matches would not only provide a Test World Champion every four years, they would also add extra interest to each individual Test series. Imagine a captain trying to work out his needs from the World Championship qualifier whilst balancing this with his requirements for the concurrent Test series. If, for instance, a team that was winning a five-Test series slipped up in trying to gain six points to help qualify for the World Championship, it could throw open the series. It would add an extra dimension to the tactical battle, and increase the competitiveness of Test cricket for the players as well as improving the entertainment for the spectators.

If you think that's overloading the players, ponder on these words of American baseball coach John McNamara: 'Pressure is NOT being in the thick of things, it's not BEING in the thick of things.' That statement could be attributed to any true competitor.

I'm sure the thought of playing off for the World Championship would excite any self-respecting Test cricketer. If it doesn't, then Test matches are doomed to die the death of the dismal draw.

Sabina Park in Kingston, Jamaica, was a Test match cauldron, up there with the MCG and the Bullring (Wanderers) in Johannesburg for electric atmosphere. The group Ten CC's hit 'Dreadlock Holiday' contained the lyrics 'I don't like cricket, oh no, I love it'. In the Jamaican home of reggae this should have been 'I don't like cricket, oh no, I love fast bowling'.

———

[*The Sun-Herald*, 24 February 1991]

On what grounds could Australia hope to claim victory over the West Indies?

Well, I think their best chance is at Sabina Park in Kingston, where the pitch has a history of favouring fast bowlers. Consequently, it's also a ground where the West Indies will expect to win.

It was at Sabina Park last season that England bowled the West Indies out cheaply twice and pulled off a surprise victory. Unfortunately for the Australians, this will make Viv's raiders wary and reduce the chances of them being over-confident.

Sabina Park is the site of the first Test and one-day International on Allan Border's tour. The ground is situated among the narrow streets of the capital city of Jamaica. The spectator facilities are the most modern in the Caribbean as they have recently built a new stand which includes corporate boxes.

Garry (now Sir Garfield) Sobers said that the Sabina Park pitch used to be like the WACA – very fast with plenty of even bounce. Obviously just how he liked it as he made his world-record score of 365 not out there against Pakistan in 1957–58.

It's not like that any more. There's still some pace but the bounce is variable. This is the worst thing a batsman can encounter when facing extreme pace.

The first look at the Sabina Park pitch is off-putting. It's a light-coloured shiny surface, which looks a lot like glass. The first thought is, 'Crikey, there's no grass, it'll break up.' However, the groundsman is adamant that there's grass under the surface; it's just that you can't see it. He knows best as the pitch generally holds together well. As with a lot of the pitches in the Caribbean he floods it and then goes over it with a trowel whilst it's still wet. It could be that a previous groundsman utilising his skills with that tool built the sightboards at the ground. They are two huge concrete walls at each end of the ground which double as sightboards and extra accomodation for the fans. They are the dominant feature as you look around Sabina Park.

In his heyday Wes Hall used to intimidate batsmen by occasionally pushing off the wall to begin his run-up. Not to be outdone, Dennis Lillee did likewise in 1973.

This is not considered unusual behaviour at Sabina Park, where they love the unexpected. In 1973 an announcement was made over the PA: 'Would Mr Weekes please return home immediately as his house has burned down.' Everyone in the ground burst out laughing but no one left. I guess Mr Weekes couldn't do much to save his house, and anyway there was a cricket match in progress.

Because of the short boundaries you can hear everything that is said from over the fence. Much of the conversation is worth hearing, whilst some of it is conducted on a higher level.

Therein lies a potential problem for Australian fast bowlers fielding on the boundary. No, not irate fans threatening with rum bottles: the problem is likely to occur when the quickie is taking a few deep breaths, trying to regain his composure. If it's true, as Peter Tosh sings, that marijuana is the only known cure for glaucoma, then I fear the fast bowlers may turn into eagle-eyed batsmen with a kind of floating footwork. Still, the thought of a new ball every seventy-five overs will quickly bring them back to earth. There seems to be some concern that this playing condition is a subversive Caribbean plot which will put voodoo dolls out of business. Rest assured, you need a new ball regularly.

The outfield at Sabina Park is fairly typical of those in the Caribbean. If it was a carpet you would describe it as threadbare. The ball doesn't retain its shine for long, and, after fifty overs, rubbing it on your creams has the same effect as using sandpaper to remove a stain.

There's another surprise in store at Sabina Park when you arrive for practice. As is the custom, net bowlers are supplied; however, Border shouldn't ask for too many. Better to rely on the fans who come to watch practice. They hang out of trees and sit on the wall and pronounce judgement on the tourists. Their next trick is to casually drop out of the trees or off the wall to field a ball. This is the only invitation they need to show off their bowling skills. Usually they charge in from a long rhythmical run and generate a fair bit of pace. Make that a lot of pace; a lot of pace, that is, for guys wearing thongs or flip-flop sandals.

If one of these 'ground bowlers' claims an Australian victim, especially bowled, all his mates fall out of the trees laughing. Soon there are more young hopefuls infiltrating the net session. It's no wonder they have a pace-bowling production line in the Caribbean.

All this makes for an interesting and varied practice session. It's also a damned good way to prepare for what lies ahead at Sabina Park.

In 1979 I was a player on the World Series Cricket tour of the Caribbean and also writing for *The Age* in Melbourne. When my opening paragraph referred to the riot at the Bourda cricket ground the telex machine sending my copy to Melbourne spluttered to a grinding halt.

[*The Age*, 20 March 1991]

As I was saying twelve years ago, before I was rudely interrupted by a telex operator, Guyana is the site of the worst cricket riot I've ever seen.

It was 1979, just a couple of months after the Jonestown mass suicides, and the local government officials were a bit touchy about adverse publicity. Hence my copy never made it to *The Age*. However, if I had my problems then, I think the West Indies cricket team has an equally big headache now.

The four-pronged pace attack is faltering. I'm not sure the West Indies hierarchy will acknowledge it; nevertheless, it's a fact. Australia could well confirm it during this series, but the return of Ian Bishop will ensure the policy is continued against England's more timid batting. Whatever the results, the halcyon days are over.

Will the Windies take remedial action? Not for some time, I fancy.

For starters, I think Viv Richards is comfortable with a pace attack. But even when Viv retires his successor may not have any choice, because spin bowling is largely scoffed at in the Caribbean. Consequently, not much thought is given to a balanced attack. Instead they continue to rely on Curtly Ambrose and Malcolm Marshall: a good young fast bowler, and an aging but shrewd customer. Nothing wrong with that combination, but they are followed by Patrick Patterson and Courtney Walsh: a pure pace bowler who relies on intimidation, and a fading work-horse who was more productive when the supporting cast was stronger.

The Australians have shown that these two lack imagination in one-day matches. If the same shortcomings are evident in the Test series they're in trouble, but I doubt it will cause a change in attitude.

The West Indies are falling for the same trap that duped the rest of the cricketing world when Clive Lloyd controlled a team that was a class above everyone else. Lloyd had on call Andy Roberts, Michael Holding and Joel Garner, three great fast bowlers, and a fourth good one in Colin Croft. When Andy retired to his fishing fleet in Antigua, he was replaced by Malcolm Marshall. Then when Croft took a sabbatical in South Africa, bowlers like Wayne Daniel fitted into the side. The status quo was retained.

With such an array of firepower the Windies blitzed the opposition on any type of pitch. Suddenly most of the cricket world equated victory with a pace attack – 'Let's nuke the bastards' – to the point that even India, previously the Fisherman's Bend of spin bowling production lines, began to search the hills for men who could bowl fast. Not a policy which would win the Professor De Bono lateral thinking award.

If anything, India should have been trying to produce more top-class spinners. This way they could have taken advantage of the fact that even the best batsmen were vulnerable to good tweakers because they faced so few of them. The opportunity to make a spin-killing went begging, but it still exists.

Whilst the rest of the world suffered from pace mania, Pakistan went about building up a well-balanced attack. It's not luck that this coincided with their most successful period in International cricket.

On the other hand, Australia fiddled whilst the ACB officials burned over the lack of success. Then the penny dropped and the selectors concentrated on fielding a balanced attack. However, Australia still lacks a top-class spinner.

At least Australia is now doing something about trying to prepare young spin bowlers for International cricket. The West Indies have concentrated on pace to the detriment of all other styles. They'll pay for their stubborn short-sightedness in the near future.

They've overlooked the fact that apart from being fast, Roberts, Holding, Garner and Marshall all had the ability to move the ball. They also used their noggin to outwit batsmen and were talented enough to perform under all conditions.

It's rare to have so many pace bowlers of that calibre for such a long period. Now there are signs that not only is the deluxe model out of production, but also the standard version is not as prolific. The Windies haven't paid heed to the warning signs and they'll soon suffer.

It took Allan Border a long time to realise the advantages of a balanced attack. He kept waiting for a battery of pace bowlers to walk into his dressing room and did little to mould the bowlers he had into a competent attack for International cricket. Realisation of his mistake has partly accounted for his improvement as a Test captain.

Now Border has the opportunity, through his strong batting

line-up, to punish the West Indies for their lack of forethought. If it happens in the second Test don't be surprised if you don't hear about it for some time – bad news doesn't travel fast from Guyana.

In 1991 the Waugh twins began a long and successful association in the Test arena, and in the process created history.

———

[*The Age*, 10 April 1991]

As Steve Waugh walked out to join his brother, Mark, for the first time in a Test, they created history by becoming the first twins to do so. However, Mark had gone to dangerous lengths to bat with his brother at Queen's Park Oval. You see, Steve came in at the fall of Allan Border's wicket, and the captain had been run out by Mark.

The only other set of Australian brothers to play together in a Test against the West Indies was Greg Chappell and yours truly. As Greg witnessed this bit of history he remarked, 'If these two have an understanding like the previous pair, then there'll be another run-out shortly.'

Greg might have had occasional problems with his calling but there was nothing wrong with his memory.

Our most celebrated mix-up was against the West Indies in 1975–76. It was the last ball of the day at the Adelaide Oval and Greg smacked one straight to Viv Richards at mid-on and took off for the run. I don't know why I agreed to the single because it was so obvious I was going to be run out that I had time to curse him (not for the last time that night) as we crossed.

Back in the dressing room there was stunned silence until I

exploded. Then the argument reached such a dangerous level that Rod Marsh had to step in and say, 'Listen, you two silly bludgers, in case you've forgotten you're on the same side.'

There were no such problems for the Waugh twins. They made a fifty-eight-run partnership and the running between wickets went smoothly.

They are different players and differ greatly in personality. Steve has the rather grim exterior of a man who has had to work hard for everything he's gained. Mark has more of the happy-go-lucky outlook of a punter to whom things come easily.

In actual fact, their Test careers took exactly the opposite paths. Steve gained his colours quickly and Mark had to wait and work very hard to gain recognition. Mark scored more than 7,000 first-class runs before he played a Test – not many players are forced to be that patient to gain International honours.

Nevertheless, I think the wait has been beneficial for Mark. He now has by far the better footwork and is at ease against Test bowling, whilst Steve, apart from a brief period in 1989 when he pulverised the English attack, has been troubled by International bowlers – this despite his natural timing and ability to score quickly.

Steve also appears to have been affected by a few dodgy decisions in the early part of his career. He seems to feel he's always on the wrong end of the umpire's judgement. When you start to think like that as a batsman, life can be a slippery dip.

If he's still thinking like a man who is hard-done-by, he'll be wondering about the vagaries of the game on the very day he helped create another bit of its history.

Not long after they joined forces, Mark was stranded by a well-flighted delivery from Carl Hooper. But Jeff Dujon gave a good impression of a keeper who has spent most of his career handling pace bowlers. He missed the ball by a wide margin and the stumping chance went begging.

Shortly afterwards Mark appeared to get a faint edge to the hardworking Courtney Walsh, and Dujon, standing in more familiar territory, intercepted the ball. However, despite a vociferous appeal, umpire Archer ruled in favour of the batsman. Mark had given the tell-tale hint of looking over his shoulder, albeit a fleeting glance, and then jerked his head around to get a better view of the umpire's reaction.

Just a few minutes later Steve went for an extravagant, firm-footed drive and edged the same bowler to Dujon. Like a man resigned to his fate, he saved Archer from any further embarrassment by tucking his bat under his arm and heading for the pavilion.

Too often Steve plays with his feet planted and hopes his bat will do the work of a magic wand. In contrast, Mark has flowing footwork that allows him to glide into the shot and caress it in any direction that catches his fancy.

At Test level the boot is now on the other foot. Things are easier for Mark, and Steve has a real battle on his hands.

I think Steve is fortunate to be playing in this match, and the selection blunder will be repeated if they pick the same side for Barbados. Steve probably has no desire and certainly has no chance of ousting his brother from the Test team. That means he has to outplay one of the other batsmen if he hopes to continue playing in the same team as Mark. At the moment that is not a viable proposition.

So Steve is finding out how tough life is for a struggling Test cricketer. If he doesn't do something to improve his footwork, he could also discover that history can be fleeting.

Allan Border was never able to beat the West Indies in a series. It was a bad combination; pairing Bob Simpson, a conservative, with Border, a pessimist, in a series which was only going to be won by Australia attacking a strong opponent.

[*The Age*, 24 April 1991]

Unless Australia's shaky batting makes a remarkable recovery, Allan Border's team is about to lose a series it could so easily have won. Why?

You don't need a Royal Commission to find the reason. Australia's thinking, which was so positive in the recent series against England, has changed into reverse gear when confronted by the powerful West Indies combination.

Uncertainty has replaced supreme confidence. Australia's batting, which was all-conquering against England in 1989, has slipped alarmingly in less than two years. There have been two costly collapses on this tour of the Caribbean: the second innings at the Bourda ground and the first dig in this (Barbados) current match.

This should be a punishable offence, especially when you consider that the Australian bowlers have initiated a number of collapses. The most recent one should have been rewarded with a victory.

Australia's batting slide has been so pronounced that the selectors have foolishly tried to correct the problem by depleting the bowling attack. Strange logic: the batsmen have let us down, so punish the bowlers.

The root of the problem can be traced back to the lack of positive thinking at the top. Just a second whilst I grab a pencil and a piece of tracing paper.

The first mistakes were made when Terry Alderman and Bruce Reid arrived in the Caribbean a little out of sorts. Sufficient time wasn't allotted to sort out their problems and reassure them their talents were desperately needed. The reason? The early success of Mike Whitney fooled the selectors into believing that he could do Reid's job. In Alderman's case his bowling was judged by Bob Simpson to have deteriorated to the point where he wasn't the same bowler he had been in England.

Then the anti–Greg Matthews feeling resurfaced. Greg hadn't bowled well since the MCG Test, where he combined beautifully with Reid to destroy England. In the meantime, however, he had contributed greatly with the bat. In his best form, his presence gave Australia batting depth and bowling variety. This was just what the team needed to guard against disintegration of the tail and predictability in attack.

He needed encouragement, but instead of working hard with Matthews to sort out his bowling problems (which mainly revolved around his thinking), the team leaders discarded him like a dirty syringe. Ironically, he hasn't bowled a ball in conflict, despite his last spell in Test cricket being the best he's bowled, since that day at the MCG.

Steve Waugh was rushed into the side to replace Matthews. Notwithstanding he was in poor batting form, his bowling skills have been eroded since his back problems and his inclusion grossly unbalanced the side.

Desperate men often make poor judgements, and the Australian hierarchy was submerged in negative thoughts. These doubts have permeated the batting. The Australian batsmen have been tentative in the Tests. They seem to have forgotten that when they attacked those same bowlers in the limited-overs series the West Indies fell apart at the seams and conceded runs easily. It's also meant that Viv Richards' shaky captaincy hasn't been put under any pressure.

There has been no move at the top to rectify this situation. In fact the opposite has happened. By picking seven batsmen they have admitted the opposition has them worried.

One of the great ironies of the tour has been the adherence to English thoughts on playing the West Indies. This is despite the fact that Australia has thrashed the old enemy seven–nil in the last eleven Tests. Suddenly England's one victory last season in the Caribbean qualifies them as experts on how to beat the West Indies. The fact that they subsequently lost the opportunity to go two up by playing conservatively has been conveniently over-looked.

In other words, the planning and thinking on this tour has been sadly astray and distinctly negative.

I've made it abundantly clear I don't agree with Australia having a coach. However, if the team is to have one foisted upon them, then his most important task is to ensure the rigours of constant toil don't wear the captain down to the point where his approach isn't positive. Simpson has failed miserably in that task in this series.

In tracing the history of the Australian team in the Caribbean, a picture of favouritism rather than selection on merit emerges. Unfortunately, Allan Border hasn't stamped out this insidious behaviour.

If Allan Border's team loses this series it will be because of a safety-first approach. It will also be the third time an Australian side has lost in the Caribbean, and Bob Simpson has been involved in the hierarchy of each of those sides.

There was a bit of history behind Viv Richards' outburst claiming 'Bob Simpson is not our cup of tea.' He said this in a press conference in 1991, but many in the Caribbean felt he'd been waiting for the right opportunity since Simpson led an Australian team, weakened by WSC defections, to the Island countries in 1977–78. The West Indies side in that series contained WSC players for the first two Tests and Simpson's comments in those lopsided contests left a sour taste in Richards' mouth.

———

[*The Sun-Herald*, 28 April 1991]

Viv Richards' captaincy is a mass of contradictions, but his thoughts on Australian coach, Bob Simpson, were straight to the point.

Simpson said he was 'amazed and shocked by this extraordinary outburst.' I wasn't.

Viv has a lot of pride in his captaincy and he would have been deeply wounded to hear his team's batting described as 'potentially fragile' by the coach of a seven-man batting side that had just collapsed twice, thus comprehensively losing the series.

In some quarters Viv's comments are being likened to his outburst over an English pressman last season. That's ludicrous. It actually reminded me of a scene I saw at school where, as a result of kid B constantly and surreptitiously annoying kid A, kid A finally turned and landed a perfect right cross on kid B's nose. At school, kid A was always punished and kid B got off scot-free.

I believe the Viv Richards' episode is now a matter of 'case closed'.

But back to Viv's captaincy. It's lethargic and vibrant, boring and inspired, illogical then totally ignoring reason, ultra-defensive and cautious, dependent on pace, but spiced with spin.

In the two West Indies Test victories in this series, Viv has displayed all of those characteristics.

In Australia's second innings at the Bourda ground he worked assiduously, in conjunction with his bowlers, to rout the top-order batting. He was radiating energy, absolutely vibrant. The next day, with just the mopping-up exercise to complete, he might as well have been playing in a beach cricket match. He was seemingly uninterested in proceedings. Lethargic.

He often allows his tail-enders to push, prod and poke and generally bring the game to a shuddering halt when the situation demands a 'hit out or get out' approach. Yet, when he comes to the crease, even with his team in deep trouble, Viv will play scintillating shots that serve as a sharp reminder that he was once THE Master Blaster.

At the Bourda ground it was Curtly Ambrose and Malcolm Marshall who set up the Windies' victory. Then, with the tail-enders at his mercy, Viv tossed the ball to Patrick Patterson and Courtney Walsh. Where were Ambrose and Marshall? Where was the logic?

It's bewildering but successful. Viv has never lost a series as West Indies captain. As he's likely to finish his Test career after the upcoming tour of England, he'll retire undefeated. No one can ask any more of a captain.

Viv has depended on pace throughout his reign. However, at

Kensington Oval, as Mark Taylor and Dean Jones threatened to save Australia's bacon on the final day, he turned to the gentle spin of Carl Hooper to break their grip. It worked. Jones played an exaggerated forward-defensive shot to a Hooper off-break and, lo and behold, the ball rolled back onto the stumps. With the breakthrough achieved and the new ball due, it appeared obvious Viv would bring on Ambrose and Patterson to blast through the struggling middle order. Wrong. Viv retained Hooper and, hallelujah, he bowled Mark Waugh, the only Australian who is batting anywhere near his best in that section of the order.

It's weird but it works.

When you stop and think about Richards' captaincy it does have a thread. Loyalty. He sticks by his players through thick and thin and even in the anorexic times. That's the big difference between Viv's leadership and that of Allan Border's on this tour.

At various times Viv has had to fight hard at the selection table to retain Gordon Greenidge, Carl Hooper and Courtney Walsh. At Kensington Oval, Gordon made a double ton, Courtney smashed through the tail-enders in both innings and Hooper took two vital wickets. Viv was rewarded with a West Indies victory.

On the contrary, Bruce Reid, who was Border's main attacking weapon against England only a couple of months back, was tossed aside like yesterday's newspaper in the early part of the tour. Greg Matthews has suffered the same treatment since Bourda, and Terry Alderman might just as well have left his creams at home and brought only shorts, suntan lotion and swimming togs.

Where Australian selection had been consistent and positive in recent seasons, suddenly on this tour it smacked of non-merit choices and was based on safety-first tactics.

This approach obviously hasn't worked.

Consequently, Viv returns triumphant to his kingdom of

Antigua, where the crowd at the St John's Recreation Ground will pay homage in one long celebration. The Australians will feel as out of place as a group of meat eaters at a Rastafarian party.

Which only confirms that the art of captaincy is full of contradictions, and the one sure way to be a success is to win.

The West Indies weren't always the easy beats they've become in the last few series. In 1991 Australia had a big chance to turn the tables on a team that had tortured and tormented them for at least a decade. In the end, as the next two columns show, Australia didn't beat the West Indies because they weren't as brave as they were in England in 1989.

———

[*The Age*, 1 May 1991]

By batting positively and well in the fifth Test, the Australians have proved that the cautious approach they adopted in the first four matches was ill-advised. They then consolidated their position by dismissing the West Indies cheaply with a balanced attack. This showed the futility of the selections in the third and fourth Tests.

So why did Australia wait until the series was all over to get their act together?

I think a conversation I had with Allan Border before the fifth Test provides a clue. In reply to a question on the Australians' needing to win the final Test for pride and to reduce the losing margin, Allan said, 'I came here hoping to win a Test. If we'd won the series that would have been great, but my aim was to win a Test.'

That over-cautious approach by the Australians was based on Border being intimidated by the West Indies' reputation. He made the mistake of playing Viv Richards' men based on what they'd done in the past rather than what they are capable of at present.

For example if, as Bob Simpson said, 'the West Indies' batting borders on fragile', why did Australia pick seven batsmen in the vital fourth Test? If he was confident Australia's batting was superior then they should have chosen four bowlers and gone for broke to level the series at Kensington Oval.

Test matches are won by brave and aggressive deeds on the field, not with statements at press conferences. The West Indies won the series by virtue of a magnificent innings from Richie Richardson at the Bourda ground and a gutsy bowling performance at Kensington Oval in the first innings. It's worth noting that both those efforts came when the momentum was with Australia.

If Australia had produced a batting performance to match Richardson's, or Mark Waugh's or Mark Taylor's in Antigua, then they would have won the Test at Kensington. But when it mattered, Australia didn't grab the initiative.

Talk is easy, but dominating a good Test attack is difficult. However, it is possible if a player is talented and he's prepared to attack when the time comes for positive action. The Australian team has the talent, but unfortunately its mental approach was astray when it counted.

In the more relaxed atmosphere of the final Test at Antigua they have played the way they should have in the middle stages of the tour, when it all fell apart.

The Australian batsmen will say that the pitch at St John's Recreation Ground was better for stroke play than the others. They are right.

The hierarchy will whisper privately of bad umpiring decisions that hampered the team. There have been incorrect decisions, but the umpiring hasn't been biased.

Against that, a top-class side will find it in their hearts to be aggressive when the game is on the line. They do so because they are aware of the value of a well-timed counterattack, rather than thinking of the consequences of it failing.

The best sides dig deep when adversity occurs. On this tour Australia was bluffed by the West Indies and suspicious of the umpiring, and this has affected their thinking.

On the tour of England in 1989, where the same hierarchy presided, the side played positively and won convincingly. They are comfortable playing against England and under the control of their umpires. This is in direct contrast to their performance in Pakistan in 1988–89, when they lost because they were suspicious of the pitch and the umpires in the first Test.

The Pakistan team is a good example of what is required to play well against the Windies. They've performed better than any other country against the West Indies in recent times. That's because of Imran Khan's leadership. He loves playing against the Windies and he wants desperately to beat them. The challenge appeals to his competitive nature. He's been the one captain who hasn't been intimidated into playing tentatively against Viv's marauders.

Clive Lloyd said the other night, 'A lot of batsmen are prepared to have an ordinary series against the West Indies. They feel they can make up for it against the other countries.'

There are two choices open to players when they come up against the Windies. They either relish the challenge, the way Imran does, or they approach the series as though they are walking through a minefield. Unfortunately the Australian team chose to sit back and wait when the situation cried out for it to strike first.

Any victory is sweet, but an Australian win at St John's will only serve to confirm the error of their earlier ways. This is one case where Australia should have learnt from their success, not their mistakes.

[*The Sun-Herald*, 5 May 1991]

It was a series that promised a lot. A skirmish for the world Test crown with a backdrop of swaying palms in the Caribbean. The champions with a strong pace attack. The challengers boasting a long batting line-up.

In this case the West Indies' good bowling beat Australia's tentative batting. When the Australians finally discarded the cloak of caution at the St John's Recreation Ground they beat the West Indies convincingly. In doing so they discovered their tactics in Guyana and Barbados were ill-advised.

The victory in Antigua should provide the blueprint for future tilts with the Windies. However, I'm not sure this will happen if we still have Allan Border and Bob Simpson dictating policy. Recognising crucial moments in a Test series is more important than knowing when to change the bowlers and move the fieldsmen, especially if it's combined with an instinct for then taking the option designed to grab the upper hand.

In this series, Border and Simpson displayed a lack of appreciation for the psychological side of Test cricket. I believe you should only have one man running a cricket team: the captain. However, if you are going to make the mistake of sharing responsibility by bringing in a coach, why compound the error by putting two conservative thinkers together?

In marriage, opposites attract. In this case they would at least bring a balance to the tactical planning.

Before the tour, I wrote that having beaten England and

Pakistan, Australia now has to prove they can beat a team that is their equal in skill and resolve. In the end the Windies were superior purely because they took the initiative when the game was on the line.

The confrontation reached a critical point before the second Test at Bourda. This was when Border needed an offsider to urge him to press on positively to keep the momentum in Australia's corner. Unfortunately this didn't happen.

I will always think of the 1991 tour of the Caribbean as a series of missed opportunities for Australia. Border's men had their chances, but when the time came they didn't have the nerve to reach out and grab for victory. Instead, they preferred to wait for it to fall into their laps.

My enduring memory will be the innings Richie Richardson played in the second Test. When Australia's batsmen failed to consolidate the momentum built up with the convincing victory in the limited-overs series, he came out, bat blazing, and took the initiative for the West Indies. It was an innings chock-full of flashing square drives, daring hook shots and delicate cuts. It was brilliant and was made more so because of the courage involved in playing such an aggressive innings at a time when a failure by Richardson could have spelt disaster for his team.

Surely, I thought, this was the innings that would show the Australians the way forward? Now they would revert to a more aggressive approach. But, horror of horrors, conservatism reigned and they went even further into their shell, overloading the team with batsmen, who then unloaded their wickets.

Kensington Oval was the killer. The Australian bowlers performed brilliantly to skittle the opposition cheaply. But the West Indies' attack, alerted to Australia's fragile state of mind by the selection of seven batsmen, bowled with great hostility to make the Frank Worrell Trophy safe for another couple of years.

Nevertheless, if you use Allan Border as a yardstick the Australians will go home happy. Border said his aim was to win a Test. He won a Test, but with a bit more emphasis on the positive he could have won the series.

Just look what happened in Antigua. Australia selected a balanced attack. Then they won the toss and batted positively, making a good score quickly. As they had at Kensington the bowlers did their job, backed by fielding that was always inspirational and at times sensational. This produced a convincing win. It's a victory which should please the Australians, but I hope it didn't satisfy them. If it did, then they don't understand the reason for playing a five-Test series. The idea is to win one Test all right – one more than your opponent.

Border won't get many more chances to battle for the title of world Test champion. He may get one more, and if he does I hope he has learnt from the mistakes he made on this tour of the Caribbean.

If he doesn't get another crack, all he'll have is a lot of pleasant memories of swaying palms, cool blue waters and refreshing pina coladas. However, they won't mix so well with a recurring nightmare of what might have been with a more positive approach.

Cricket grounds in the Caribbean are full of characters, and their sense of humour is legendary, as I found out on Australia's 1990–91 tour.

[*Laugh on Us*, Swan Publishing, 1991]

Think of the Caribbean and it conjures up a vision of swaying palms, blue skies and crystal-clear waters, which provide welcome relief from the constant heat.

Not true. Well, not in Trinidad in 1991. During the third Test between the West Indies and Australia, the rain in Port of Spain fell mainly at Queen's Park Oval.

Rain is the bane of a cricketer's life, but what about the poor spectator who has to sit around and watch the rain tumble down, or witness a cricket match ruined by inclement weather?

With the Test meandering to a draw in between stoppages for rain, I decided to see what the fans did in the Caribbean to keep themselves entertained when the cricket was less than riveting. This exercise promised to be fun, as I'd noticed a noisy but interesting group of characters in the Learie Constantine stand.

First up there was 'Big Tony', a giant of a man who had a voice like rolling thunder. He also had a ready smile, a sharp wit and a mind which harboured enough cricket information to earn him a fortune on *Sale of the Century*. Every time I walked up or down the stairs to the commentary box, Big Tony informed me that my fellow cricket caller Michael Holding 'is your father'.

Eventually I queried him: 'How do you work that out, Tony?'

'He get you, Greg 'n' Trevor out in de one innings at Queen's Park in '79,' he said in his Trinidadian lilt, 'dat make him your father.'

The Constantine stand erupted. Out in the middle, the players must have wondered what all the commotion was about. For the last hour, Mark Taylor and David Boon had been giving their impression of a Chris 'The Tortoise' Tavare innings, as they took the opportunity to get some centre wicket practice.

My next excursion to the Learie Constantine stand brought me in contact with Gabriel Belfon. He's better known to his mates in that section as 'Blue Food' the conch-shell trumpeter.

Blue food is a Caribbean term for fast food, and the conch is a ten- to twelve-inch-long shell from carnivorous snails. Belfon has a different sound on his conch shell for almost everything that happens on the field, and each time he trumpets his 'commentary' he's answered by a lady with a conch shell in another part of Queen's Park Oval. By listening to their expert commentary, a blind man could spend a day at the ground and know exactly what happened.

As I finished an interview with Blue Food, another member of the Constantine group came over to me with a bottle. He wasn't trying to do me any harm – well, not with the object but maybe with its contents.

'Have a bloody drink,' he yelled, dropping quickly into the Australian vernacular.

I tried to explain that I don't drink whilst I'm working. However, equating cricket with work to a Trinidadian is like telling an alcoholic a soft drink will quench his thirst. 'Have a bloody drink,' he repeated.

I figured this guy was going to be as hard to despatch as a

'Deadly' Derek Underwood delivery, so I muttered, 'If you insist. What is it?'

With that, a smile came over his face and he tilted his head back and roared, 'Fibreglass.' This brought guffaws from his mates who had gathered round.

I made out to take a quick swig from the bottle, putting on what I thought was a good show. I wiped my lips and said, 'Ah, that's great.'

'Drink the bloody stuff,' he ordered, and made a quick hand gesture which suggested it was meant to be downed in a hurry.

Resigned to my fate, I closed my eyes and swallowed. In retrospect I should have closed my mouth and kept my eyes wide open.

It was horrible. It burned the whole way down and kept on burning – for the next hour. Even the beer chaser, which I accepted in the naïve hope that it would put the fire out, tasted bad. When a beer doesn't fix the problem, you know you're in trouble.

I thanked the guy for his generous hospitality and quickly headed for the safety of the commentary box. But I wasn't quick enough. With the timing of a Mark Waugh on-drive, Big Tony caught me as I lurched past brother Greg on the stairs. He called out, 'Which one of you ordered Trevor to bowl underarm?'

'It was him,' said Greg with a huge grin on his face as he pointed at my rum-riddled form. Despite walking doubled over in agony because of the burning in my belly, a hundred people in the Constantine stand now believed I was the one who ordered the underarm.

Meanwhile, out in the middle, another pair of brothers had problems not of their own making.

Mark and Steve Waugh had just made history by becoming the first twins to play together in a Test match. But even this momentous event brought only a ripple of applause from the fans in the

Constantine stand. Having given up hope of witnessing any exciting cricket, the Constantine characters were now heavily involved in their own game – a game of five-card brag.

So involved were they in their card game that even the advent of another character, 'Nutslanding', with his constant banter, couldn't disturb their concentration. Still, the perambulating peanut-seller soon found other fans willing to take the bait, if not a bag of his nuts. When one guy had the temerity to compare the nattering nutsman with his rival, Jumbo, he was quick to take umbrage. 'I a better nutsman than Jumbo,' he explained, 'dere are Jumbos crashin' all over de world, while I still landing.'

The card players laughed, but still didn't shift their attention from their game to the one in the middle.

Just then, Mark Waugh danced down the track intent on dealing with part-time off spinner Carl Hooper. Mark missed by the proverbial mile and looked back in time to see the ball pass Jeff Dujon's gloves by about the same margin and wend its way to the boundary.

At that precise moment the brag dealer, with his back to the game, said, 'Who blind?'

Without appearing to notice what had happened out in the middle, Big Tony casually picked up his cards and answered, 'Dujon. He just missed stumping Mark Waugh.'

In the late Eighties and early Nineties the administrators made a mess of the legislation on bouncers, but fortunately the ludicrous limitation didn't last long. However, the ICC did rectify the problem of too many drawn Tests by sensibly ensuring time that was lost to bad weather was ostensibly made up during the game. Unfortunately they have not built on that good work by cracking down on the disgracefully slow over rates. They have also contributed to the increased incidence of one-sided and quick-finishing matches by granting one sub-standard team (Bangladesh) Test status and allowing another (Zimbabwe) to retain theirs, when it was obvious they weren't up to the mark.

———

[*The Age*, 19 July 1991]

I f Test cricket is killed off, it'll be an inside job.

The International Cricket Council (ICC), the administrators who are supposedly appointed to protect the interests of the game, will be guilty of the murder. The weapon they use is a slow poison administered in the form of lethal doses of lunatic legislation.

With the victim ailing, they could well have dispensed the fatal dose with their mind-boggling effort on short-pitched bowling. From 1 October this year only one bouncer per batsman per over will be allowed in Test cricket.

Just in case that doesn't do the trick, they have defined a bouncer as a ball that passes above the shoulder of a batsman standing upright. If a bowler transgresses he'll be no-balled on the first two occasions in an over and the third time he's out of the attack for the rest of the innings.

This legislation will outlaw good deliveries and make sightings of the hook shot as rare as those of the Tasmanian tiger. It will increase the incidence of that mindless tactic – bowling short of a length to a ring field. And finally, it'll create enormous problems for the umpires, especially if a batsman is caught off a bouncer that is deemed a no-ball.

What a pity the West Indies aren't playing a Test at the WACA ground in early October. With Curtly Ambrose, Ian Bishop and Courtney Walsh bowling fast on a bouncy pitch they could all be ordered out of the attack in the first half-dozen overs and the game reduced to a farce.

It will only be a comedy of this magnitude that will save us from the tragedy that lies ahead.

At a time when followers of Test cricket are crying out for fewer draws and more activity, the administrators have produced a piece of legislation which is totally in favour of batsmen. This will result in more big first-innings scores, which (unless they are amassed quickly) are the prime cause of drawn games.

The most damaging aspect of a bouncer is not necessarily the delivery itself, but the uncertainty it creates in a batsman's mind. If he's unsure whether the bouncer is going to be 'this one, the next one or the one after', it can derail his train of thought and leave him vulnerable to an assortment of other deliveries.

Knowing only one bouncer an over is permissible takes a lot of the anxiety out of batting and reduces a fast bowler's potency by about fifty per cent. The uncertainty placed in the mind of England's Graeme Hick by the West Indies' pacemen is the reason he's currently a struggling Test player when he appeared to be a world-beater at county level.

Batting at the top level should always be a test of skill, intelligence and courage. By markedly decreasing the need for the latter, you dilute the first two and diminish the spectacle.

Nevertheless, the introduction of this ludicrous law and needless definition is consistent with the ICC's lacklustre performance over the years. First, there was the introduction of the front-foot no-ball law. Then they decided the punishment for disgracefully slow over rates was to introduce overtime. Now this. In each case the corrective action creates more boredom than the perceived crime.

A properly punitive scheme which greatly improves over rates and the strict enforcement of the current law on intimidatory bowling would have done a lot to reduce any surplus bouncers. That, in conjunction with a crackdown on deliveries that pass way over the batsman's head, and some forceful backing for the umpires from the administrators, would have put Test cricket well on the road to recovery.

These facets of cricket are important because they all involve the balance between bat and ball. If the scales are tentatively balanced between the two, then a competitive match is guaranteed.

Because of unrealistically slow over rates, the balance has recently been far too much in favour of the fast bowler. At least that meant lower scores and the chance of a result. This latest monstrosity tips the scales to the opposite extreme in favouring batsmen, and greatly increases the chances of a draw under normal Test match conditions.

Test cricket is ailing because the ICC is so immersed in political manoeuvring that it is totally incapable of administrating solely on the basis of what is in the best interests of cricket.

The ICC should be put to rest immediately and replaced by a

ruling body that a) is accountable for its actions and b) rules on a global rather than self-interest basis, with the overriding factor being the good of the game.

That is the only antidote to the poison that has been administered, and the only way the game is going to survive and thrive in the next century.

Allan Border passed Sunil Gavaskar's run-aggregate record of 10,122 on 26 February 1993, in the first innings of the first Test at Christchurch.

[*Today UK*, February 1993]

A llan Border became only the second man to reach ten thousand Test runs, by simply pushing a single at the SCG. It was no different when he finally passed India's Sunil Gavaskar to become the highest scorer in Test history. No frills, no flamboyance, just the little Aussie battler doing his job.

Allan Robert Border has always been a 'never mind the quality, look at the aggregate' player. That doesn't mean there's no quality to his batting, just that it runs a distant second to making runs as far as Allan's concerned.

The quality of Border's batting is in his grit and determination, his one-two punch, the cut and pull shots, and his remarkably straight bat when he drives through the off-side. Even at the age of thirty-seven he's still the hardest man in Test cricket to dismiss when his team is in trouble.

One of the endearing qualities about Border is his love for playing cricket. He tries his hardest no matter what the standard or the situation in the match.

There's a story that sums up Border's approach to cricket. After the Australians had a resounding victory in the first Test on the 1989 tour, the team embarked on an equally noisy celebration. Border wasn't playing in the following day's match against Lancashire at Old Trafford, but he went to the ground to watch proceedings. He lasted no longer than it took for a tardy David Boon to spill a simple chance. 'It was pitiful to see,' said the skipper. 'I couldn't bear to watch any more.'

Border expects the best all the time, and gives his best under all circumstances. That's why it was so hard for him in the early days of his captaincy when Australia kept crashing to defeat. Border wanted his team to be the best. Now he is the best in statistical terms.

Allan is pleased with his feat. He even allowed himself the luxury of a raised-arms salute after passing Gavaskar's mammoth aggregate. But he took only a few seconds to soak up the standing ovation, to experience the Australian fans' love for their skipper, before it was back to the job.

The captaincy is a job that Border inherited from Kim Hughes in the 1984–85 season. For a long time Allan was a reluctant captain, who used to get very grumpy when Australia lost or made silly mistakes. In the early days there was much grumpiness and on two occasions he offered to quit if things didn't improve quickly.

However, right from the start of his term he was a competent limited-overs captain. His expertise in this area gained him a taste of glory in the form of the 1987 World Cup. Australia maintained superiority in this form of the game up until their defence of the Cup on home territory, when the weight of expectancy seemed to weigh Border and his team down.

Border finally came of age as a Test captain on the 1989 tour of England. I will never forget his innings at Leeds in the first Test. Australia, a mixture of new faces and some familiar ones who were probably on their last chance, were in early trouble at

2 for 57. Border came to the crease and instead of embarking on a reconstruction job he took the attack to the English bowlers.

This resulted in some fierce pull and cut shots, and when he departed for sixty-six Australia was well and truly on top. They never looked back from that moment and Border's captaincy quickly grew in stature. He formulated an on-side field placing in conjunction with Terry Alderman that brought Graham Gooch undone, and by the end of the tour Australia had won the series four–nil, to regain the Ashes in England for the first time since Bill Woodfull did it in 1934.

Border's century at the MCG in the current series, which helped Australia to victory and a one–nil lead over the West Indies for the first time since the 1981–82 season, was another attacking gem. He will never play a better one-day innings than his undefeated 127 against the West Indies to help Australia to a shock victory in the first World Series final of 1984–85. He came in with his team reeling at 2 for 7 and buckled at the legs as he was hit a sickening blow in the ribs by Joel Garner. By the end of the innings, Border had brought the West Indies' bowlers to their knees with his scintillating stroke play.

I'm sure Border could have played this type of innings more often during his career, but his naturally pessimistic outlook generally saw him resort to the backs-to-the-wall approach. No one has played that style of innings better and his defiance at Old Trafford in 1981, when he posted an unconquered century despite having a fractured finger, epitomised his willingness to fight to the bitter end.

Border has remained at the top of his profession for nigh on fourteen years, with a batting average in excess of fifty. For over eight years he has been captain of a country that demands success from its skippers, and despite fluctuations in the team's fortunes his form has rarely dipped. When he has been criticised he has inevitably bounced back with a performance of consequence.

All of these feats have called for a remarkable mental strength. When I think of Allan Border I think of a man who loves playing cricket, who is extremely hard to dismiss when the chips are down, and who has a toughness about him that would serve an endangered black rhino well.

The 1992–93 series in Australia was Allan Border's last chance to beat the West Indies in a series. He failed, but only by the barest margin.

[Today UK, February 1993]

The West Indies dramatically dismissed any suggestion of a recession in their cricket with a convincing display in the second half of the Australian season.

Richie Richardson's recession-busters included a positive personal approach, a great fast bowler and an exciting young batting prospect.

Most important was the strike bowler. From the moment Dean Jones had a mental aberration in the first World Series final and asked Curtly Ambrose to remove his sweat band, the Antiguan assassin took aim and kept firing. Despite his obvious anger, Ambrose continued to think clearly and maintained an easy rhythm.

Having reached that plateau, he held his form for the two finals and then the final two Tests. He bowled at extreme pace, and most importantly discovered the perfect length for wicket-taking in Australia. Armed with that knowledge he took nineteen wickets in two Tests, including the ultimate humiliation of Australia: he took 7 for 1 in an amazing spell at the WACA.

In spite of those incredible figures, Ambrose's most significant dismissal was to bring about David Boon's demise on the final day of the dramatic Adelaide Oval Test. Ambrose got Boon for a duck, and this made possible Courtney Walsh's last-gasp heroics, which brought victory with only one run to spare. If Boon had lingered to play his normal sheet-anchor role, Australia probably would've won with a few wickets to spare.

Richardson deserves a lot of credit for his positive outlook, which in the end proved vital. In the first Test, when Australia was pushing for victory, they tended to get angry and lose their way as a stream of lbw appeals were turned down. On the last day at the Adelaide Oval the West Indies had reason to be upset at two lbw appeals that were knocked back, including one against Craig McDermott in the hectic final stages. However, Richardson didn't complain and kept his troops on the job, to be ultimately rewarded with an amazing victory.

As a captain, Allan Border is more capable than the inexperienced Richardson. However, when it comes to being positive and keeping his players focused, Richie is in front. Whilst Richardson was completing the odd handstand at the Adelaide Oval in the heat of battle, Border blew his top in Brisbane and was reported.

Another West Indies' asset was the supremely confident batting of Brian Lara. Brian's brilliant double century in the third Test at the SCG, and his fine batting in the World Series finals, rank with Ambrose's bowling as a catalyst for the West Indies' mid-series revival.

At one down in the Tests and 2 for 31 chasing 503, the West Indies were looking down the barrel as Lara strode onto the SCG. His innings of 277 was an example of elegant dominance and it robbed the Australian bowlers of the momentum they'd carried with them from the MCG. Most importantly, his confident handling of Shane Warne's deliveries had a similar revealing effect on his team-mates as someone explaining a magician's tricks.

From the time he flayed the Australian bowling all over the SCG, the West Indies' fortunes changed dramatically and they didn't lose another match on the tour.

The most amazing turnaround came in the limited-overs game. Under the captaincy of Viv Richards the West Indies had slipped from a position of world dominance to a world of disasters. Apart from a more enthusiastic outlook, there were no signs during last season's World Series and World Cup competitions that much had changed under Richardson's leadership. However, this enthusiasm, combined with a return to former expertise in bowling, plus Lara's batting, saw a big change this summer. The bowlers curtailed their generosity with no-balls and wides, and the fielding, which had become sloppy and at times panic-stricken, was suddenly competent and reasonably calm. Despite Lara's excellent form there were still moments of panic among the batsmen and this cost the Windies one win against Australia and very nearly the second final.

However, Richardson can be well pleased with the improvement in the West Indies' batting in the Tests. There were three first-time century-makers in the series: Lara, Keith Arthurton and Phil Simmons.

Arthurton's form during the Test series was a revelation. He displayed great maturity during his century at the Gabba, and despite a couple of aberrations in Melbourne and Adelaide he continued to show that he's a good Test-match batsman. His fighting knock at the WACA confirmed his growing confidence and commonsense, and he and Lara, plus Jimmy Adams, inspire confidence for the future.

Simmons is an interesting case. With a couple of simple adjustments to his batting he could be a valuable, dangerous and permanent member of the side. A successful attacking opener can do untold damage to the opposition as well as boost his team's confidence. Apart from this ability, Phil has the added attributes of playing spin well, being a brilliant catcher and a useful medium-pacer. He's an exciting player to watch and one who could play a prominent part in the next phase of West Indies cricket.

Ian Bishop is an important part of that future. Whilst his bowling was largely inconsistent and at times disappointing, there were signs in Perth that he might be coming to grips with the mental side of his recovery from a back injury. At the WACA he appeared to at last trust his re-formed action and his back. If that is the case, he should be able to shed all inhibitions and bowl with similar efficiency, even on less helpful pitches.

For the Australians it was another case of missed opportunities. In the Caribbean in 1991 they failed to dictate terms after holding the upper hand in the limited-overs series. This time it was a similar story after taking the lead with a good win at the MCG.

The complete breakdown of their top-order batting in the last four innings was even more perplexing following the aggressive display in their MCG victory. Unfortunately, they didn't repeat that form in the series, despite having a wonderful opportunity to demoralise the West Indies' attack on a flat wicket at the SCG. This was the only time Richardson struck a negative chord, when he suggested that the only way the pitch would bounce was if they used a tennis ball. That should have been the signal for Australia to go for the jugular, but instead they were cautious.

The main reason for this approach is Allan Border. He's become so used to defeat against the West Indies that he's almost expecting the worst. It was as though the loss in Adelaide confirmed his fears and knocked the stuffing out of the Australian side.

The one batsman who didn't capitulate in Perth was the tough

Tasmanian David Boon. He has been Australia's best batsman for the last three summers at home, and it would be wise for the other players to take note of his methods. He uses a full range of shots off both back and front foot, backed by a solid defence and a resolute approach.

Mark Waugh, on the other hand, has most of the shots, but he indulges in antics that don't befit his ability. He can call it innovation, he can explain it as his method of taking the attack to the pace bowlers, but it's still backing away. The problem with Mark's habit of retreating to leg and cutting the ball over the off-side field is that it encourages the opposition pace bowlers and also sets a bad example for his team-mates. When Damien Martyn started emulating him at the WACA, it was an indication that the bad habit had to be stopped.

Border's team hasn't prospered from its victories. Their most aggressive batting displays against the West Indies were in Antigua (1991) and Melbourne. They won on both occasions, but, curiously, Border has been reluctant to issue the order that this is the preferred course of action.

On the other hand, the Australian bowlers have played their part. Merv Hughes was the most consistent, and his first-innings spell at the MCG, where he got rid of Haynes, Simmons and Richardson cheaply, was inspiring. From there, Australia went on to claim victory, with Shane Warne taking seven second-innings wickets. Merv laid the charges and Shane pushed the plunger.

Craig McDermott's form was erratic, but his best was very good. The loss of Bruce Reid after the first Test was a blow the team could ill afford as Australia's stock of replacement fast bowlers is low. Nevertheless, this provides an opportunity for the spinners and I think Warne and Tim May could become a good combination. Warne is a much-improved leg spinner and his match-winning effort at the MCG did a lot for his confidence.

May has all the skill, but his biggest problem is staying fully fit for any length of time.

In this series Australia prepared for their future, and as well as Warne they blooded two good young batsmen in Martyn and Justin Langer. Langer is a hard-working and gutsy top-order player, whilst Martyn is an exciting stroke player who could eventually be a match-winner at number four. Together, they epitomise what we've come to expect of Australian batting – tough and aggressive. I just hope when the two sides meet again in 1995 that their team-mates are convinced that this is the only way to beat the West Indies: by batting in the traditional Australian manner.

Former captain Ted Dexter was chairman of the England selectors; former batsman Keith Fletcher, the coach; and Graham Gooch, the captain. This trio was a big help to Australia on the 1993 tour.

[*The Bulletin*, May 1993]

For a long time the most annoying thing about the Ashes was that even after a series win you never actually got your hands on the blasted urn.

Recently, the administrators have come up with a compromise and a replica urn is presented to the members of the winning team. I expect to see a repeat of the 1989 scenes with Allan Border kissing the imitation urn on the balcony at The Oval.

Four years ago Border became the first Australian skipper to regain the Ashes in England for fifty years. It was a comprehensive victory. Despite England's drubbing in India and then being humbled by Sri Lanka on their recent tour, I believe they'll provide stronger opposition this time, if they pick the right team.

Australia will start as favourites in their own right, but they'll also get some help from the England hierarchy of Ted Dexter, Keith Fletcher and Graham Gooch. Lord Ted has made some mystifying statements lately, which have been echoed by coach Fletcher. As long as these two continue to make flimsy excuses for England's failings and avoid facing reality, their chances of winning will be diminished. Gooch is an admirable leader in many ways, but his judgement of some players is questionable, because he places too much emphasis on conforming and not enough on performing: for example, choosing moderate performers ahead of a world-class player in David Gower.

Australia do have a few worries, but these pale in comparison to England's problems. Australia's meagre haul of victories during the summer of 1992–93 was a result of too many batting collapses. These stem from a sequence of moderate scores from batsmen who got a start and didn't capitalise. No Australian batsman scored a Test century after Steve Waugh's at the SCG, and in that period the team lost two Tests to the West Indies and one to New Zealand whilst chalking up a solitary victory over the Kiwis.

The formation of a sound opening partnership is the first priority. This provides an opportunity for either Michael Slater or Matthew Hayden to team up with the left-handed Mark Taylor. I'd favour Slater at this stage, because he's a right-hander and also a more complete batsman.

If one of these combinations clicks, it will allow Australia the luxury of moving David Boon back to number three. Boon has been the side's best batsman over the last few summers and he's so often the foundation on which Australia's big scores are built. When Boon is not at three the batting order looks like Sydney Harbour without the bridge.

A settling of the top order should allow Mark Waugh the freedom to fully harness his enormous talent. He sometimes plays like a batsman whose instincts conflict with the instructions. However, he does have a tendency to try to hit through the on-side too often, and on other occasions he loses his wicket in a 'soft' fashion, because of mental lapses. He has to learn to be more ruthless without sacrificing his flair.

I think Border also needs to change his batting order. Allan should separate Mark Waugh and either his brother, Steve, or Damien Martyn by batting himself at five. This is the ideal way to blend stroke play with solidarity, as well as a right- and left-hander.

With some fine tuning to the order and more attention paid to turning moderate scores into match-winning contributions, the Australian batting should once again be a force.

The bowling will be adequate as long as Craig McDermott and Merv Hughes remain healthy. They are constantly probing for wickets in their role as spearheads, whilst Hughes has the added advantage of being an enforcer who can be used to shake up batsmen when things are stagnating.

The selection of the tearaway Wayne Holdsworth is a good one. As the fastest bowler in Australia he will be the ideal back-up if either McDermott or Hughes is injured. If he really clicks he'll add further to English woes with his outswing at genuine pace. At worst he'll be handy against the counties, as he will intimidate some of those batsmen, thus taking the onus off McDermott and Hughes to bowl sides out in the minor matches as well as in the Tests.

The other bowling plus is Shane Warne. He's gone from being a bowler with potential, when he was first picked, to a potential match-winner. He's already had a hand in three Australian victories and his variety, accuracy and persistence will cause batsmen who are notorious for being over-anxious about wrist-spinners a few restless nights. In particular, he could reduce Robin Smith's effectiveness, and this is important as Smith has the shots to change the course of a game quickly.

The biggest worry for Australia would be to encounter a damp summer. On seaming pitches they struggled recently in both Sri Lanka and New Zealand. Nevertheless, under those conditions

I think this batting line-up will cope better than their predecessors, and the Australian bowlers will also be a handful for England's batsmen.

For Graham Gooch to get his hands on the imitation urn, Australia will have to play poorly and England improve markedly.

In light of the 2005 Ashes loss the question posed here should be: 'Why do Australia beat England most of the time?'

[*Wisden*, 1994]

Why do Australia beat England?

In general, because Australia play an aggressive brand of cricket, and when the talent is there they win more regularly than England because they are in a position to seek victory more often.

Notwithstanding, Australia couldn't have lost the last three Ashes series, even if they'd bet heavily on England. The pride of the Lions was largely absent on the prairie and they played badly, often. In particular, the bowling was abysmal and at times totally inadequate against an Australian side that was on the rise after a period in the doldrums.

During the summer of 1993 I constantly heard the lament, 'What is wrong with English cricket?'

If you work on the premise that many of the people who run the game either haven't realised or don't accept that England no longer rules the world, then you'll better understand the predicament.

In part, the answer is the inability of people directing the game to recognise the good in English cricket. For instance, some of the more common moans were, 'Where are all the England fast bowlers?'

Answer: Where was Devon Malcolm for the first five Tests?

And, 'What has happened to the old-fashioned English seamer?'

Answer: Steve Watkin was busy plying his trade with Glamorgan for the first five Tests.

Or, 'Why were England four–nil down after five Tests?'

Answer: From the time of the second Texaco Trophy match when, as captain, Graham Gooch froze like a rabbit caught in the headlights, it was obvious he wasn't the man to lead England to an Ashes victory.

Get the picture?

England's ability to over-theorise and complicate the game of cricket is legendary. Ever since I became involved in Ashes battles, I've felt that Australia could rely on some assistance from the England selectors. So far their form has been better than many of the players they've picked.

In 1993 they were in a magnanimous mood, giving Australia a four-game start before the penny dropped. They then promoted Mike Atherton to the captaincy, and in no time England picked a reasonably well-balanced side, with an attack that bore some semblance of hostility.

Atherton had one piece of good fortune, which every captain needs to be successful. Angus Fraser chose the appropriate moment to return to full form and fitness. With a stunning Man of the Match comeback to Test cricket, he helped lift England to the victory Atherton's team so desperately needed to boost their confidence.

Displaying infinite cricket wisdom, Atherton said at Edgbaston after only three days in the job, 'Our most important task is to identify the talent to win games. Then we must be prepared to stick with them.'

He was as good as his word in helping to select the touring

party for the Caribbean, and in addition he cleverly used his newfound power to make important adjustments to the balance of the side.

Up until the advent of Atherton, England's selections had often lacked rhyme or reason. A classic case was the predicament of dashing twenty-one-year-old Mark Lathwell in the Texaco Trophy series. At Lord's, Australia had an unbeatable two–nil lead, so the selectors took the opportunity to play their talented twenty-one-year-old Damien Martyn. As he made mincemeat of the bowling on his way to a glorious half-century, a Marylebone Cricket Club member said to me, 'How come you Australians always produce good young batsmen?'

With Lathwell needlessly sitting in the pavilion watching his third match in a row, the answer wasn't difficult. 'We play them,' I replied.

One can only assume that either Atherton immediately had a large influence in choosing teams, or his commonsense approach rubbed off on his fellow selectors. Whichever way, England can only be grateful for his presence, both on and off the field.

However, victory and some much-improved showings by England shouldn't induce an air of complacency, because Atherton needs plenty of support.

Whilst Atherton needs assistance, he doesn't need assistants like Keith Fletcher. The England cricket manager is typical of a mentality that pervades county cricket – if it's difficult, take the easy way out.

Fletcher's illogical call during the Ashes series for groundsmen to help England by producing seaming pitches went as it should have: unheeded. However, Fletcher's behaviour should have caught the attention of the officials and received a reprimand. Not only was Fletcher's suggestion unfair, his reasoning was also astray. This was proved at The Oval, where a well-balanced side, capably led and playing good aggressive cricket, beat Australia on one of the best cricket wickets I've seen in England. There was pace and bounce in Harry Brind's pitch (as usual) and it produced the best match of the series.

If the counties followed the shining examples of Brind and Old Trafford's Peter Marron and, where possible, produced pitches of a similar ilk, then England's good cricketers would benefit substantially at International level. Unfortunately, the county mentality is often similar to Fletcher's, where pitches are either prepared to assist the home side or to blunt a strength of the opposition.

Fletcher compounded his misdemeanour by arrogantly and incorrectly suggesting that England is the only country where helping the home side with pitch preparation isn't accepted practice. I haven't played on or seen any green-top flyers in the Caribbean and my brother Greg has often said, 'If you have to bat against four West Indies pace bowlers then the best place to do it is on their own turf.' And in more than thirty years of playing and watching cricket in Australia, I can honestly say that I've never seen a Test pitch that varies greatly from its behaviour during the Sheffield Shield season. In fact, one of the strengths of the Shield competition is that the players perform on pitches which are very close to Test standard. Under this system it's easy to identify the good players who stand a chance at Test level, the ones who are capable of playing only first-class cricket and also those who will soon return to club cricket.

England needs to do some fine tuning to the county system, so that it constantly produces a surplus of Test-standard players.

When Australia hit rock bottom through the 1984–87 period, the standard of Sheffield Shield cricket was low. The problem was addressed and now it's a vibrant competition and an excellent breeding ground.

England is on the right track with four-day first-class games, but it will take time for the benefits to accrue. I think they should go a step further and reduce the number of teams to make it more competitive, as there are players in the county structure who are not up to first-class standard. Any system that protects incompetence needs fine tuning, and if this means having a first and second division then that could be the way to accommodate part-time players who want to combine business and cricket. These changes could be part of a package to convince the counties to put England's needs at the top of their list, rather than on the same level as: 'Which colour will we paint the pavilion roof?'

Any move to improve the structure should be aimed at increasing pride in playing for England. Encouragingly, since Atherton has become involved in the selection process I detect a move back to the feeling that the England team is for English players. If this is the case it's good news, as England was in danger of becoming a haven for career cricketers who were unsure of making it in their own country.

Lack of pride manifests itself in a number of ways, and in England's case the most serious has been to capitulate in a Test when trouble loomed. England used to be the best side in the world at extricating itself from trouble and living to fight another day. The players need to rediscover that urge.

The inability to save Tests must also have something to do with technique and mental strength. In an age where we have more coaches, not only in England but throughout the cricket world, I query how much good they are doing. I believe in good coaching, but I think players are better to have none (that is, work it out for themselves) than to have bad coaching.

In Australia I believe the cricket academy could be run more effectively by not removing the young players from their home environment. However, many of the players leaving the academy are mentally tough and primed for first-class cricket. This is exactly what you'd expect with the no-nonsense Rod Marsh as head coach and there's no doubt it is having a positive effect on the depth of Australian first-class cricketers.

Also, apart from a brief period when Australia, like other teams, was bluffed by the West Indies into thinking that pace was the almighty weapon, there has been a broad-brush approach to bowling the opposition out. This includes leg spinners, and in the period when they were forgotten in Australia, Bill 'Tiger' O'Reilly, a great leggie in his time, was quick to unleash his wrath at this failing.

But Tiger, just as he did in his playing days, saved his most lethal delivery for the old enemy. 'I can never forgive English cricket,' said Bill, 'for attempting to kill off leg spin bowling.'

No type of bowling should ever be discarded; it only needs to be bowled well and accurately to have a place in International cricket. Hopefully Shane Warne's electrifying success in the Ashes series will have proved once and for all that there is a place for leg spin in the game if it's bowled well. Yes, even in England. Atherton is one who seems convinced, judging by Ian Salisbury's selection for the Caribbean tour.

The subject of leg spinners brings me in a roundabout way to uncovered pitches. This is often suggested as a recipe for helping English cricket. I say codswallop. Uncovered pitches at first-class level would encourage the expectancy of easy pickings for the bowlers. Leg spinners are the antithesis of easy pickings. They are at their best when the going is tough and all they ask is a bit of turn and plenty of bounce. The occasional uncovered pitch at club level isn't a bad thing because it does a young batsman good to discover how to play when the ball is misbehaving. But pitches must either be fully covered or totally uncovered, so that you don't have the ludicrous situation where fast bowlers are running up on dry ground, banging the ball into a wet pitch.

The lack of experience in handling erratic bounce is one reason put forward for poor technique in Test-match batsmen. Another is too much one-day cricket. To the latter I say bollocks. On the contrary, a lot of one-day cricket is the saviour of an ordinary player because his poor technique will be found wanting at Test level. If young players are taught PROPERLY, as they progress in the game the smarter ones learn to adapt their thinking to all sorts of different pitches, bowlers and playing conditions. They become really good players because they adapt and bat well in any type of cricket.

Still on the subject of one-day cricket: prior to the 1993–94 season the Australian Cricket Board (ACB) gave the selectors power to 'rest a jaded or slightly injured player from One Day Internationals, while still receiving full pay'. This is recognition that Test cricket is the true measuring stick for a player's skill, but also acknowledges the contribution made by Internationals to the game's finances and spreading popularity. It could also be a solution to the vexing problem of the right balance between Tests and one-day games in an International itinerary.

The ACB's edict is an interesting development in the gradual evolution of the professional game in parts other than England. Like so many aspects of the game, the English invented it and other countries have improved on their system, leaving them languishing.

However, there are some signs of modern thinking in the marketing of English cricket and the game is currently in good financial shape. This is encouraging in tough economic times, but it should never be forgotten that in the end the only thing that will allow the marketing men to flex their muscles is a strong England side.

Marketing is just one area of positive change in English cricket recently, but it has taken an inordinate amount of time to occur.

Perhaps if Atherton proves to be a successful captain and there's a continued good showing on the field as England put their faith in youth, it'll have a flow-on effect among the administration. It's to be hoped so, because cricket needs a competitive England side.

Prior to this trip in 1994 I'd last visited South Africa on an International Wanderers tour that Richie Benaud managed, in 1976. The change from player to a journalist and commentator wasn't the only big difference I noticed this time around.

[*Wide World of Sports Year Book*, February 1994]

Everyone was talking about the new South Africa that would follow the 26 to 28 April elections. Notwithstanding that event, arriving in South Africa in February 1994 after an absence of eighteen years, I found a distinctly different country. For starters, there were no 'Nie Blankes' and 'Slegs Blankes' signs, nominating which were the non-white and whites-only areas. That had to be an improvement.

After a few days, the overall impression I gained was two-fold. First, the bulk of the population wanted the 'new' South Africa to work, and secondly, they were delighted an Australian touring side was once again in the country.

When I asked Kepler Wessels in Australia what South Africa was like these days, he replied, 'It's good, but you'll find it a bit Third Worldish.'

At the time I thought, 'That's a strange description.' On reflection, after nearly three months in South Africa I felt it was an accurate one.

Climbing aboard yet another bus parked out on the tarmac,

this time to take us to the distant terminal at Jan Smuts Airport, an Australian journalist wearily asked, 'What was it like when you toured here?'

I replied, 'Good. In those days South Africa was up with and in many cases ahead of the developed world.'

I came to the conclusion that in isolation what had happened was not much. Sure, there had been cosmetic changes. In Johannesburg a lot of companies had moved their offices out of the city into security-conscious, low-rise areas like Sandton City. These are serviced by a large, self-contained shopping mall where customer safety is a priority. But little appeared to have been done to update a lot of the 'infrastructure'.

The Australian team and the media were housed at Sandton City, sheltered from the real South Africa. Even so, go for a walk and it pays to be constantly on the alert. It's a bit like batting: one lapse in concentration and it could spell trouble.

On the contrary, most of the batting in the first four one-day internationals was of such a high calibre that it was the bowlers who were in strife.

The first one was played in the Wanderers Bullring, and Hansie Cronje inspired his team-mates and fuelled an already excitable crowd with a marvellous display of controlled aggression. This resulted in an innings of 112 off just 120 balls, with three sixes and seven fours.

Hansie's scintillating century took a toll on the bowling of Shane Warne and also set up an exciting finish. Chasing 232, Australia got away to a solid start. Commencing the forty-eighth over with only twenty-four runs required and wickets in hand, it appeared they had a good chance of victory. Fifteen minutes later South Africa had won by five runs and the Bullring was reverberating to the chant of 'Fanie, Fanie', as the crowd acknowledged their second hero that afternoon.

In the midst of all the excitement, a remarkably calm Fanie de Villiers had bowled six deliveries which only cost two runs and claimed the wicket of the dangerous Allan Border. It was the best over I've seen in a tense one-day match and 'Fast' Fanie had shown that he's also amazingly accurate.

That set the scene for more heroics in the Highveld as the teams travelled to Pretoria.

The morning followed a remarkably similar pattern to the one in Johannesburg. Kepler Wessels won the toss and his vice-captain, Cronje, responded with another confident display of strokes, which produced three sixes, but this time fell three runs short of his century. Cronje had again enlisted the aid of Jonty Rhodes to boost the total, but their partnership proved to be just an entree before Adrian Kuiper gorged himself in a run feast.

Kuiper had closely watched Cronje's method until he was run out by a bullet-like throw from Border. Suitably impressed, he began launching balls into the thin atmosphere that surrounds the administrative capital. His forty-seven not out came off just twenty-two balls and included four sixes and two fours, with twenty-six precious runs blasted off Craig McDermott's final over.

The crowd loved it when Kuiper lofted sixes off the final two balls, but when they discovered the last one was a no-ball they went into a frenzy. As the extra delivery disappeared into the masses around mid-on, Kuiper ran off the field waving his bat in triumph and the crowd gave him a standing ovation.

This was a mighty display of hitting as McDermott had entered his final over with the highly respectable figures of 0 for 20 including two maidens. He was powerless to halt the carnage and it resulted in the sign of the tour appearing at the next match: 'Who needs a Reiffel, when you've got an AK-47.'

The Adrian Kuiper caper had helped South Africa post a total of 265, which ensured they'd take a two–nil lead. Australia only reached 209, but it allowed Border the luxury of a rehearsal for one of his most devastating one-day innings.

Two days after scoring forty-one off forty-nine balls in Pretoria, Border strode onto St George's Park in Port Elizabeth with his team well placed at 5 for 233 in the forty-sixth over. What followed was every bit as spectacular as Kuiper's innings, although being played by an intruder meant it wouldn't be similarly acclaimed.

Border clobbered three sixes and four fours from the seventeen balls he faced, and finished on forty not out. His innings was a masterful combination of cricket stroke play and his skill as a baseball hitter. Whilst his shots didn't have the elevation of Kuiper's, Border hit the ball just as hard without anything like the effort. Anyone in the crowd who wasn't watching Border's every move was crazy. Not only was it worth the entrance money just to see those seventeen deliveries, but it was also downright dangerous to be looking elsewhere.

Border's bashing had knocked South Africa senseless and they capitulated in chasing 281. That reduced the leeway to 2–1, but Australia's joy was short-lived as Craig Matthews shattered their batting on a lively Kingsmead pitch in Durban. He took 4 for 10 from eight overs, five of them maidens, and South Africa finished the day section of the limited-overs matches with a 3–1 advantage.

It had been good to get back to the coast and enjoy the smell of salt water. But wandering back from the beach in Port Elizabeth I was reminded how much South Africa had changed from the days when the non-whites used to step off the footpath to let the 'honkies' past.

On the path from the beach to the hotel I came within a few metres of an elderly white lady sitting in her car. As I approached she put down her book, slammed the door and locked it until I'd passed. Yes, things had changed in South Africa, mostly for the better.

At the one-day matches in Durban and Port Elizabeth there was a wide cross-section of races in attendance. At Kingsmead I noticed an African guy acting as a cheerleader, which was a far cry from when they were penned up in small 'segregated' sections of the ground and expected to be 'seen and not heard'.

For an outsider, the most difficult thing to comprehend was the senseless violence in the lead-up to the elections. Despite the air of inevitability with which the locals accepted the bad news there were odd occasions when you glimpsed how it touched people.

On Good Friday we visited the King William's Town golf course, which was kindly opened for us by a staunch and proud member. Some months before, terrorists had fired a number of rounds with AK-47s and detonated a few hand-grenades in the club's two lounges, which had resulted in some members dying.

A member showed us the grim reminders of the tragedy: the spot in the changing room where a hole had been blown in the ceiling by a grenade explosion, and the bullet holes in the roof. When he pointed to damage on the veranda, he muttered, 'The cowardly bastards.'

It was still a friendly club, but it was now screened by a security camera perched above the barred and bolted door. Fortunately, the spirit was locked in, not out, and we were made most welcome by people who epitomised the resilience of the human spirit.

It's people like them and John, the driver for the United Cricket Board's vice-president, Ray White, who I think of as we enter the period of the 'new' South Africa. Their spirit and dreams are going to be needed in plentiful supply, but they must be encouraged by (and thankful for) the dramatic drop-off in the violence since the elections.

There are many who want South Africa to prosper and few ignoramuses like the two who boasted to some Australian players in a Bloemfontein night spot that, 'We've killed more Kaffirs than anyone else in the country.' When I heard that these two Afrikaner Resistance Front supporters had concluded the evening by head-butting a local journalist, I assumed it was the first time all night that they'd used their craniums.

At the opposite end of the scale there were the deep thinkers. One gentleman likened the new Bill of Rights and Constitution to 'a hundred passengers waiting to board a train and when it departs thirty-seven people are left behind.'

That analogy took on more significance when Mr Buthelezi allowed the Inkatha Freedom Party to participate in the election. To have more passengers boarding the train no matter how late in the journey must have been welcomed by Nelson Mandela and F. W. de Klerk.

The (then) State President took time out from his arduous election schedule to enjoy the Test at the Wanderers. Mr de Klerk was amazingly relaxed and he chose wisely. It was one of the best Tests I've watched, nearly matching the game at the Adelaide Oval (1992–93) when for four days the tension level remained high as the West Indies defeated Australia by one run.

The first day was full of shots and surprises. The South African batsmen scored 126 in boundaries, and whilst all the top-order players got a start, only Jonty Rhodes passed the half-century mark.

And it wasn't until Jonty was joined by keeper David Richardson that a half-century partnership was posted. Their sixty-eight runs came quickly, and when added to the forty-six run liaison between Rhodes and de Villiers, it gave the South African total a hint of respectability.

Their 251 was scored at such a clip that Michael Slater and Test debutant Matt Hayden still had time to thrash thirty-four from some wayward bowling. It had been a day of excitement and drama and despite the three wickets to both McDermott and Merv Hughes, the most significant dismissal was that of Cronje.

Hansie had plundered the Australian bowling to that point and capped it with a double century for Orange Free State. However, Cronje committed the cardinal sin of not starting his innings from nought and played as though he was continuing on from his recent 250. He paid the penalty when he over-confidently slashed at a Steve Waugh delivery and it ended in Border's hands at second slip.

The next day Australia made a dismal start which they could only blame on their muddled thinking. Slater, who had been in spectacular form the night before, perished at third man, and the normally reliable David Boon was caught at fine leg. Not rash cut and hook shots, but poorly executed ones. In between time, Hayden, who was a last-minute replacement for an ill Mark Taylor, was Donald's first victim when he edged to Richardson.

Those self-inflicted dismissals were then compounded by the needless run-outs of Mark Waugh and Border in two overs. These misjudgements changed the course of the match as the pair had begun to look comfortable in a sixty-six-run partnership. In the end that stood alone as the only half-century liaison for the innings, and even Steve Waugh's stubborn resistance wasn't enough to gain Australia a lead.

Once again the pace had been hectic and Hudson and Gary Kirsten had time to add to South Africa's three-run advantage with a further sparkling forty-two. Despite the hard-working efforts of the bowlers, it was the run-outs that won South Africa their edge.

After two exciting days of cut-and-thrust cricket, with the low scores setting the scene for a result, the third day produced a contribution which left one team as favourite. Cronje, in partnership with his captain, Wessels, had pushed South Africa to a position of security, when suddenly the vice-captain took the game by the scruff of the neck. He launched an assault that took his score from sixty-two to eighty-six with five fours. This was no message in a bottle asking for help; rather, a bold declaration to the opposition that, 'We intend to win this game.'

Cronje went on to record his third Test century, with the message being every bit as important as the runs.

For some time it appeared that Cronje hadn't got through to his skipper. However, if Wessels did leave the declaration a bit late, he at least chose an appropriate psychological moment. Matthews and Donald had respectively executed an exquisite off-drive for six and a square drive that rattled into the fence, both off the bowling of Warne. If that didn't have them in the mood to bowl then they're not genuine number ten and eleven batsmen. Australia needed 454 for victory and to save the match they had to bat for more than a day.

Whilst Slater was at the crease victory was always a possibility as the pitch was still playing well. Before the match the curator was roundly criticised for his preparation, but he confided, 'I don't care what other people say. I've made a pitch that hopefully will bring a result around tea on the final day.'

By tea on the fourth day, Hayden, batting with a broken thumb, had been bowled by de Villiers, but Slater and Boon were matching each other shot for shot and the total had raced to forty-nine.

When Slater was bowled by de Villiers the chances of victory were reduced, but Mark Waugh, with his delightfully simple stroke play, kept the flame of hope flickering. However, that hope was quickly snuffed out by Donald on the final morning. Then when those two stalwarts in a sticky situation, Boon and Border, also buckled in the same session, even hopes of a stirring defiance seemed to have disappeared.

Nevertheless, Hughes and Healy's resolve was boosted by a darkening sky. No, Merv hadn't blotted out the sun, it really was a thunderstorm on the way.

Healy perished and McDermott failed to heed the thunder, but Tim May proved to be a capable ally for Monstrous Merv. They stuck together for over an hour, in which time the crowd became agitated as the wind whipped through the stadium and light rain sent the players briefly from the field. In desperation Wessels threw the ball to Cronje. With his third ball he finished the match that he'd indicated by his actions two days earlier could be won.

It was a relieved and delighted South African team and crowd that applauded Man of the Match Cronje from the field. However, one fan reserved his attention for Merv and the big fellow reacted angrily to the mindless abuse.

Hughes' actions, coming on top of the reporting of both him and Warne earlier in the match, caused a furore. The match referee, Donald Carr, had fined both Warne (for abusing Hudson) and Hughes (for similar treatment of Gary Kirsten) about 250 Australian dollars. Not satisfied, the ACB weighed in with another 4,000 dollars. And for Hughes' angry response to the fan there was also a suspended fine of 2,000 dollars.

If Merv doesn't feel enamoured of the Wanderers, then he's not on his own. In 1966–67 Transvaal became the first team to beat Australia on South African soil. A few weeks later Bob Simpson's touring side became our first to lose a Test in the Republic. Now Allan Border's men had become the first Australian side to lose a Test to the Proteas in South Africa. All these calamities occurred at the Wanderers. Yes, Merv, I agree, bugger the Bullring.

Australia's litany of disasters at the Wanderers is only matched by the ACB's mishandling of player relations. The Hughes–Warne affair added to an already long list. And the ICC is no better. If the referee decreed that both players were guilty, then how on earth could Carr fine Warne the same amount as Hughes? Merv's offence made him a three-time loser, whilst Warne was guilty of a first offence. There's no way that adds up to a fine of equal amounts.

However, the ACB then compounded matters by fining the players a second time for the same offence and from the seclusion of Australia. Surely the ACB either abides by the International system (which it agitated for) or it makes Australian players exempt and metes out the punishment itself.

On the positive side, the messy affair had the desired effect on Warne. In the second Test at Newlands he bowled with great control of each delivery and his emotions, to help propel his team to victory. This took a lot of courage and determination. Hudson started as though he was intent on making a century before lunch, and South Africa appeared to be cruising after winning the toss. However, just as had happened at the Wanderers, a couple of run-outs changed the course of the game. Gary Kirsten took off for a senseless single and was brilliantly run out by Slater diving *à la* Jonty style. That prompted a mini-collapse in which Cronje and Wessels fell in quick succession.

However, the advent of Peter Kirsten settled things down as Hudson went merrily on his way to a second Test century. The right-hander pierced the field regularly with well-timed drives and the odd fierce cut and pull shot.

Then, just when South Africa appeared to be on the road to recovery, a magnificent sliding save and accurate throw from Steve Waugh produced a sleight of hand run-out to match any rabbit-out-of-the-hat trick. Hudson waited for an eternity to discover his fate from the video replay, which was in line with the many long hold-ups at the Wanderers, caused by indecision over whether a ball had crossed the boundary or not.

Over rates are slow enough now without the administrators' increasing tardiness. Surely the umpires have to use their own judgement wherever possible, and if there must be video replays for run-outs and stumpings, then ensure the cameras are perfectly positioned. On too many occasions during the tour a batsman's fate was decided by a head-on replay rather than one that was in line with the relevant crease. That brings an element of guessing to the decision, which videotape was employed to eradicate.

With Hudson gone South Africa appeared to be content to play for a draw. This approach got them into trouble at the picturesque Adelaide Oval and now it cost them dearly at the second prettiest Test ground in the world.

The recent changes to Newlands caused much debate. I think they've done a good job in providing modern accommodation whilst still retaining a link with the past. For the night game, Newlands was a great sight with the powerful lights enhancing its stadium-like qualities, as the subtly lit Table Mountain towered over it. During the Test there was ample time to view the changes as the South African batsmen plodded on to 361, a score that they must have thought made them safe from defeat.

Australia's innings progressed steadily as Boon and Taylor provided a good platform with a century partnership. This pattern continued when Border joined the squat Tasmanian, and South Africa's conservative approach was becoming more and more apparent. The advent of Steve Waugh and Ian Healy moved the match into another gear, and when they took Australia into the lead early on the fourth morning, alarm bells started to ring in the South African camp.

Their anxiety was calmed by a fine spell of bowling from Matthews which helped to restrict Australia's lead to seventy-four.

However, that figure grew in importance when Warne and Steve Waugh combined to send back two batsmen before it was erased.

South Africa had eked out a lead of twenty when the folly of their conservative tactics was laid bare. Wessels was run out by some smart work from Border, and once again the Warne–Steve Waugh combination struck. Three wickets fell for the cost of only a run apiece and when, shortly afterwards, nightwatchman de Villiers and McMillan also perished, lbw to the deadly two W's combination, the South African innings was in tatters.

A match that had meandered along at a leisurely pace for more than two days suddenly came alive thanks to three of Australia's most positive cricketers. Steve Waugh, Warne and Healy all contributed to changing the course of the match.

On the final morning Rhodes and Richardson made a determined effort to stave off defeat by surviving the first session. However, the advent of the second new ball broke the partnership and the South African resistance crumbled.

Steve Waugh had added five victims to his eighty-six runs, as his superb form with bat and ball continued. He was well supported by a patient Warne, who worked very hard for his wickets in a display that emphasised his ability to learn quickly.

Needing only ninety-one runs to win, Australia didn't fall into the SCG trap, as first Slater and then Boon picked off regular boundaries and brought the target down quickly.

The series was levelled, and in the process Australia stretched their record at Newlands to seven wins and only one loss. After their earlier inland ineptitude, it wouldn't have surprised me if the Australians opted for a celebratory verse of 'Oh, I do like to be beside the seaside.'

As a result of a combination of mental fatigue and South Africa's apparent satisfaction with a drawn series, the Kingsmead Test quickly became a bore. Not even a Mark Waugh century on the final day could relieve the tedium and all that remained was to observe the last day of Allan Border's Test career.

It was spent like so many others, with Border playing a backs-to-the-wall innings to ensure his team was safe from danger. There were no frills, but plenty of concentration.

One of the most endearing things about Allan's cricket was his ability to compete day after day and never lose his appetite for battle. He fought it out right to the very end, playing a maiden from Jonty Rhodes, and then it was handshakes all round.

But Allan still had some unfinished business: the day/night section of the limited-overs series. At 3–1 down with four to play, he'd need every ounce of that competitive spirit.

Border took the Man of the Match award as Steve Waugh hit off the winning runs peering through the gloom provided by the poor lights at Buffalo Park in East London. South Africa 3–2. However, if the lights were under strength in East London they were puerile at St George's Park in Port Elizabeth. At first they were only on at thirty per cent, but even at full strength they provided less illumination than a candlelight dinner. Australia had no chance chasing on a pitch that became a minefield after the break. South Africa now led 4–2 and Australia couldn't win the series. However, they kept alive their hopes of drawing it with a good win under the excellent lights at Newlands. South Africa 4–3 with one to play.

Springbok Park in Bloemfontein was the venue for one last act of drama between these two evenly matched and highly competitive sides.

Australia seemed a little light on for runs when they only set South Africa 204 for victory. This appeared to be confirmed when Hudson took control from the outset and the Proteas were cruising towards the win. However, a couple of wickets to Reiffel and a run-out quickly put Australia in the box seat as South

Africa still required twenty-nine to win with only three overs remaining. The game took another sudden turn as Eric Simons and Richardson hit out to reduce the final over to a quest for six runs.

Border threw the ball to rookie Damien Fleming, who was a replacement for the injured McDermott. His previous over had cost him twelve so it was a bold gamble by the Australian skipper. Rising to the challenge, Fleming produced a final over that only cost four runs. He and the rest of the Australian team had really buckled down to work, even when many were suffering from battle fatigue. It was a tribute to their competitive spirit, exemplified by the captain and the keeper.

Fleming's marvellous match-saving over was reminiscent of Fanie's amazing effort in the first match at the Wanderers and was a fitting finale to what had been a gripping series.

So ended a slogging six months of cricket between two ideally matched sides. It had been like witnessing two heavyweights trade punches for fifteen rounds, and in the end neither had the strength left to put their opponent away. A tough, uncompromising battle, played in the true tradition of Australia versus South Africa contests.

This was the beginning of Mark Taylor's highly successful captaincy reign. He began with a pair in his first Test and the team lost by one wicket thanks to an unfinished fifty-seven-run partnership between Inzamam ul-Haq and Mushtaq Ahmed. However, Mark showed his resilience by persevering and becoming the best of the four Australian captains in this golden period.

———

[*The Bulletin*, November 1994]

The tour of Pakistan has been an eventful one for Mark Taylor's Australian team. A riot a day keeps boredom at bay.

In the years to come, Pakistan 1994, with its riots, an earthquake and other assorted mishaps, will be remembered fondly by the resilient Australian players, because as someone once shrewdly observed, 'adventure is discomfort recollected in tranquillity'.

Meanwhile, the team's short-term recall should focus on the way they pressured Pakistan on the field. Mark Taylor made a bold start to his captaincy career by embarking on a laudable policy of batting aggressively, and the Australians scored in excess of three hundred on the opening day of each of the first two Tests.

Unfortunately, their enterprise didn't pay immediate dividends and they found themselves one–nil down. However, there was some consolation in that the limited-overs final was won comfortably as the Australian batsmen posted a large total that placed an intolerable burden on the equally aggressive Pakistani top-order batsmen.

By relentlessly pursuing a policy of aggression, even in times of adversity, the Australian batsmen were able to avoid being dominated by the Pakistan pace pair, Wasim Akram and Waqar Younis. Consequently, the team made reasonable totals in good time, which meant they were competitive and there was always the likelihood of a result.

The other encouraging aspect of the tour was the development of the young players Michael Bevan, Damien Fleming and Glenn McGrath. They shouldered their increased responsibility as though it were an empty school knapsack and performed well at important times during the tour. This meant it wasn't always left to Shane Warne and Craig McDermott, plus the senior batsmen, to pull Australia out of trouble or provide the impetus when victory beckoned.

The results in Pakistan may have disappointed the Australian team because they could so easily have been much better. However, persevering with the aggressive approach could result in some handsome rewards being reaped shortly. England's fragile bowling attack could disintegrate when confronted by such an onslaught.

Despite the vociferous early claims about the English pace bowlers and Devon Malcolm's impressive start to the tour, their ability to maintain control under attack from the best Australian batsmen must still be in dispute. Coach Keith Fletcher's statement that the English fast bowlers are similar in speed to Dennis Lillee and even Jeff Thomson – that's 1974 vintage, not circa 1994 – is as irrelevant as it is extravagant.

I can understand Thommo in particular leaving a lasting impression on Keith, as one of Jeffrey's lethal deliveries hit the Englishman right on the badge of his cap. I can only assume that blow at the SCG in 1975 did more damage than initially appeared to be the case. If Fletcher seriously thinks that any of his present crop of fast bowlers can generate the speed or create the havoc that Jeff Thomson did in 1974–75 then they had better start testing cricketers for anabolic steroids.

Pace is dangerous, but if it's not well directed the only damage done is to the bowling figures. Anyone who bowls with controlled pace, backed with aggression and a smidgeon of movement, is going to make it tough for the best of batsmen. If Malcolm and Darren Gough can produce and maintain that standard then the Ashes series will be a humdinger.

That's where the doubt creeps in with this England side – IF. With the exception of Angus Fraser there's no doubt that the England selectors, led by their crafty chairman Ray Illingworth, have picked the right types to succeed in Australia. The question is whether they can play or if indeed they are allowed to play at their best by Australia. So we have the chance of a close, hard-fought series if England plays at their best, or, if they don't, Australia winning by a comfortable margin.

In addition to the prospect of some close contests, there's also the possibility of individual stories of bravery and controversy. Tantalising tales, tall and true, about such issues as: Who will win the captaincy battle? Who will win the race if Gatting and Gooch have to chase a ball from cover and mid-off respectively? How quickly will Ian Heal(y)? Will Graeme Hick survive the onslaught if Merv makes a comeback? And can Australia produce a medical miracle and reactivate Bruce 'Broken' Reid?

Therein lies the potential to make the revelations of 'the silver-haired bodgie' and 'Richo', in cricketers' language, 'irrelevant, immaterial, and what's more they don't even matter'.

Taylor's captaincy survived a rigorous test in Pakistan, to the point where he began to flourish. He overcame serious personal setbacks, like making a pair in his first Test as captain and dropping the catch that cost Australia a victory, to prove that he's mentally resilient. We already know that Michael Atherton is similarly endowed, so a titanic struggle looms in the battle of wills. The general with the superior troops will prevail.

I have the distinct impression that Mike 'The Gut' Gatting is here as experienced back-up if Graham 'The Guv'nor' Gooch should be injured or old age gets the better of him in the heat. I doubt that they'll often be in the team together and I'll guarantee that if they are they won't be on the same side of the infield. Sorry to disappoint, but you can put the glasses down, there won't be a running race or a run chase between The Gut and The Guv'nor.

The injuries to Healy and Steve Waugh coming at the end of the Pakistan tour are a headache for Australia. Both are tough competitors and, because of their versatility, hard to replace. It takes time for a new keeper to 'blend in' with the team and it will hurt Australia if they have to chop and change throughout the Ashes series, especially as Healy is the vice-captain.

The same applies to Waugh. His all-round skills allow the selectors to balance the team for a variety of conditions and his prolonged absence would weaken the side.

When the Australian pace bowlers first saw the name Hick at number three, they must have immediately started forming plans to 'terrorise' him. This would've been based on their own experience during the last Ashes series and when he played for Queensland, and also on what they'd witnessed when he faced Curtly Ambrose and company from the West Indies. However, Hick has made a confident start to the tour and a continuation of that form would see him do a bit of terrorising of his own as he's a powerful striker of the ball. A decisive victory either way in this psychological battle will contribute greatly to a series win.

It will make life a lot more difficult for Hick if Merv Hughes is fit and in form. Merv is an enforcer and there's no one who does the job better under Australian conditions. I'd have him in the team if he's bowling well.

I'd also include the thin Reid, certainly for the MCG and WACA Tests, if his body holds together. With Hughes and Reid thrust into battle it may look like a re-run of 'Fat and Skinny went to War', but their presence could help Australia win two Tests, which would be enough to retain that confounded urn.

The prospects are fascinating even without the spice of a riot or two. This will be Ashes adventure in the comfort of your lounge room or the tranquillity of a nearby cricket ground.

I played for Ramsbottom in the Lancashire League in 1963. During that season I met Raymond Patrick Hogan, an Australian who was selected in the NSW State squad in the early Fifties and then played for Northamptonshire in the English County competition. By 1963 Hogan was playing with Heywood in the Central Lancashire League and we often used to meet for a drink in Manchester during the week. After a few drinks we would have a meal at the Kazi Indian restaurant and Hogan would occasionally stand up and recite 'Under the Southern Cross' and finish with 'Australia you bloody beauty' if there were still some other patrons present, or the slightly more risqué version if we were the only people left in the restaurant.

I'm not sure where the ditty came from, although I suspect Hogan learnt it from John McMahon, a South Australian who played for Somerset and Surrey before retiring to live in Lancashire. 'Macca' was an avid reader and loved Banjo Paterson, and I assumed it was from his writings. I used to recite it every now and then – usually when we were celebrating – and Rod Marsh heard it and liked the rhyme so much that he stood on the table and recited it after we won the first Test against England in 1974–75. That is the first time it got a public airing as the team's victory song, and after Rodney retired in 1983–84 he passed it on to Allan Border to continue the tradition.

[*ACB* magazine, 9 January 1995]

When Allan Border became captain of Australia he passed the baton to David Boon to lead the team in singing 'Under the Southern Cross' every time they won an important victory. In the early stages of Border's captaincy reign Boon would have needed a song sheet to recall the words. However, Border's boys grew into men with Boon leading the way as the side's most consistent batsman and they began to win regularly. After a while, 'Australia you bloody beauty' became a familiar catchcry of David Boon and his team-mates as the song rang out in dressing rooms all round the cricketing world.

Boon's solidarity in the important number-three spot was the foundation on which Australia's batting was built. So much so that for a short period almost every time Boon went cheaply the opposition dismissed Australia for a meagre total. Fortunately for Australia, Boon's batting was as solid as his own undercarriage and there were few collapses and much after-match singing.

These days there isn't the same reliance on a big score from Boon. Sure, if David goes cheaply there's always a feeling of apprehension in the crowd and he still has an anguished look on his face as he belts his chewing gum towards the boundary on departure, but the dressing room is more relaxed now with the likes of the Waugh twins and Ian Healy ready, willing and able to come to the rescue, just as they did in the Caribbean. And recently another name has been added to the list which inspires even more confidence: the dashing right-hander Greg Blewett.

Blewett's arrival on the Test scene was as spectacular as a Sydney Harbour fireworks display. His bold approach to batting and a century in his second Test following a brilliant debut hundred suggested a career for Greg that was more likely to be a lingering sky-lighting rocket rather than a short-fused squib. Nevertheless, that fairytale beginning was followed by a long struggle in the Caribbean until Blewett broke the drought in the series-deciding final Test to put the icing on the cake already baked by the Waugh twins. So enthused was Mark Taylor by the young South Australian's style that he likened him to Doug Walters in his ability to change the course of a match by accelerating the scoring rate. No higher praise can come from a New South Welshman.

Adding to the glow of Blewett's meteoric rise to fame was the fact that it was so unexpected. Just a few months earlier it appeared that left-hander Michael Bevan had secured the middle-order spot vacated by Border, following a string of good scores in Pakistan. Instead, Bevan's failure to capitalise against a generally moderate English attack left the way open for Blewett, who grabbed his opportunity after some impressive innings for the Australia A side. Bevan's demise could so easily have unsettled the batting line-up as it upset the ideal balance between left- and right-handers, and the loss of his exciting stroke play and gazelle-like running between wickets could have meant a diminishing of Australia's attacking potential in the middle order. On the contrary, Blewett, with his elegant driving and powerful pulling, actually enhanced Australia's scoring-rate potential and hence his captain's delight.

Unlike Walters, who plied his trade almost exclusively from the number-six spot, Blewett, with his background as an opener for South Australia, has the credentials to bat anywhere. He could succeed Boon at three when the old stager decides to put his feet up and keep the doctor at bay by munching an apple a day. Blewett would be a different style of player to Boon, more spectacular than safe, but he would do a good job.

However, he might have to beat off a challenge from Ricky

Ponting, who like Boon hails from the Apple Isle. Ricky made the tour to the Caribbean as a reserve batsman and has the potential to be an excellent number three with his sound technique, good temperament and the ability to dominate an attack. I prefer Ponting as the man to eventually take over from Boon, with Blewett either inheriting the number four spot if he wants to stay down the order or succeeding Taylor as an opener when the skipper decides he's had enough. The thought of Michael Slater and Blewett marching out to launch Australia's onslaught should be enough to induce a few loose deliveries from the best of opening bowlers.

Gone are the days when Border and Boon used to be the B for Backbone in Australia's batting. But there is still one job where they rely heavily on the stocky Tasmanian and that's as choirmaster: it's David Boon's job until he retires. However, there's a fair chance when he does depart that having gone from Border to Boon the baton will no longer be wielded by a B, as Blewett will still be regarded as an apprentice in such matters. With singing talent being a minimal requirement in leading 'Under the Southern Cross' and pride in playing for the baggy green cap a prerequisite, it could become a Waugh cry, with Steve calling the tune.

Boy, how things were to change ten years later in 2005.

[*The Bulletin*, January 1995]

Australia has retained the Ashes they regained in England in 1989. In that period Australia have dominated with thirteen wins to one. Ashes to ashes, dust to dust; these ancient clashes, are they a must?

There will be horrified gasps in England at the temerity of the suggestion. Why, in 1933, when the Australian Cricket Board sent a telegram to the MCC complaining about the 'unsportsman-like' nature of Bodyline bowling, diplomatic relations between the two countries were threatened.

Notwithstanding the repercussions, something drastic has to be done to improve English cricket. The decline is the result of negligence in a number of areas, including the game being near extinction in the schools, an archaic club system, and a first-class structure that boosts the finances of the counties and ignores England's best interests. Perhaps a gentle hint from the ACB suggesting England's permanent spot on the tour roster every four years is in jeopardy would have the desired effect.

The gap between the two teams has been widening since Australia was jolted out of their lethargy by two catastrophic series losses in the mid-Eighties. These setbacks prompted remedial measures such as the opening of an academy, the organisation of regular spin schools around the country, specialised coaching for fast bowlers, and the implementation of schemes to rejuvenate interest among youngsters.

In their hour of need England's officials have dithered and dallied and done a lot of window-dressing whilst achieving little. A recent comment by one of their highest ranking administrators encapsulates the English approach. Following England's second-innings demise in the MCG Test, a former Australian player asked what could be done to improve English cricket. The official shrugged his shoulders and replied, 'You tell me.'

For heaven's sake, England's collapse for ninety-two was not the result of a sudden bout of complacency in a hitherto supreme batting line-up. This was the third occasion in less than twelve months that this hapless bunch had crumbled for under a hundred; it followed a total of forty-six against the West Indies and a ninety-nine against South Africa. When England slumped to 3 for 20 in their first innings at the SCG it appeared they'd made a New Year's resolution to maintain batting form.

Despite these capitulations, it's the fielding rather than the batting which best indicates the gap between the two teams. In a one hundred-over one-day contest the combined difference in fielding and running between wickets is as much as forty. This is terminal on all but the odd occasion when an individual's brilliance papers over the cracks.

When England bowl well and find the edge of the bat and the ball flies into the slip cordon there's a fair chance it'll be grasped. If the Australians hit the ball in the air anywhere else it's almost certain to be grassed. Hence the variation in England's performance in the third Test. They bowled Australia out for 116 in the first innings, but found themselves on the rack when Mark Taylor and Michael Slater amassed a double-century opening stand in the second.

There were screams about umpire Darrell Hair not calling for the third umpire, who would surely have given Taylor run out. The complaints were not unreasonable; however, they shouldn't cloud the real issue. If John Crawley and Devon Malcolm had hung on to the sitters they were offered by Slater and Shane Warne then England probably would've won anyhow. When I described England's fielding as abysmal, former captain David Gower, only half-joking, said, 'You think it's that good?'

There are precious few athletes in the England side and the Australian batsmen can run virtually any time they want. The catch that got England back on the rails at the SCG was taken on the run by Phil Tufnell. This was hailed as one of the modern miracles, ranking up there with the Salk vaccine and splitting the atom. In actual fact, Michael Bevan in the same situation would've been in position and had time for a glance at his watch before taking the catch. With England, there's no lack of endeavour in the field, just a lack of mobility.

However, the intent is often missing in their batting. In the first innings at the SCG the Englishmen (apart from Mike Atherton and Crawley) played Craig McDermott as though he was delivering hand grenades. Then along came Darren Gough, armed only with a bat and abundant confidence, and he started hammering the same bowler to all parts. Buoyed by such a spirited display, Malcolm, a virtual rabbit with the bat, bludgeoned two sixes off Shane Warne. In the previous two Tests Warne's twenty wickets had cost a mere nine runs each.

Despite these obvious failings, England has the nucleus of a good side. Atherton is right when he says England need to pursue a youth policy, but he's likely to find himself in hot water for daring to say so publicly.

The England tour party was selected with very little concern for the World Series competition. One glance at the Australian cricket calendar, with the Tests and one-day games interwoven, is enough to reveal the folly of this ploy. It has resulted in some huge discrepancies in England's results, ranging from consecutive losses against the cricket academy to almost forcing Australia to follow-on in the third Test.

England's best is very good, but their worst is horrible. It must frustrate and embarrass Atherton that there's rarely anything in between.

Atherton himself is an excellent cricketer, with a lot of skill and loads of determination. However, like Allan Border in the mid-Eighties when the Australian team was struggling, Atherton is naïve when it comes to Test-match captaincy and he's had to keep the team afloat by maintaining his own personal batting standard. Like Border, he's averaged over fifty in a time of team crisis.

However, in Border's case the Australian selectors and the administrators set about improving the situation, whilst their English counterparts have done little to help Atherton's cause. If England's administrators keep shrugging their shoulders and blaming their lack of initiative on the insular outlook of the counties then the gap between the two countries will continue to widen.

For quite some time now an Ashes series has been useless as a guide to rankings in world cricket. In recent times England must accept full blame for this situation, which has arisen primarily because many of their officials refuse to accept that they no longer rule world cricket. Someone needs to explain that the days of Guy Fawkes are past, and if they're not careful someone will put a bomb under them.

No visiting team had won a series in the Caribbean since Australia in 1972–73; a visit by a cricket team to the Island countries of swaying palms was the equivalent of a trip to Death Valley. Mark Taylor's team was about to embark on that daunting tour in 1995, and so began the Australian team's ascent to the number one ranking.

[*Tony Cozier* magazine, January 1995]

In the four years since Australia was last in the Caribbean the team has changed dramatically and they have a realistic chance of reclaiming the elusive Frank Worrell Trophy.

The three most important changes, which have resulted in Australia becoming a more aggressive team, are the appointment of Mark Taylor as captain, the emergence of Shane Warne with his bamboozling leg spin, and the amazing opening onslaughts of Michael Slater.

Having not been on the receiving end, Taylor is not affected like Allan Border was by the endless beatings the West Indies handed Australia in the Eighties. Consequently he's less likely to be inhibited by his opponents and more likely to attack them at the appropriate time.

Border tended to approach the West Indies in the Nineties as though he was still playing the invincible juggernaut of the Eighties. There were times when he should've issued the order for full-scale attack, but because of past thrashings he couldn't quite bring himself to believe he had the upper hand. As a result he occasionally let the Windies off the hook, notably on the last tour at both Bourda and Kensington. It wasn't until it was too late that Australia went on the attack and won at St John's.

Taylor has wisely adopted his own style, and that includes encouraging players to bat naturally. Slater and Mark Waugh are the main beneficiaries of this approach. In addition, Taylor is a 'hands on the levers at all times' leader, and hence the predominately conservative views of coach Bob Simpson don't permeate the side as they did when Border allowed him a fair degree of control.

Slater's arrival on the scene has proved to be a blast of fresh air resembling Warne's cyclonic effect on the cricket world. He attacks from the outset and is as good as any batsman I've seen at dealing out equal portions of punishment from either the back or front foot. Even the best of players seem to favour one or the other, but in Slater's case he drives his opponents to distraction in a wide arc in front of the wicket, but also has the same effect with ferocious pulls and cuts.

'Slat the Bat' is as refreshing as a cold Banks. He hates to be tied down and rather than waiting for bowlers to err in line or length he sets out to provoke a few mistakes. However, it's wrong to think of him as purely an aggressive opener. Slater is amazingly consistent for one who attacks the new ball with such verve, collecting only six single-figure scores in his first thirty-six Test innings, whilst complementing that with an equally impressive conversion rate of five centuries.

Slater can be exasperating, but when he's exhilarating Australia usually win.

To his credit, Taylor appears happy to live with the odd 'head in the air swipe' which blots the otherwise brilliant Slater landscape, even if it brings about his downfall when he has the opposition at his mercy. The ultra-aggressive right-hander has benefited from Taylor's broad-minded approach, and in a reasonably short time they've become a formidable opening partnership.

And on the subject of formidable, there's Shane Warne, the blond bamboozler.

When Warne returned from a youth tour of the Caribbean, some Australian officials were critical of his relaxed manner off the field. Nowadays, administrators are perturbed there aren't more Shane Warnes in Australian cricket.

Warne is not only an excellent leg spinner, he also has a very wise head on young shoulders. He has wonderful control of all his deliveries (bar the wrong-un, which is his weakest) and on the odd occasion when he has been attacked he's relished the challenge. Along with Craig McDermott he is the most potent force in the Australian attack and between them they comprise about seventy-five per cent of the firepower. Dominate those two bowlers and Australia has the destructive capability of a blunt arrow.

Warne is not a one-day (or even a five-day) wonder: he's the real thing. He'll be around for as long as he wants or at least until his overworked shoulder gives way. He has the ability to turn the ball a long way on almost any pitch, but he does it with control and subtle variation. Richie Benaud describes Warne as 'the best young leg spinner I've ever seen', and goes on to add that he has mastered the difficult art by always having his hand in the right place for each delivery at the moment the ball is released. Add to that courage and a shrewd cricket brain, and the best the opposition can hope for is to make Warne pay a reasonable price for his wickets.

The West Indies' best hope of blunting Warne lies with the three left-handers in the middle order as his most dangerous delivery will be spinning into their pads. As one of the left-handers also happens to be the talented world-record holder Brian Lara, their battle could well decide which team takes the upper hand in the contest. It will be important, however, that the Windies' left-handers make the bulk of their runs in the first innings, as they will have enormous problems coping with Warne's prodigious spin out of the footmarks as the game nears its conclusion.

No doubt the West Indies will pursue their normal course in targeting the opposition captain for special 'treatment'. Overseeing the doses will be that prominent ear, nose and throat specialist Curtly Ambrose, who will trouble Taylor because of his ability to move the ball both back into and away from the left-handed opener off the pitch. If Ambrose's lifting deliveries result in Taylor's footwork becoming the shuffling variety rather than a positive movement either forward or back, then the 'treatment' will be deemed a success.

Because Ambrose is the West Indies bowler best equipped to maintain line and length under fire, he'll also be the toughest opponent Slater has yet encountered. Australia's ability to weather the new-ball onslaught will, along with the Warne–Lara contest, be the most important factor in deciding the fate of the Frank Worrell Trophy.

Another new player in the Australian line-up is swing bowler Damien Fleming. He is predominantly an outswing bowler and will trouble the West Indies' right-handers in particular if he can achieve what neither Bob Massie nor Terry Alderman (two noted swing bowlers) could in the Caribbean, and that is to get the ball to deviate late in its travels. If Fleming fails it will probably fall to Glenn McGrath – a stock rather than shock bowler, who bangs the ball into the pitch and tries to move it off the seam – to provide adequate support for McDermott's excellent all-round fast bowling.

The other influential players in the Australian side are likely to be Mark Waugh and Old Reliable, David Boon. Waugh, with his gliding footwork and graceful style, is well equipped to cope with the West Indies' pacemen. He'll be troubled occasionally by the short-pitched ball, but he more than any other Australian has the range of shots against top-class bowling to extract some retribution for any embarrassment. Boon, with his unflappable temperament and ability to play off both back and front foot, is often the solid platform on which respectable Australian scores are built. It's interesting to note how often Australia collapses if Boon is dismissed cheaply. It happens too often to be a coincidence.

Whilst Australia is heavily reliant on McDermott and Warne when bowling, they do have an excellent fielding side, headed by the genius of Mark Waugh. His marvellous catching, plus the efficiency of Ian Healy, Taylor and Steve Waugh, tends to make any bowling side better.

I see Australia having a slight advantage in batting if Desmond Haynes doesn't play, as his experience would balance the scales. On the other hand the West Indies have a distinct advantage in pace bowling which will be enhanced if Ian Bishop makes a successful comeback. However, Warne is a potent weapon and his ability to run through the Windies' tail like a raging bushfire will help to right this imbalance.

Any captaincy advantage is difficult to determine because of the uncertainty about whether the West Indies will have Courtney Walsh or Richie Richardson in charge. On the little I've seen, Australia will be better suited if Walsh is skipper.

The biggest question mark hanging over Australia is their abysmal record overseas since the beginning of the Eighties. In recent times it has been boosted by wins over England (1989 and 1993) and Sri Lanka, but the record still doesn't match the talent. However, on the recent tour of Pakistan they played aggressive cricket and were unlucky to lose a tight series one–nil. This was

Taylor's first venture as a captain and it was a promising start, providing optimism that Australia can play to their potential in the Caribbean. Whether that is good enough to beat the West Indies is another matter, but it would be an improvement on 1991.

When Tim May, Shane Warne and Mark Waugh named Pakistan captain Salim Malik as the player who had offered them money on the 1994–95 tour to perform below their best, it opened a bubbling pot on cricket corruption. There had been rumours flying around for some time about match-fixing, but in their inimitable fashion the administrators had turned a blind eye.

Now cricket has an anti-corruption unit (ACU), and yet with all the investigations only Malik, former South African captain Hansie Cronje, former Indian captain Mohammad Azharuddin, former Indian batsman Ajay Jadega, and former Pakistani fast bowler Ata-ur-Rehman have received any lengthy sentences. There can be no doubt that others have been extremely fortunate to escape serious punishment.

It is hard not to be cynical about the bias in the process when Herschelle Gibbs and Nicky Boje, still playing for South Africa, refuse to tour India because the Central Bureau of Investigation there won't rule out further questioning of those players. That tour of India took place in late 2005, but I still haven't heard any report of the ACU questioning the two South African players concerned. I would have thought this would be an automatic response to the players' refusal to tour, unless there was a reason for the Indian board to not want this to happen.

[*The Bulletin*, 16 February 1995]

The public naming of Pakistan captain Salim Malik as the person who allegedly offered substantial amounts to a number of Australian players to perform below their best in Pakistan has ensured the 'bribes affair' will not die quickly.

At first glance it's easy to blame greed when the captain of an International cricket team risks criminal charges, as well as bringing the game into disrepute. However, substantial rewards are given to players on the subcontinent for performing well on the cricket field, and this can have a profound influence on judgement.

For instance, former Pakistan captain Javed Miandad reportedly received valuable gifts including an expensive car when he slammed a six off the last ball to win a final against India in Sharjah. In the past it was safe to assume that these gifts were from rich, fanatical supporters, but now, with big money and a criminal element involved in some of the gambling on cricket, it's unwise to assume that any such 'reward' is offered without a future 'dividend' in mind.

In the Pakistan case it's highly unlikely that the player who allegedly offered the bribes was dealing with his own currency. That then begs the question: is he in the 'debt' of illegal gamblers? If so, the man is in trouble and his destiny, at least on the cricket field, is not in his own hands. The headline-grabbing 'Bribes Affair', plus a number of other unrelated but disturbing incidents, means it's imperative that there's a thorough investigation into the matter of gambling on cricket.

Those other events include India being docked two points by International referee Raman Subba Row after losing a one-day game to the West Indies. Subba Row explained his actions by saying India didn't 'play to its full potential'.

Recently in England two Essex players confessed that in 1991 they conspired to allow Lancashire to win a Sunday League (one-day) game in return for a generous declaration the next day in the county match against the same opposition. The two captains involved in the game denied the claims and after an investigation both clubs said they couldn't find any evidence to support the allegations.

And then there's former Pakistan captain Mushtaq Mohammad's 'joking reference' to Allan Border at Edgbaston in 1993. If Border had expressed interest rather than downright disgust when he was asked, 'What happens if someone offers you big money (to lose)?' it doesn't need too vivid an imagination to envisage Border's reply being relayed to another party.

So far it's been all allegations and no proof, and until a vigorous investigation is underway innocent parties will suffer. Already Warne, May, Mark Waugh and possibly one other Australian player have been put in the invidious position of having to 'shop' a fellow cricketer. The fact that they did so in dangerous circumstances is a credit to them and says much about their feeling for the game. And now Zimbabwe's historic first ever Test win is tainted, because it was at the expense of Pakistan.

The job of giving the game a thorough going-over in relation to these matters is not one for cricket officials. It needs to be conducted by someone with a background in criminal investigation who is not directly associated with any country's cricket administration. It would be a disaster if such an investigation was overshadowed by claims of bias or racist insinuations.

Cricket administrators the world over have a history of burying their heads in the sand when a problem occurs, in the hope that it will magically disappear. The fact that the Australian Cricket Board (ACB) passed to the International Cricket Council (ICC) some five months ago information relating to the attempts to bribe Australian players, suggests that London is currently the best viewing spot for ostrich impersonations.

The ACB, perhaps reacting to Dennis Lillee and Rod Marsh's successful betting coup on England at Headingley in 1981, does at least preclude players from betting on cricket matches or series in which they are participating. Surely the time is right for the players' behaviour code to exclude all International cricketers from betting on the game at all times during their playing career.

This may sound like a draconian measure, but by removing the temptation it lessens the chances of a player falling in debt to any shady characters. It's also exactly what is expected of professional baseball players in America. They are expelled if caught gambling on the game, and this clause was enacted in 1989 when Pete Rose, one of the game's heroes, was banned for life for betting on baseball. Almost seventy years prior to his sad demise, eight members of the 1919 Chicago White Sox team were banned for life after it was alleged they accepted bribes to throw the World Series against the Cincinnati Reds.

Gambling is a slow-spreading tumour in sport. Officials may not be able to cut out the cancer, but they should at least attempt to starve it by quarantining the healthy areas.

So far, the bribery targets revealed in cricket only involve experienced players. But imagine the predicament of a young player from a poor background, without the profile and the prospective riches of Shane Warne, being confronted with a proposition similar to the one Warne rejected in Pakistan. There's a time in every cricketer's life when he wonders if he's going to be good enough to make it at the top level. If a lucrative offer is put to a player grappling with those doubts it could prove tempting.

A young International player should be encouraged to dismiss such offers out of hand. To do so he needs to be aware that the penalty for doing otherwise is so great as to make it absolute stupidity. In addition, he also requires the assurance of knowing he's not on his own in such circumstances. He must feel secure in going straight to his captain or an administrator for assistance and guidance, knowing that he'll be fully protected.

It's not enough for the administrators to be fairly sure that any attempts by players to 'throw' a game of cricket will be obvious, or to assume that it's impossible to rig a Test match because there are too many players to buy off. As Rod Marsh once said, 'A drowning man will clutch at a serpent.' Desperate, greedy men will stop at nothing, and if players won't bite, then umpires could become a target.

Crooked gamblers don't care about sport or the people involved. They only care about money. The ICC must act quickly and firmly in this matter to protect the players and force these criminals to look elsewhere for their ill-gotten gains.

After a ding-dong battle the Australians finally conquered the Caribbean hoodoo and now ranked as the best Test team in the world.

[*The Bulletin*, 4 May 1995]

At first glance Australia's long-awaited triumph over the West Indies could be attributed to simply having the right man at the crease at the crucial time.

Steve Waugh is a battle-hardened cricketer who was hand-picked as a young player for his substantial talent but also because he had plenty of 'character'. For the past eighteen months he's been the side's most consistent batsman, and when Australia was tottering at 3 for 73 he marched into the Sabina Park cauldron and provided exactly the backbone the innings needed. His double century in the deciding Test of this enthralling series was not his most flamboyant contribution, but it was easily his most important.

Steve provided the stiffening, and his twin brother, Mark, the elegant stroke play, in a partnership that finally tilted this seesawing series in Australia's favour. In a low-scoring series it was always likely that one worthwhile partnership could make the difference, and the Waughs' efforts effectively ended hostilities. However, to make absolutely certain Australia gained the victory needed to reclaim the Frank Worrell Trophy, Steve pushed on to completely break the Windies' spirit.

It's ironic that Steve Waugh should be the man to defy the Windies and ultimately bring them to their knees. The West Indies became obsessed with a juggling catch Steve took in Barbados, believing he'd cheated local hero Brian Lara. They've also had a long-term fixation about his discomfort with the short-pitched delivery. During his marathon innings at Sabina Park it appeared these feelings took over to a point where the bowlers preferred to injure Waugh rather than inflict the worst pain – dismissal.

Through all the conflict Steve Waugh kept his concentration at a peak. He never missed an opportunity to remind the Windies of his presence, whether it was by taking a cheeky single after defending his face from a rising ball, or rifling a return to the keeper and sending the batsman scurrying back to his crease after he'd played a good shot. It was as if Steve decided in Barbados, 'If you're annoyed now, you're going to be sick to death of me by the time we finish at Sabina Park.'

Waugh won the battle and eventually the grudging respect of his opponents. A number of them gathered to shake his hand as he left the ground, last man out, having compiled two hundred and helping to double the Windies' first-innings score. There's no more humbling experience than having to shake the hand of an opponent you've ridiculed.

Despite Waugh's mammoth contribution, it would be unfair to the Australian team to imply that it was solely Steve's innings and his partnership with brother Mark that won the series. It was a gradual build-up of momentum by the Australians as they first outwitted the West Indies and then out-batted, out-bowled and out-fielded their opponents.

Captain Mark Taylor must take a lot of credit for the team's demeanour. He began his captaincy reign in Pakistan, where he instilled a different approach to touring, and it almost clinched victory on that tour. However, the plan finally gelled in the

Caribbean, where Australia showed what a good team they are by hitting back after a horrendous defeat in Trinidad.

Just as important as the positive mental approach when playing overseas, Taylor also implemented a policy of more aggressive batting. On many occasions under Taylor the Australians have scored at a rate in excess of three hundred runs per day, thereby increasing the opportunities to win. This ploy also delivers the message to the opposition: 'We want to be in a contest, because we fancy we can win.'

In the end Taylor's confident and positive approach, plus a superior tactical awareness, led the Australians to believe they were better than the West Indies. They were proved right.

The sign that the West Indies had finally wilted quickly followed the end of Steve Waugh's innings. No sooner had they congratulated Steve than they were wringing their hands at the quick loss of three second-innings wickets to the persistent Paul Reiffel.

The accurate Reiffel epitomised the Australians' performance in the Caribbean. There was nothing fancy: a few runs here, a catch there, the odd wicket as a result of some tidy bowling and a few runs saved by virtue of an ambling gait that's quicker than it looks and a strong throw. Reiffel, like so many other Australians in the series, contributed to an overall team effort.

The bowling was a shining example. At best the Australian attack was varied and persistent, but it also carried the twin threat of Shane Warne's magic and a fielding side that excelled. Warne's figures may not reveal a lot of wickets, but his presence resulted in a few falling at the other end, and the mental damage done by the brilliant fielding was untold. In addition, Taylor fully utilised his resources, ensuring at all times he had the right bowler on for each batsman and constantly adjusting his field placings to exert maximum pressure.

As well as defeating the West Indies, Taylor's team has finally exposed a number of shortcomings in the side that has been threatening to end its amazing winning run for a couple of years. In the recent past the Windies have escaped defeat thanks to the individual brilliance of Curtly Ambrose and Courtney Walsh with the ball and Richardson and Lara with the bat. However, at Sabina Park the individual efforts were insufficient and the team wilted.

There's now a sameness about the Windies' attack, with the ball predominantly coming into the right-handers, but I fancy that too many of the decision-makers in the Caribbean have prospered from the all-pace policy to be willing to make a change. The four-pronged pace attack has been dying a slow death ever since the balance slipped below the exceptional level of three great ones and one good one.

The loss to Australia signals the right time to abandon the life-support system and search for a balanced attack. This will require a major change of thinking in the Caribbean, from the selectors right down through the captain to the players. For a man like Richardson, who has prospered through two generations of pure pace, this would be asking a lot. The time will be right after the England tour to elevate Brian Lara to the captaincy, as he's worked with a balanced attack when leading Trinidad.

As well as lacking any great variety, the West Indies' bowling lacked a persistent performer who could 'bottle' things up for a while and allow the captain to exert some pressure on the Australian batsmen. The inconsistency of the two Benjamins was patently obvious during the Waugh twins' partnership, and the Windies can't afford the luxury of both of them, especially when neither contributes much with the bat to a tail that doesn't even twitch, never mind wag.

Australia must be delighted with the tour. Not only have they won the series and finally taken the step which proves they are the best side in the game, but they've also boosted prospects for a prosperous future. Suddenly the bowling resources don't look nearly so thin, with Glenn McGrath growing in stature and Reiffel proving he's a man who can be relied upon. And the three young batsmen, Greg Blewett, Ricky Ponting and Justin Langer, have just seen at close quarters what is required to win vital Test matches. Having witnessed Steve Waugh's epic fight to drag Australia to the top of world cricket, the young players are now better equipped to play with a similar pride and determination to retain that exalted position.

The first World Cup was a cricketing experiment held in England in 1975. Twenty years on the one-day game had become the financial lifeblood of cricket and the World Cup tournament was evolving into a licence to print money.

[*Wills Souvenir*, 6 October 1995]

Limited-overs cricket has evolved as the public's game, the entertainment that keeps the turnstiles clicking so that Test matches can retain their favoured position among players as the true test of a cricketer's worth.

There is no doubt that since the Eighties limited-overs cricket has been the financial buoy that has kept the game afloat. In many parts of the world Test-match popularity has displayed all the tendencies of a ship in rough seas, dipping one moment and then rising slowly, sometimes appearing ready to founder, but in the end surviving. Despite or perhaps because of these differences, the two versions of the game complement each other well, helping to maintain cricket's reputation as one of the most discussed and dissected pastimes in the world.

The evolution of the one-day game has coincided with a vast improvement in fielding and running between wickets. As a consequence, there has been some exciting contests between fielders and batsmen, which have added new dimensions to the game in both crowd enjoyment and umpiring headaches. Spectacular sights like

South African livewire Jonty Rhodes diving headlong at the stumps to bring about the downfall of an opponent are great entertainment, but they don't make an umpire's job any easier. This has resulted in the advent of the off-field video-replay decision, but instead of the delay detracting from the game, it has the effect, especially in a tight contest, of adding to the dramatic build-up of tension.

There is no doubt that the show-piece of the limited-overs game is the World Cup. It was launched in 1975, and after an enthralling final between Australia and the eventual winners, the West Indies, the concept was assured of success. That future now looks very bright indeed, and not just because of the introduction of flood-lit cricket.

Cricket at night, with its coloured clothing and white balls, produces a spectacle that provides the right mix of competitive entertainment. But, more than that, the idea of playing outside working hours has unveiled cricket to a whole new audience who now embrace the game, either by attending matches or watching on television.

Despite these important innovations, the most radical change has been the attitude of the players towards the shortened version of the game. This is not necessarily a change in tactical appreciation (which tends to be cyclical and oscillate between attack and containment, depending on things like the field-restricting circles or whether Shane Warne is playing or resting), but rather a professional need as compared with a cavalier approach.

In the early Seventies the players looked upon limited-overs cricket as the sideshow, with Test cricket the main attraction. Whilst the present players are conscious that the ultimate test of skill, cricket intelligence and courage is still the five-day game, they are also cognisant of the need to be classed as a competent one-day player or else face extinction as an international competitor.

The power of limited-overs cricket can be gauged from a glance at Zimbabwe's progress in the international arena. They weren't invited to either of the first two World Cups and registered their disapproval by upsetting Australia in their opening match of the 1983 tournament, which also happened to be their official debut at that level. There were no such upset victories for them in 1987, but in their final contest of the 1992 World Cup, with an application for Test status languishing among a pile of papers at ICC headquarters, they inflicted a surprise defeat on the eventual runners-up, England. That made it difficult for England to vote against Zimbabwe's entry into Test cricket and so, via the short route, they entered cricket for the long haul.

Fortunately the Zimbabweans weren't the only ones to grasp the importance of the World Cup. Building on that first success in 1975, the promoters have wisely used it as a vehicle to promote the game to a wider audience. So, from a meagre beginning as an eight-team tournament that wasn't a viable proposition outside the UK, the World Cup has grown into a twelve-team extravaganza, which includes cricketing minnows like the United Arab Emirates, Kenya and Holland. It will be watched by millions on television and played simultaneously in three different countries, all of which are a long plane flight from London, even allowing for the speed of Concorde.

The advancement of technology in the lifetime of the World Cup has outstripped the speed of even the fastest jet, and this has also added to the image of the tournament. In 1975 the final was watched by a full house at Lord's and a television audience of maybe two million, with the number boosted by some poor misguided souls in Australia who thought themselves privileged to stay up until six a.m. to see their team lose. In 1996, a player who experiences the joy of being part of the winning team and holding aloft the trophy at the Gaddafi Stadium in Lahore will do so in the knowledge that not only are the folks at home basking in the glory, but that tens of millions of cricket fans, some recently acquired and others of long standing, will have witnessed the entertainment.

This ill-considered decision taken during the 1996 World Cup, played in India, Pakistan and Sri Lanka, hasn't come back to haunt Australia as much as I thought it would. However, it did strain relations between the Australian and Indian administrations for a few years.

The following two columns describe the build-up to and confirmation of one of the Australian Cricket Board's (ACB) most controversial decisions.

[*The Bulletin*, 7 February 1996]

Sometimes a team has to play to win in trying circumstances, and if they don't succeed there is at least the satisfaction of having lost with honour. There is no honour in conceding.

The ACB would be wrong to forfeit an international match. I have no doubt that conceding the two points would not be the biggest penalty the Australian team suffers if the ACB continues to refuse to play in Colombo. A decision to forfeit would haunt the Australian team more than the underarm delivery has shadowed Greg Chappell.

Once the ACB had unsuccessfully attempted to have the match against Sri Lanka rescheduled, I don't see how they could avoid playing in Colombo. The offer to fly the Australian team in and out of the country in the shortest possible time has to be acceptable in these circumstances. It may not be the ideal preparation for a World Cup match, but at least the two points will have been fought for and won or lost, not conceded.

If Australia forfeit to Sri Lanka, the question arises: where will they tour in the future?

Lives are being lost in Karachi on a regular basis. South Africa is still far from a safe country. Kingston, Jamaica, is a dangerous city if you travel to the wrong area. The list is a lot longer. What happens if a disaster occurs in one of those countries just prior to an Australian tour? Does the ACB then call off the tour? The IRA bombings in London didn't stop Australian teams touring England.

Having wavered on this occasion the ACB has left itself wide open to every crank who wants to put the fear of death into an Australian cricketer. If, for instance, a fanatical supporter in another country feels he can keep Shane Warne and Craig McDermott at home by writing threatening letters, isn't he now going to be encouraged to do so, on the basis that if successful it might help his team?

I can understand the ACB being fearful of sending the Australian team to Sri Lanka. Who wants to be responsible for sending a team into a war zone and then have a player injured or worse? However, this is not a lengthy tour. The ACB could not be blamed if it decides to cancel the tour planned for later this year if the same tension prevails, but for one match it's a different proposition.

I think the ACB has tended to concentrate on the worst-case scenario rather than giving the situation balanced appraisal. The Australian and West Indies' boards have asked for their matches to be rescheduled. Zimbabwe and Kenya, two countries that have experienced war conditions, have indicated their preparedness to play in Colombo. Somewhere in the middle must be a compromise, and I think the Sri Lankan authorities have come up with a reasonable one.

In 1994 New Zealand were touring Sri Lanka and a serious bomb blast occurred in Colombo. Five of the Kiwi team asked to return home and they were replaced so that New Zealand could complete the tour. This they did without further incident. Sometimes cricketers are asked to go above and beyond the line of duty. How the individuals handle those tense situations is often influenced by the leadership at the time.

I have been on the field whilst four riots have occurred. These were serious enough for the field to be littered with bottles and in some cases for the stands to be on fire; and on one occasion the Indian dressing room was full of bloodied casualties. I have been in the dressing room whilst the stands at the Bourda ground in Guyana were smashed. An Australian player was hit by a deck-chair thrown from the members' stand and I've seen an Indian captain pelted with chairs from above by an irate crowd in Calcutta. I have been in a room when the two umpires have spoken about fearing for their lives if they officiated the next day.

None of which was much fun. However, in virtually all cases the game went on and afterwards everyone felt stronger for having weathered the storm.

I was fortunate. The first two riots I witnessed at close quarters, when Bill Lawry was Australia's captain. As the stands burned in Bombay's Brabourne Stadium, the official scorers came onto the field to tell the umpires that they couldn't see because of the smoke and the game had to be stopped. Bill Lawry's response was to get on with it: 'We need a wicket badly.' From his outward appearance Bill might easily have been in charge of a Northcote XI in a pre-season tussle with Essendon where the umpires were worried about the bails constantly blowing off at Windy Hill.

The Australian team was fortified by Bill's approach and it had an effect on the way I looked at future dangerous situations. In contrast, Ray Illingworth took his team off the field when a few bottles came over the fence at the SCG, and I remember thinking it was an overreaction.

It is hard to equate bottle-throwing and burning stands with suicide bombers. However, Sri Lanka's offer of a brief stay for the Australian team would only involve the players in exposure at the ground. At worst this should be no more dangerous than what is often experienced at a number of the volatile cricket centres in the world.

A lot of the game of cricket has to do with perception. The ACB will show itself to be vulnerable if it resorts to a forfeit, and having been thus exposed it will find it difficult to win back that ground.

[*Indian Express*, 12 February 1996]

The decision of Australia and the West Indies to forfeit a game at the World Cup is a regrettable one, but rather than being a move that splits the cricketing world asunder, let's hope it turns out to be the one which brings the administrators to their senses.

The offer made by Sri Lanka to fly Australia and the West Indies in and out quickly, spending precious little time in the danger zone of Colombo, was one that should have been accepted.

Unfortunately it appears that having taken its original stance, the ACB was not prepared to change. Administrators should be like players; they should be prepared to adapt to changing conditions, and on this occasion I think the ACB has been too inflexible.

Sadly, cricket administration has become increasingly political. Too often the best interests of the game are sacrificed in the efforts of the officials either to gain an advantage for their board or to score points off another country's board. It is on the field that the game should be ultra-competitive, not around the board-room table.

For many years now cricket has been crying out for a governing body that administers the game on a global basis. No issue makes this point better than the shambles we've seen in the last twelve months, which is being passed off as running the game. A bribery scandal, ball-tampering accusations, a chucking incident and now two forfeits at cricket's premier spectacle suggest that it is in need of some healing medicine. What has been administered is pure quackery.

The ICC complains that it has been powerless to step in and take control in virtually all of these controversies. If this is the case then the individual boards should immediately vote to give the ICC power to run cricket on a global basis. They should also add a rider that all decisions should be taken in the best interests of the game. If this isn't done quickly then it will continue to rip itself apart and the result won't be a pretty sight for cricket fans.

The decision to forfeit has caused anger and resentment. Dav Whatmore, the Sri Lankan coach who played his Test cricket for Australia, spoke of an 'empty feeling' on hearing the news that Sri Lanka had received a four-point gift. When you have anger and resentment in the air, that is when people are likely to strike out in trying to seek retribution, and the position only worsens.

It is a pity the administrators from around the world couldn't have been in the cavalcade that went from Salt Lake Stadium in Calcutta through the city on the day preceding the World Cup opening ceremony. The ex-captains of World Cups gone by experienced the warmth of the reception from the people of Calcutta. It's unfortunate the officials who are attempting to run this game weren't there to experience how deep the love for cricket is in India. It was exactly the experience they need to make them sit up and say, 'Hang on, it is time we fixed what ails this game and made it better for the people who matter most; those who pay their money at the turnstiles.'

It is going to take a strong hand and a cool head – it always does in a crisis, and that is what cricket has on its hands. The decision of Australia and the West Indies to become the first teams to forfeit a one-day International has the potential to ruin a tournament that had all the signs of being the best World Cup yet. The tournament probably won't be ruined because the administrators somehow have the knack of 'muddling through'. Perhaps it is because cricket is too strong for even the worst of administrators to ruin, but it deserves better than just 'muddling through'.

I am not happy that Australia has forfeited a cricket match. I believe that to fight bravely for the two points even in adversity and lose brings honour. The only redeeming feature of the decision made by Australia and the West Indies could be that it has such an effect on the cricket world that it forces the administrators to take a look at the job they are doing and realise that they need to do it a whole lot better.

In 1996 Chennai was still Madras and Mark Waugh was . . . well he was always worth watching. On a hot, humid night Mark played a gem to push those pesky Kiwis out of the World Cup.

[*Indian Express*, 11 March 1996]

Australia overcame their deepest fears to defeat arch rivals New Zealand in a magnificent run chase and set up a meeting with the West Indies in the semi-finals.

In recent times the Australian team has had the most difficulty in the one-day game when confronted with a stiff run chase. They put that bogey to rest with a commanding performance from Mark Waugh and cool contributions from his brother, Steve, and Stuart Law.

Although their batting session was full of tension, the Australians must have thought Christmas had come early when they commenced bowling at the Chidambaram Stadium in Madras. The pitch was a bouncy one, similar to what they are used to at home, thus ensuring that any edges would carry to the catching fieldsmen. As Paul Reiffel and Damien Fleming were both able to make the ball swing away from the right-handers they must have been licking their lips as the ball carried through to Ian Healy.

Unfortunately for Australia the pitch was also to the liking of New Zealand's Lee Germon and Chris Harris. In New Zealand's flexible batting order they came together after Stephen Fleming was out to Glenn McGrath and Australia were on top having taken three wickets in only 8.3 overs. Germon and Harris based their resurrection job on all-out aggression.

This approach unsettled the Australian bowlers, who were unusually loose in both line and length. It was almost as though the Australians, having been away from home for a month, became so excited at the sight of some bounce in the pitch that their train of thought was derailed. It wasn't until well after the thirty-over mark that the Australians got back on track and began to concentrate on keeping the ball full and at the stumps. However, by that stage of the innings the Kiwis were well and truly in control.

New Zealand's superiority was established during a record-breaking partnership of 168 between Germon and Harris. Their batting was at times audacious, often brilliant and occasionally fortunate. However, it was a case of fortune favouring the brave and Germon deserves credit for the approach of the New Zealand team. It takes a lot of courage to continue playing aggressively when early wickets have been lost, but fortified by the thought of a long batting order, that is exactly what the skipper did.

Amazingly, the scintillating batting of Germon and Harris wasn't heralded by any prior form. Germon hadn't made a half-century in a limited-overs international and Harris had only twenty-six runs to his name in the Wills World Cup and hadn't played in the two previous games. This was a typical Kiwi response – save your best for Australia.

In the end it wasn't good enough, only because of yet another magnificent century by Mark Waugh. He became the first player to score three centuries in a World Cup tournament and paced himself beautifully in pursuit of an extremely difficult target. So elegant is Waugh's batting that his centuries have a tendency to creep up on you. It came as a mild surprise when a lofted on-drive landed in the crowd, taking Waugh to within one of his century. After passing the three figures Waugh perished more from exhaustion than any devil in the bowling, but he had left his team-mates with no more than the mopping-up.

On a day where Brian Lara had set the standard in the morning, Mark Waugh at least equalled that performance under lights. Mark's batting was silky smooth and the Kiwi attack, depleted by injury, was powerless to stop the elegant assassin.

Whilst Australia succeeded in putting their chasing bogey to rest, they need to improve their bowling. McGrath continues to take a pounding, conceding far too many boundaries for comfort. And in a most untypical display, Reiffel struggled to maintain line and length under fire. Shane Warne, hampered by a finger injury, was also below his usually high standard.

Nevertheless, the Australians survived another torrid encounter with their trans-Tasman rivals. Thanks to Mark Waugh they now get the chance to exact revenge for the loss to the Windies in Jaipur, and Mark's personal reward is a head-to-head battle with Brian Lara.

Shane Warne has always been at his best as a bowler when the team needs him most. This was the first of two super-human performances Warne contributed to the Australian cause in consecutive World Cup semi-finals.

[*Indian Express*, 14 March 1996]

Talk about snatching defeat from the jaws of victory. It was even worse: the West Indies were guilty of first-degree murder at Chandigarh.

As Mark Taylor said at the presentation, 'They won ninety-five per cent of the match and we won the last five.' The Windies had played themselves into a winning position through good bowling and sensible batting, and then for no reason at all they started swinging for the fences when all that was required was more of what they had been doing. Unfortunately, the West Indies team appears incapable of maintaining its standard for fifty overs, when either batting or bowling.

What ended so disastrously for the West Indies had all begun so gloriously, thanks to Curtly Ambrose. In the last couple of years I have had Wasim Akram slightly ahead of Ambrose as the best strike force among the pace bowlers. After this performance I'm not so sure. I can't remember Curtly ever letting the Windies down when they required wickets, endowed as he is with a big-match temperament. He struck a decisive blow with his second delivery, getting an off-cutter to snake back and trap Mark Waugh lbw. Ambrose then added to his contribution by producing a similar delivery to ambush Ricky Ponting.

At the other end, in an inspired move Richie Richardson gave the new ball to Ian Bishop and he performed like an Archbishop. Where the tall, well-built fast bowler had struggled at first change, only taking one wicket in the tournament, he suddenly sliced through the defences of Mark Taylor and Steve Waugh to add to Australia's early misery.

However, the difference between Richardson's West Indies side and the great ones of the past is that this team allowed Australia to clamber back to their feet after being knocked down. At 4 for 26 Stuart Law was caught off a Bishop no-ball, and then at 4 for 78 came an even bigger blunder: the dangerous Michael Bevan was left stranded by Roger Harper and Courtney Browne fumbled the stumping opportunity. Browne makes a bad habit of missing the vital ones: Steve Waugh in the Sabina Park Test, Sachin Tendulkar in the Gwalior loss, and now Bevan.

Law and Bevan made the most of those escapes and posted Australia's best fifth-wicket partnership in World Cup matches. Law is a serene player often underestimated at international level, but he's highly rated by his team-mates. Bevan is more spectacular and hence his reputation at this level has preceded him.

Despite their fumbling in the field the West Indies had given themselves a chance to go to Lahore by restricting Australia to only 207. The Australians were going to need every ounce of their famed determination and a spot of magic from Shane Warne to extricate themselves from this mess.

They showed their intentions early when Taylor didn't waste any time in calling on his trump. Browne and Shivnarine Chanderpaul started confidently against the pace bowlers, but Warne broke that promising partnership with his first delivery – an ordinary one, but enhanced by a sharp catch. That brought Lara out to face Warne, and the animated crowd that had been busy doing the wave stopped immediately and concentrated solely on cricket.

They were rewarded with an absorbing battle, but eventually Lara's class started to tell and the target began to look within easy reach. However, this Australian team never concedes easily, and after being flayed through the covers, Steve Waugh produced a gem to bowl the little master. For a time that changed the complexion of the game, as Richardson struggled, but eventually Chanderpaul, who had gone quietly about his job, got the momentum back into the Windies' innings.

The pair added seventy-two in fine style and then, out of the blue, suddenly started playing shots as though they required ten an over. Taylor was quick to sense the hint of panic, and when Glenn McGrath had picked up two wickets he brought Warne back into the fray.

What followed was a blur of wickets and batting that was as reckless as the driving of a Calcutta cabbie. The West Indies managed to squander eight wickets for thirty-seven in fifty-one balls in a criminal act that would have made Jack the Ripper blush. They had wilted under the pressure applied by Australia, and the Sri Lankans had their wish – another crack at Taylor's team.

Arjuna Ranatunga needled Australia right up to the eve of the 1996 World Cup final. In a television preview of the match he described Warne as 'a media myth'. When Shane came up for his interview he asked, 'What has that fat bastard said about me now?' It was rare in this period for an Australian opponent to have the upper hand psychologically, but Ranatunga had grabbed the high ground the moment he stated, 'We want Australia in the final,' after they had forfeited their preliminary match.

[*Indian Express*, 16 March 1996]

The 1996 Wills World Cup final is a classic showdown between the two best sides in the competition. And just to add a bit of needle, there are a few recent scores to be settled between Australia and Sri Lanka.

From Sri Lanka's point of view they believe they were hard-done-by on the recent tour of Australia. They were accused of ball tampering, which was later rescinded, then had their premier spinner no-balled for throwing, and just for good measure the players consider they were on the wrong end of a few crucial umpiring decisions. For their part the Australians were aggravated by the Sri Lankan time-wasting tactics and the way they believe some players, particularly the skipper, Arjuna Ranatunga, manipulated the law concerning the use of a runner. As keeper

Ian Healy bluntly informed Ranatunga in a heated moment during the World Series Competition (WSC) final, 'The reason you need a runner is because you are unfit, not injured.'

All of this may seem like petty stuff when there are bombs killing people, rampant AIDS epidemics in some countries and millions starving, but to a professional cricketer these irritations matter. Niggling, ongoing things are often used as motivation against an opponent and in the end one of these annoyances may cause the final to be lost.

Which finalist is most likely to wilt? The answer twelve months ago would certainly have been Sri Lanka. However, after a highly successful period where the Sri Lankans have beaten all the top sides at one-day cricket, the answer is not so clear cut.

These are the two best batting sides in the competition, with depth and a nice blending of aggression and solidarity. They also field well, although Australia has a slight edge. The rapid improvement of Chaminda Vaas and the injury to Craig McDermott have narrowed the gap between the bowling attacks, and the teams are well led. Both captains maintain their composure under pressure, but Mark Taylor's leadership relies on more flair than Ranatunga. Nevertheless, none of this adds up to a distinct edge, until you reach the name Shane Warne.

The Sri Lankans play Warne as well as any team, but still the blond bamboozler managed to bowl a match-turning spell in each of the two WSC finals. The main reason Warne plays such an influential part in so many games is because Taylor always turns to his leggie when the match is on the line. He did so against the West Indies in Australia's incredible semi-final win, and with devastating effect. And, just as importantly, Warne succeeds because he enjoys bowling at the point where the match will be decided.

With that in mind it may not hurt the Sri Lankans to bat first as it is not so easy to pinpoint the defining moment in an innings when the target is not set. However, that would mean changing Sri Lanka's favoured formula, which is to chase. Despite the accepted wisdom that it is folly to alter a plan that is working, there is one other compelling reason to bat first: no team has won a World Cup final chasing.

On the score of World Cup experience the Australians are ahead, with Steve Waugh having played in the 1987 winning side, but this is not a significant advantage. As this game will be won by the team that is mentally stronger, a key factor may be the mental state of two of Australia's most important players, Warne and Mark Waugh. With the final being played in Pakistan, the Salim Malik 'bribes affair' enters the equation, and if this has an effect on two of Malik's accusers it will hamper Australia's chances. Warne has the added mental hurdle of a sore spinning finger which restricts the use of his most effective delivery, the leg break.

Both teams have proved themselves in the lead-up to the final, with Australia treading a slightly more harrowing path. Sri Lanka has brushed aside the challenges of England and India as they single-mindedly headed for the showdown they have been eagerly awaiting.

In the process, Sri Lanka has shown they fear no player or team, whilst the Australians have displayed enormous courage in fighting every game out to the end. It is tough on the nervous system to win three close encounters in the knockout stage, but if any team has the nerve to succeed, it is Australia under Mark Taylor.

In 1975 Sri Lanka was one of only eight teams competing in the inaugural cricket World Cup. It was their first one-day competition and they were still almost seven years away from playing their first Test match. Their sudden and exciting rise to the pinnacle of the one-day game was a remarkable feat.

———

[*Indian Express*, 17 June 1996]

Just twenty-one years after they were thrashed by the West Indies in their first Cup match, the Sri Lankans rose to the pinnacle of one-day cricket by pulling off a magnificent victory against Australia in the 1996 World Cup final.

For Sri Lanka this was the story of how de Silva turned to gold. Aravinda de Silva, for so long an under-achiever, harnessed his concentration to the point where it matched his talent, scoring a century that will rank with those of Clive Lloyd and Viv Richards in World Cup folklore. To complete his remarkable day of achievement, de Silva was there at the end when his captain, Arjuna Ranatunga, hit the winning runs.

This was the culmination of a remarkable gamble by Ranatunga, who won the toss and decided to defy history by trying to become the first team to bat second and win a World Cup. It hadn't happened in the five previous tournaments, but that didn't deter the Sri Lankan captain, who stuck with his favoured method of chasing a target.

By the way Mark Taylor commenced his innings it appeared that he had a target of three hundred in mind. Taylor has a fondness for Lahore, having already made two half-centuries at the ground, and following a series of pull shots and drives he quickly made it a hat-trick.

The runs flowed quickly and easily, but Ranatunga is not one to allow a game to slip away without a fight. He called on de Silva to break this dangerous liaison, who then not only rid Sri Lanka of the Taylor menace, but also brought about Ponting's downfall with one that turned appreciably. This handy spell of bowling set the tone for Aravinda's greatest day in cricket.

That flurry of wickets brought the crowd alive and put a spring in the step of the Sri Lankans. De Silva then pulled off another coup when he took a good running catch to get rid of the dogged Steve Waugh. The Australians had faltered against some persistent spin bowling and a potential huge total evaporated. So tight was the Sri Lankan stranglehold that when Stuart Law lofted Kumar Dharmasena for six in the forty-third over it was the first boundary for 113 balls.

Despite the hiccups, the innovative Michael Bevan managed to scrape together a few boundaries and pushed the target to a respectable 242. This would be a difficult chase against a fighting bunch like Taylor's team, but the fact that the Sri Lankans eagerly applauded each other off the field suggested they were confident of the chase.

This wasn't reflected by the Sri Lankan openers, who made a jittery start. Sanath Jayasuriya ran between wickets as though he'd had a pep talk from a kamikaze pilot, and he paid the penalty. However, he was unlucky to be given out by the third umpire. I'd hate to be hung on such evidence: it was flimsy. Kaluwitharana looked very tense, and without a lot of runs to his name he perished trying to play an ambitious pull shot.

That brought together the in-form de Silva and Asanka Gurus-inha, and they proceeded to put together a steadying partnership. They did so with a mixture of good shots and a bit of good fortune. The best break looked to be a sub-par Warne. He was really struggling to bowl his leg breaks with any bite and his sore finger also caused him to pitch short too often.

Despite Warne's problem and a couple of uncharacteristic dropped catches, the Australians had one last chance when Gurusinha threw his head in the air and lost his wicket. This was the point in the semi-final where the West Indies panicked; however, the Sri Lankan resolve was far stronger.

De Silva concentrated fiercely and Ranatunga worked the ball into the gaps until the target was within sight. The clincher came, appropriately, when the skipper lofted Warne for six over square-leg. That relieved any final tension that could have been Australia's saviour, and, incredibly, Sri Lanka were rulers of World Cup cricket.

It has been a remarkable climb from the bottom to the top in twenty-one years. Sri Lankan cricket has certainly come of age.

It is rare for Australian cricket to adopt the English method of selecting the captain first and then the other ten players. However, for a while that is what the Australian selectors did and it caused quite a few headaches.

[*The Bulletin*, 17 March 1997]

There is no doubt Australia has won Test matches courtesy of Mark Taylor's cool calculating captaincy. On the other hand it must be of concern that the team has experienced far too many batting collapses, and Taylor's miserable form is a contributing factor.

The moment of truth is not far away for the selectors. They cannot keep picking an unbalanced side in addition to having Matthew Elliott, potentially one of the best openers in the game, languishing at number three. In the Port Elizabeth Test it could be fairly argued that South Africa would not have reached anywhere near two hundred in the first innings if Paul Reiffel had played. Equally, Australia may then not have disintegrated so badly in reply if Elliott had opened. There is a lot to be said for ensuring trouble rarely occurs rather than trying to mount a rear-guard action following early failures.

There is also another reason why the selectors face a dilemma over Taylor, even though Australia has generally outplayed South Africa. Despite numerous opportunities, he shows no signs of coming out of his prolonged slump. Even with Shaun Pollock, his most dangerous new-ball opponent, missing from the action in the second innings at St George's Park, Taylor gave no indication that a big score was just a few well-timed shots away. Apart from his cool leadership the thing that may save his neck is the fact that Matthew Hayden is not looking any more convincing than Taylor.

Whatever the touring selectors decide for the third Test, it can't include the luxury of Elliott batting at three and only two front-line pacemen. To overcome these problems one batsman has to go, and it must be either Taylor or Hayden. If it is Hayden – and that is logical, considering that the captain's current contribution to the team effort is the greater of the two – Taylor's problem doesn't completely disappear. What then happens to him for the limited-overs series?

Bearing in mind Australia's dismal record at the shortened version of the game lately, there is no way a horribly out-of-form Taylor can occupy a vital spot in the order. If Mark doesn't open the batting then there's no place for him in the one-day side.

So, despite Australia's dominance at the Wanderers and the courageous fightback in Port Elizabeth, it's an extremely harrowing time for the selectors. There have also been some rather anxious moments for Australian supporters, who have been on an emotional roller-coaster ride with the team this summer.

If you're searching for reasons why Australia is inconsistent, then look no further than the batting line-up. They are prone to collapses on anything but a good pitch, as we've seen on the dust bowl at Delhi, the wide cracks at the WACA and an underprepared St George's Park. The comforting news is Australia bats well on good pitches, and because the attack is penetrating and varied they regularly win in those circumstances. Also providing a crumb of comfort is the fact that Australia are slightly less vulnerable than all the other sides, as the game goes through a phase where the bowling is far superior to the batting.

Australia has the opportunity to strengthen their batting by coming up with a well-balanced line-up for the tour of England. This must involve Elliott playing as an opener and recalling both Michael Slater and Ricky Ponting. Australia would then have its best six batsmen in England and it becomes a ding-dong fight to find out who are the top six.

More than likely Taylor will make the tour of England, then it will be a matter of whether he survives the cut-throat battle for a place in the Test side. The issue of his inclusion in the best six batsmen shouldn't be clouded by the misguided assumption that Australia only has one player who can captain the team success-fully. I have no doubt that either of the Waugh twins could do the job efficiently and that Shane Warne has the potential to be an excellent and aggressive captain. So, Mark's selection should not be dependent on the fact that he is tailor-made for the captaincy, but on whether his batting is cut from inferior cloth.

This was written before text messaging had become a way of life. However, I still enjoy Shane Warne's company, and despite a few indiscretions on his part I still regard him as an honest and straightforward character. And what a pity he never captained Australia in Test matches – he would have made the cricket a joy to behold for both his players and the fans.

[Foreword in *My Own Story*, Swan Publishing, 1997]

The first time I heard about Shane Warne was from former Australian wicket-keeper Brian Taber. As manager of the Australian Youth team that toured the Caribbean in 1990, Brian summed up the young Shane this way: 'Most of the other guys [in the team] didn't want to know about drinking with the opposition after facing a few bouncers, but Shane would always grab a bottle of beer and march into their room and chat away happily after a day's play. He's also not a bad leg spinner.'

Apart from developing into one of cricket's finest leg spinners, not much about Shane has changed since those days in the Caribbean. He still has a great love for the game and its traditions and he enjoys talking about cricket as well as playing it to the best of his ability. Warne, along with Sachin Tendulkar, has handled fame and adulation in an extremely mature fashion. The way Shane treats young fans is indicative of a man who still vividly recalls his own cricketing roots.

I have enjoyed watching the development of Shane Warne into a great Test match bowler, possessed of a keen cricket brain and a strong competitive spirit. My only disappointment would be if he shied away from taking on the Australian captaincy whilst he is still at his peak as a player. I think he would make a fine leader in the most difficult category of all, a bowling captain.

I have gained equal pleasure in getting to know Shane Warne the man. I admire him and enjoy his company. It is not sufficient to utilise a God-given talent to its fullest, a sportsman must also conduct himself as a decent human being. Shane Warne has succeeded admirably in both categories.

I still regard the dropping of Michael Slater as one of the poorest selections since Keith Miller was left out of the 1949–50 touring party to South Africa.

———

[*The Daily Telegraph* UK, 28 May 1997]

A ustralia is outright favourite for the Ashes series on the basis of excellent wins against strong opposition from the West Indies and South Africa. However, the Australian players won those two Test series despite the selectors. The panel stumbled into the quicksand when it took the ridiculous step of dropping Michael Slater, and every move it has made since has sunk it deeper in the mire. Poor selections eventually hurt a team, and in the Texaco series Australia fiddled whilst England was on fire. Now it is again up to the players to display their resilience by ensuring they don't allow England to maintain the upper-hand in the Test series.

Australia has the talent and the mental strength to re-group for Edgbaston, but they need to quickly sort out the top-order batting and get their front-line fast bowlers into form. The major obstacle in Australia's way is the molehill that has turned into a mountain – what to do with Mark Taylor?

I see no other solution for Australia but to discard Taylor as the skipper – unlike the Rolling Stones – he no longer has time on his side. There has been no sign that Taylor's form is emerging from hibernation, and to continue with a selection policy which puts the captain ahead of the team risks creating further uncertainty in a side that came close to disarray during the Texaco series. The selectors are responsible for this mess; therefore, they should take on an unaccustomed role of leadership and tell Taylor to step down. If they continue to remain silent then it puts Steve Waugh, the man who will inherit Taylor's job, in the unenviable position of having to wield the hatchet. Despite Taylor's undoubted ability as an aggressive captain, Australia cannot keep performing Houdini-style escapes if they continue to play ten men against the opposition's eleven.

The priority must be to ensure that a combination of three of Matthew Elliott, Michael Slater, Greg Blewett and Ricky Ponting is quickly in form. Australia has a talented middle order, but they are also vulnerable against top-class pace and spin bowling. Therefore it is imperative that Mark and Steve Waugh and Michael Bevan get some protection so they are free to play their natural game on most occasions.

Elliott is potentially a top-class batsman, but he badly needs to acclimatise to English conditions. He is a born opener who bases his game on a good defence, spiced with the ability to drive and pull anything not pitched on a good length. As a combination he and Slater can quickly assert control and with a star-studded cast to follow that spells trouble for the opposition. Every time this Australian side posts a large total it capitalises, which is exactly the method used to bring England to its knees in the last two Ashes series in this country.

If Australia do lose early wickets then the job of resurrecting the innings falls to the Waugh twins. Mark, with his twinkle-toes footwork and graceful timing, is the best equipped to handle any crisis, but Steve is not far behind with his steely determination and incisive punishment of any loose delivery. However, even their God-given talent can be nullified if they constantly have to face fresh new-ball bowlers. They need some help from above – not religious, but reliable opening stands.

Australia's best-balanced side has Bevan at number six, which means Blewett batting at three. This isn't a hardship as Blewett is a good player of pace bowling and he's endowed with an excellent temperament. Like Elliott, Blewett drives well and plays the pull shot, which makes him a difficult customer to tie down. Bevan at his aggressive best is the ideal number six, as it gives him a chance to survive the ball moving towards the slips, where he was often caught when England last toured Australia.

In addition to his batting, Bevan becomes a bonus bowler to complement the three pacemen and the spin of Shane Warne. Australia's other priority besides settling the top order is for the fast bowlers to take some wickets before they play in the Edgbaston Test. Despite the pedigree of Glenn McGrath, only Brendon Julian of the pace quintet has a Test wicket (five) in this country.

There were signs in the one-day series that the pacemen need to adapt to bowling the right length in England. McGrath relies a lot on steep lift to 'set up' his dismissals. However, he may have to unearth an alternative method of softening up the batsmen on the less bouncy pitches in England. He has the class and the accuracy to do so as long as his volatile temper doesn't preclude him from out-thinking the batsmen rather than resorting to the big-bully approach.

Jason Gillespie is another young pace bowler with a lot of talent, but so far he has bowled an 'Australian' length on English pitches. If he and McGrath bowl well and make early inroads then it will greatly enhance the effectiveness of Warne. Too often in the Texaco series it was the blond bamboozler who was called on when Australia was in trouble, and this load needs to be shared. Like the Waugh twins, the third of the Australian three W's needs some assistance.

Australia's favouritism has waned since the Texaco whitewash, but with due diligence they can regroup for the Ashes series. However, if the hard decisions aren't taken immediately there is a danger that where Australia won the last two series despite the selectors, this time they might lose because of them.

Mark Taylor had gone through an excruciating dry spell of twenty Test innings where he hadn't scored a half-century. This had caused a lot of consternation about the Australian captain's ability to hold his spot as an opening batsman. The continuing vacillation over Taylor's position in the team finally took its toll in the opening Test of the 1997 series in England.

———

[*The Daily Telegraph* UK, 5 June 1997]

S hane Warne dominated the first session for Australia at Edgbaston; a fairly normal experience, except that this time he was trying to extricate his side from a batting mess rather than being involved in a bowling onslaught.

Australia paid a heavy penalty for dithering at the selection table, which left their batting under-prepared and short on confidence. The top-order players were no match for an England bowling side that had a battle plan which it followed meticulously and that was backed by good fielding. If the Australian selectors weren't convinced their inaction over the Mark Taylor controversy was having a disruptive effect on the team, they had irrefutable evidence with the score board showing 8 for 54.

That is when Warne came to the rescue. Striking out boldly he hit a number of boundaries, the bulk of them coming from the early destroyer Darren Gough, emphasising Warne's aggressive approach to all facets of this game. Often a low-scoring match is won by such a contribution from a tail-ender, and at least Warne had given his side a chance to claw its way back into the match.

Australia's situation was improved by some good early bowling, but they tended to lose concentration for a short while after they bounced out Alec Stewart. For a period after that success the length was too short as the bowlers tried to intimidate the English batsmen. Graham Thorpe was able to take advantage of these lapses to relieve the desperation of England's situation. Concentration is just as important for bowlers as batsmen in this type of game, and even the smallest of slip-ups can be terminal.

Currently there is a lot of pressure on the Australian bowlers. With all the controversy over selection the top order is unsettled and not contributing much to the cause. This means collapses are always a chance, and that often requires bowling at meagre totals, which isn't ideal for an attack that is aggressive by nature.

The mental battle was well and truly won by England on the first day. Australia wilted under the pressure of good, aggressive and thoughtful cricket from England, but all the problems commenced with another poor start to the innings. Too often in this period of uncertainty Australia has been forced to fight a lot harder than they should have for victory. This is a result of poor selection, and on this forgettable day at Edgbaston they paid the ultimate price for constantly opening the door for the opposition.

After a shaky start to the 1997 Ashes series the Australians began the fightback at Old Trafford. The story of this dramatic match unfolds in the following four *Daily Telegraph* reports.

[*The Daily Telegraph* UK, 3 July 1997]

The Australian batsmen were made to struggle on the first day at Old Trafford, but it was a battle they must have expected after Mark Taylor won the toss.

Although Taylor is a captain who loves to bat first, he would have been sorely tempted to send England in on a slightly moist Old Trafford pitch. Perhaps the sight of a few bare patches at each end of the pitch and the thought of Shane Warne weaving his magic later in the game swayed Taylor. However, at lunch, with three top-order batsmen back in the pavilion, he was probably wondering if it was the right decision.

The one bright spot in the pre-lunch struggle was the continuing good form of Matthew Elliott. The conditions meant that Elliott had to play in a totally different manner to his innings at Lord's, and it was a tribute to his skill that he was able to cope with this dramatic change in technique. Matthew would have taken great satisfaction from surviving the two hours until lunch, but he was disappointed with his dismissal on resumption.

Elliott perished in similar fashion to his two left-handed team-mates, caught behind the wicket from the capable seam bowling

223

of debutant Dean Headley. Whereas both Taylor and Michael Bevan quite obviously edged off-cutters, there was some doubt about Elliott's demise, especially as he rubbed his elbow whilst departing more slowly than the eleven o'clock from Warwick Road Station. It was the sort of action that wouldn't have put him in the good books of umpire Venkataraghavan.

The other Australian player who found a way to survive under the difficult conditions was the redoubtable Steve Waugh. He displayed great concentration and determination as always, and presented a broad bat more often than his team-mates. The drastic improvement in Steve's batting since reclaiming his Test spot has coincided with constant fine tuning to his technique. Waugh is the type of player who is never happy with good; he always wants to make it better, and his hard work has paid off handsomely.

His effort and that of Elliott has kept Australia in the game on a day when the England bowlers threatened to break the match open quickly. However, I'm sure the Australians will feel that under conditions that are likely to prevail for at least another day, any first-innings total over two hundred will keep them competitive and give Warne a chance to bring them victory.

[*The Daily Telegraph* UK, 4 July 1997]

Australia's hard men came to the fore on a day when the boys of the baggy green needed something special to put themselves into a winning position.

For Australia it was a case of anything England's seamers can do our spinners can do better. Shane Warne took his team to a position of dominance at Old Trafford with a wonderful spell of leg spin bowling reminiscent of his efforts at the same ground four years ago. Warne said before the Test that he was feeling good about the way the ball was 'coming out'. He confirmed with the number of deliveries that swerved in the air and those that spun quite sharply that what he was feeling was indeed happening.

It's amazing what motivates cricketers to give their best. In Warne's case his constant motivation is pride in his performance and a desire to do well for his team. However, at Old Trafford there was the extra incentive of doing well in the first Test after the birth of his daughter, Brooke. In years to come, Shane and wife Simone will look back on the way the birth of their first child was celebrated with a good personal performance and an Australian victory. In picking up five wickets, Warne equalled Richie Benaud as Australia's leading spin-bowler, with 248 Test wickets.

The other man who contributed much to Australia's position of dominance after two days was the ebullient Ian Healy. He really set his team alight with a magnificent leg-side stumping to get rid of the stubborn Mark Butcher. This was Healy's hundredth Ashes victim and a marvellous way to mark a milestone. It was Healy at his best, collecting a half-volley outside leg stump and then his eagle eye spotting that Butcher had lost his balance and stepped out of his crease. Healy didn't stop there – he picked up a couple more difficult catches and also imparted some soothing and wise words to his team-mates at the appropriate moment.

Warne and Healy were responsible for the perfect follow-up to the impetus that had been provided on day one by Steve Waugh's best Test innings. It was fitting that three of Australia's toughest competitors should be the men at the forefront on such an important day in this Ashes series.

[*The Daily Telegraph* UK, 6 July 1997]

Australia is left with only the mopping-up to do at Old Trafford after Steve Waugh produced his second epic innings in a match dominated by the bowlers.

Waugh became the first Australian right-hander and only the third in all to score a century in each innings of an Ashes Test. Typical of the man, there was very little emotion after Steve pushed off spinner Robert Croft through mid-wicket for three to attain this remarkable goal. He just took the helmet off, lifted the bat to all sections of the crowd, and after a quick handshake from Paul Reiffel it was back to business. That is the way of Steve Waugh: he is a dogged, determined and calculating cricketer and there is no room for becoming over-excited, it might bring about an error of judgement.

Look at a graph of Waugh's innings and it's rare that there are two the same. That is one of the great things about Waugh's batting: he nearly always finds a way to beat his opponents. 'Whatever it takes' could well be Steve's motto as he goes about the business of driving the opposition mad before he drives them into the turf.

However, once Waugh was dismissed, caught off another nasty lifting delivery from Dean Headley, the continuation of the Australian innings seemed superfluous. The lead was 406, which was ample sufficiency, and there is always the threat of rain in Manchester.

This was soon to be academic after Jason Gillespie made the initial breakthrough. It was an important wicket for Australia: not only did it get the demolition process underway but it also meant Alec Stewart would be confronted by Shane Warne almost immediately. For the second time this summer Stewart was playing for a leg break when Warne had in fact delivered the over-spinner. That left a gap wide enough for a Manchester canal barge and the cricket ball sailed comfortably through to disturb the furniture. Once again Warne was on top and England was on the defensive.

At this point Gillespie rammed home the advantage, bowling with pace and movement off the seam. The gangly young speed-ster has rewarded the selectors' faith with steady improvement and the ability to strike at a good rate. His fiery spell and the wizardry of Warne has Australia hoping that the mopping-up will entail only wickets and not water.

[*The Daily Telegraph* UK, 7 July 1997]

A score line of one all after three Tests suggests the two teams are on parity, but in reality Australia is now in front in the series.

England has some regrouping to do and some selection worries. Australia, on the other hand, have sorted out most of the problems that were afflicting them in the lead-up to Edgbaston and only have the suitability of Michael Bevan at number six to worry about. In saying that is the only selection problem I am assuming the tour management will ignore Mark Taylor's insecurity as an opener, because they did for so long before the first Test century that it would be a complete back-flip to now do otherwise. Taylor is still a long way from in form, and were it not for Steve Waugh's obduracy and skill, particularly in the first innings, then the constant loss of an early wicket would be a more glaring problem than it is currently.

Australia's victory and Taylor's sound judgement as a captain, particularly at the toss, will save him, but I can't see how the selectors can continue to overlook Bevan's batting deficiencies.

Whilst the two W's, Waugh and Warne, played the major roles in winning the Test for Australia, it would be unfair to overlook the work of Ian Healy. He had a tremendous match, keeping immaculately, including a marvellous leg-side stumping and an acrobatic diving catch to dismiss Mark Ealham. In addition Healy contributed a fast forty-seven in the second innings when that was exactly what was required. That is the hallmark of Healy's play: he produces at the appropriate time. The stumping came when the game was in the balance, but within an hour of that alert piece of work Australia was well and truly on top.

To complete a remarkable Australian revival since the first Test, Jason Gillespie bowled with fire and skill to give the attack a bit of extra bite. He and the fiery Glenn McGrath, who not only bowled well on the final morning but also struck a few psychological blows, can be an irrepressible pair in this form.

So the Australians are on the rise, and with a bit of common-sense at the selection table they have the opportunity to improve further. There will be a certain amount of relief in the Australian camp that the series has been levelled, and with their aggressive style of play they must feel confident that there is at least one more victory just around the corner.

Finally, two young men who were destined to play a big part in Australia's fifth Golden Era staked their claim as fully fledged members of the team. Ricky Ponting had been dropped in the previous series against the West Indies and his omission was nearly as bad as Slater's in 1996.

[*The Bulletin*, 1 August 1997]

After the part they played in Australia's comprehensive victory at Headingley, the motto of the young guns could well be: 'Anything you can do, we can do better.'

Predictably, it was the senior members and Australia's hard men who won the third Test to level the series at Old Trafford. Steve Waugh, Shane Warne, Ian Healy and Glenn McGrath all played their part in putting the skids under England, then, whilst Mike Atherton's men were flailing about trying to regain their balance, Jason Gillespie, Matthew Elliott and Ricky Ponting slipped them a brand-new banana skin. The trio's match-winning efforts brought England down and Australia will put them out of their misery in the next Test.

Trent Bridge, the venue for the fifth Test, is regarded in England as a 'draw pitch', but Australia plays the brand of cricket that produces results even on a flat surface. Given anywhere near the thirty hours of allocated playing time, Australia will beat England to retain the Ashes because they have the match-winners. At the start of the series they numbered five (add Mark Waugh to the third Test list), but judging by the form of the talented trio at Headingley that may have to be revised upwards.

Gillespie has shown himself to be a quick learner as well as a fast bowler. Jason enjoys playing cricket, but he doesn't add to the pleasure his opponents derive from the game. His lively pace has been complemented by a ball that swings away from right-handers, and his display at Headingley indicated he's ready to be classified with McGrath as a dual strike force.

This is a far cry from the lad with a ponytail and potential who graduated from the academy just a couple of years ago. Jason had a haircut immediately he was drafted in to the Australian side at the 1996 World Cup and the ponytail has not reappeared. However, he is still his own man, with a golden pirate earring dangling from each side as he bounds in on his rhythmical run. The way he plundered wickets at Headingley indicates there will be plenty more big hauls in his career.

Elliott, the exciting left-hand opener, drives handsomely through the off-side and pulls and hooks powerfully through the on-side. His placement suggests that although he didn't attend the cricket academy he had more than a passing interest in geometry at school. He hits the gaps precisely, ensuring that none of his good shots are wasted, and this is why he produces big scores. It also allows him to avoid the frustration that normally builds up when a batsman has periods of scoring inactivity. Matthew missed a double century by one run at Headingley, but he'll soon correct that anomaly as he doesn't become bored with batting.

Ponting is another with more than a passing interest in the art. He was the perfect partner for Elliott, and the features of Ponting's play are similar to the left-hander's, except that Ricky is a better driver off the back foot and through the on-side. Ponting couldn't have had time for geometry at school as he is a low marker at golf, a good Australian Rules footballer, and if someone explained the rules he would excel at Crown Green Bowls. Ponting didn't learn placement, he was born with a talent.

Not surprisingly, many thousands of Australians were confused when Ponting was dropped from the Test side, and after his dashing display at Headingley there is an equal number of Englishmen who are now similarly miffed. They can only be thankful there was no mental scarring as Ponting has now re-established himself in the side by playing his natural counter-attacking game.

If Ponting hadn't been harshly and ridiculously dealt with by the selectors, he'd now be the established number three. That would give Australia the ideal batting order, with the two best players of pace bowling leading the onslaught.

Thanks to the initiative and skill of these three, Australia should dominate the rest of the series. At the same time as these young players are learning from the older brigade, they are also pushing them, thus ensuring the team is constantly operating at full power. This spells trouble for teams far more talented than England.

**Considering the turmoil surrounding the team's early prepara-
tion in 1997, two horrific losses by Australia wasn't surprising.
However, despite all the problems they still managed to retain
the Ashes.**

[*The Daily Telegraph* UK, 24 August 1997]

Australia finished the series as they started it – in disarray.
Fortunately, against a notoriously inconsistent England,
their play in between was top-class and sufficiently sustained to
retain the Ashes.

The first Test loss had little to do with Australia being under-
prepared; it was more like ripe for the picking. The raging controversy surrounding Mark Taylor and poor selections combined
to siphon the spirit from the Australian tank. For a while it
appeared England had been the one sucking on the hose, as they
won the Texaco Trophy and the first Test by overwhelming
Australia with a combination of aggression and flair. However,
from the moment Taylor scored a century at Edgbaston and put
an end to all the conjecture, Australia was refuelled and on the
road to rehabilitation.

Whilst Taylor's hundred ensured he retained his place for the
series, his future as Australian captain is far from assured. His
form, despite an improvement at Trent Bridge and The Oval, is
still patchy and there are too many good batsmen on the verge of

breaking through to keep selecting a struggling player. It all depends on Taylor's priority – does he want to go out on his terms or is he prepared to risk the embarrassment of being dropped? In recent times the selectors have treated Taylor the batsman generously, but he may be unwise to push his luck, especially with a tough series looming against South Africa. Depending on his preference, a dignified retirement may be his best option.

The emergence of Matthew Elliott as a top-class opening bat has added to Taylor's dilemma. The ideal opening combination is a left- and right-hander and Elliott's place is now secure. On this tour Elliott and Jason Gillespie were Australia's two big improvers, and, combined with the resurgence of Ricky Ponting and the continued good form of Greg Blewett, there is the nucleus of a good side when the present hard men retire.

Not that there are any signs that Ian Healy or Steve Waugh are on the wane. Waugh was at his mind-controlling best at Old Trafford, where his two centuries shone like a miner's lamp, but few of his work-mates were in the same tunnel. Healy's glove-work was impeccable and his leg-side stumping at Old Trafford was the highlight in a series containing plenty of excellent deeds. Typical of a great player and top-class team man, Healy's timing is precise, and that stumping ignited a flurry of wickets which put Australia on top in the pivotal Test. From that moment they forged ahead of England, but Healy, not content to rest on his laurels, then produced an innings in that game and another at Trent Bridge designed to dishearten the toughest of opponents.

Shane Warne showed that he will be very much a part of Australia's future and may even lead the 'next generation'. His contribution along with the pinpoint accuracy and penetration of Glenn McGrath meant they were the potent attacking force. They provided the important breakthroughs for Australia –

McGrath having the better of his duel with Mike Atherton and, similarly, Warne with Nasser Hussain.

For a bowler who is often described as 'not as good as he used to be', Warne had a very good series. There is no doubt he still has a strong grip on English batsmen and in wrestling parlance it's a sleeper hold – they didn't molest him much. Nevertheless, Australia's spin bowling shortcomings will be exposed when Warne retires as the back-up is virtually non-existent. There shouldn't be any such worry in the pace department, as Gillespie and Michael Kasprowicz have both learnt a lot on the tour of England.

The Tests Australia won they did so by a wide margin, but the first three days at Trent Bridge and The Oval match were extremely competitive and typical of the Ashes tradition. Australia was the better side and the margin is most evident in fielding and athleticism. Nevertheless, England's best is a big improvement from when Mike Atherton took over the captaincy; the problem is their worst is seen too often and it's not a pretty sight.

I found it an entertaining series, helped by the fact that the gap between the two teams is narrowing.

This was written in the period when Mark Taylor had been omitted from the Australian one-day side and Steve Waugh had taken over as captain. The idea of Australia having separate captains for Test and one-day international matches wasn't a resounding success in the early stages.

[*The Bulletin*, 26 January 1998]

Australia's recent losing trend in limited-overs cricket has occurred as a result of ABC – no, not a subversive plot by the national broadcaster, but simply Australia's Blunders Costly.

Mistakes made off the field usually manifest themselves in on-field problems. The Australian selectors have ignored a number of golden rules in choosing the one-day side and this has resulted in the team stumbling into the Carlton & United finals' series on the basis of three wins over a lacklustre New Zealand team. The situation is made less palatable when a comparison of the two sides suggests that Australia should be pushing South Africa rather than being a pushover. A vast improvement in form during the first final was diluted by yet another batting collapse, which led to Australia folding meekly when they had a morale-boosting victory in their grasp.

There are certain rules of selection that are best adhered to, and by breaking them this panel has put itself in jeopardy.

1) Avoid choosing a self-centred player as captain whenever there is an alternative.

Steve Waugh has been an extremely successful cricketer because of his ability to focus on his own game and entirely block out any other influences. Whilst this has helped him to play match-winning innings in demanding circumstances like Sabina Park and Old Trafford, his single-mindedness is his Achilles heel as a captain. Situations such as those which occurred in the Hobart Test against New Zealand and during the final overs of Australia's innings in the last qualifying match of the Carlton & United series (where he scored predominantly singles when quick runs were the order of the day) make it difficult when he places demands on his players.

Twenty-eight runs off the last five overs with seven wickets in hand was not good enough against New Zealand, even if Steve did feel Australia was already in possession of a winning total. If a team has a chance to make 270 why settle for 250? To compound matters, in the after-match interview Waugh blamed wayward bowling and dropped catches for the unexpected loss to New Zealand, saying that 230 should have been a defendable total. I can't imagine this would have gone down well in a dressing room already deflated by a debilitating defeat.

There has been too much selfish batting in the Australian team, going back to the Allan Border era. In recent Test matches it has been left to the younger players to take the risks when the scoring rate needed a boost, with Matthew Elliott at Lord's, Ricky Ponting at the Gabba and Greg Blewett at Bellerive all obliging. The fact that the selectors have not responded to this worrying trend means they are condoning the behaviour.

It was interesting to note the players' response to Shane Warne's captaincy at the SCG in the win over New Zealand. They were sharp in the field and for the first time in a long while

Australia won without a big score from Mark Waugh (out injured) after Ponting and the fast-maturing Darren Lehmann overcame a poor start by building a big partnership.

2) Getting the combinations right is another must at the selection table.

If the selectors chose the side with a view to beefing up the batting when the occasion demanded, then they needed to go the whole way by appointing a captain with a gambler's approach. In the current side that is Warne rather than Steve Waugh.

3) A good cricketer is a good cricketer.

The best players adapt to the length of the game because they have desire and pride in their performance, in addition to skill. They don't want to lose their place in any team, working on the premise that 'you never give a sucker an even break'.

The best bowlers are wicket-takers and they don't concede runs easily – the ideal combination for success in a game of cricket no matter what the duration. The best batsmen make big scores because they are not easily tied down, due to the wide range and placement of their shots – again the ideal recipe for any game of cricket. As a rule, the top four batsmen and the best three bowlers in the good Test sides should be automatic selections in the limited-overs squad.

Players become topnotch Test-match cricketers because they learn to cope with challenging situations. Greg Blewett, Michael Slater and Matthew Elliott have all proved they can play fast bowling successfully in a Test match and yet not one of them has opened in a series where Australia has used five different combinations at the top of the order. Apart from Elliott's slowness in the outfield due to wonky knees, there is no good reason for their absence.

Any list of the best performers in one-day cricket is littered with the names of good Test-match players, along with a smattering of one-day specialists. The all-conquering West Indies of the late Seventies and early Eighties and the current Sri Lankan and South African sides are among the best ever limited-overs teams, and in each case the changes made from the Test line-up have been minimal.

4) Keep both eyes on the present and restrict yourself to an occasional peek into the crystal ball.

Good cricket teams evolve from selectors picking the best available talent and meticulously fine tuning the combination. However, following a declaration by the ACB at the start of the summer, this panel has become so engrossed in building a team to win the 1999 World Cup that its pre-occupation has been detrimental to the performance in the Carlton & United series.

The only time wholesale changes or radical moves are in order is when a team is faltering. Sure, Australia's one-day record in recent times has been abysmal and some experimentation was acceptable. However, when things started to go wrong the selectors' search for answers took them further away from the players who were part of a highly successful Test line-up and this was a major blunder. For instance, with the team losing and Adam Gilchrist's batting talents being misused, it was time to reinstate Ian Healy to bolster the team for the finals.

Time and again in the recent past there has been no discernible pattern to selection. This has caused confusion among the players and hindered the smooth build-up of team spirit, which has been the foundation stone in many good Australian teams. The selectors may have been blinded by Australia's reputedly deep pool of talent, which is exaggerated in a Shield competition often played without the challenging presence of international players. In addition they have relied too heavily on the 'jack of all trades, master of none' type of all-rounder.

As often happens, the panel has been unlucky, with major

injuries to Glenn McGrath and, to a lesser extent, Jason Gillespie. However, the weakness of the current selection panel is the lack of a former top-class cricketer in its ranks. The Australian panel should always include a former player of the calibre of Bradman, Harvey, Lindwall, Davidson or Greg Chappell, and that is a golden rule to which the ACB should adhere.

This is one of my treasured moments in Test cricket. Fourth day, and the match was still evenly poised, with Australia's champion (Warne) bowling to India's champion (Tendulkar). Whichever player won the battle, his team would claim victory in the war.

[*Indian Express*, 9 March 1998]

Indian captain Mohammad Azharuddin has a well-developed sense of history, setting Australia 348 for victory, exactly the same figure required in the tied Test at this ground almost twelve years ago. He can thank his predecessor as skipper for India's position of dominance.

Navjot Sidhu would have been annoyed with himself, losing his wicket in the sixties twice in the Test match. It is vital that Sidhu converts a few of his good starts into big innings, because he is such a competent player of spin bowling that whilst he's at the crease batting is made easier for his partner. In the first innings he was unlucky to be dismissed, but on the second occasion Sidhu was lured to his downfall by a well-flighted delivery from Gavin Robertson.

His dismissal brought Sachin Tendulkar to the crease, and Shane Warne's ultra-competitive approach was immediately on display. He probed with some spitting deliveries and it required all the skill of the Indian maestro just to survive. However, once he'd negotiated this awkward period, Tendulkar set the ground alight with some marvellous pull and cut shots to race to fifty by lunch. If, as they say, the Masters golf tournament starts on the back nine on Sunday, the defining period in this Test commenced when Tendulkar was threatening to change the course of the match.

In an effort to provide the vital breakthrough Warne changed to around the wicket, but Tendulkar refused to remain becalmed. He went for the deliveries pitched outside leg stump like a kid offered an ice cream. This onslaught was designed to demoralise the Australians and set up a victory opportunity, something India weren't able to achieve in all of 1997. Tendulkar charged to his first century against Australia in his own country, a milestone he celebrated with two horizontal bat shots, one on either side of the wicket, which absolutely blazed their way to the boundary.

As India pressed on to build a big lead it was appropriate to ponder the vagaries of this incredible game. When Warne dismissed Tendulkar for a personal cost of four in the first innings, the batsman was able to mull over his downfall in the privacy of the pavilion. No such joy for Warne, who had to stay on the field and suffer his punishment in front of a crowd that had built substantially on the news that the Indian champion was on fire.

Nevertheless, Warne coped better than some of his team-mates as the Australian fielding standard started to slip as India piled on the agony. Thanks to Tendulkar's magic the Australians had yielded, and Mohammad Azharuddin grabbed the opportunity to rub salt into the wound by blazing a quick-fire half-century. Azharuddin is one of the most fluent players in the world and he was able to keep the scoring rate up as Tendulkar tired a little. The Indian skipper's boundary-studded innings paved the way for a late-evening declaration, a positive move as the Australians had wilted.

Their stocks would have slumped even further by stumps as India removed three top-order batsmen whilst only conceding thirty-one runs. The first to go was Michael Slater, a trifle ambitious in his attempt to drive a wide ball. Slater has looked extremely edgy in his return to Test cricket and appears to be trying too hard to prove a point.

Azharuddin preferred Rajesh Chauhan to Anil Kumble in his choice of first spinner and for that the Australians can be thankful. Kumble's quick leg spinner immediately disposed of Greg Blewett, who prefers to face pace early in his innings, and then he got the bonus wicket of Mark Taylor. The Australian captain is struggling for form and was obviously disappointed at missing a short delivery that should have been put away.

Having claimed three victims Azharuddin ensured there would be no repeat of history in Chennai. It was going to take a masterful innings for Australia to survive, let alone win, and it's long odds on another knock of Tendulkar's magnificence in this match.

When he retired in 1965, with the world record of 307 Test wickets, forthright English fast bowler Fred Trueman said, 'Whoever passes me will be tired.' Well in 1976 West Indian off spinner Lance Gibbs retired, having bowled 27,115 balls to take 309 Test wickets. If the blond bamboozler was tired when he passed Gibbs in 1998, it hasn't stopped him.

[*Indian Express*, 26 March 1998]

Shane Warne is now the most successful spin bowler in the history of the game, having passed Lance Gibbs' former world record of 309 Test wickets.

It will suit Shane that he attained the record without any fuss or fanfare as he's always been more interested in team success than that of the individual. Nevertheless, it will please him that he achieved the mark with a classic leg spinner's dismissal, pitching leg stump and turning past the edge of Rahul Dravid's bat to knock down off-stump. It will also matter to him, perhaps later rather than right now, that it was a top-order batsman rather than a tail-ender who was on strike when he reached the spin bowling pinnacle.

Other than that Warne won't be feeling much joy tonight as his team is in dire straits and he'll be blaming himself for not contributing more. 'I've never been cut so much as I have on this tour,' he mused before the first day's play in Bangalore. Then, typical of the man's positive outlook on life, he quipped, 'I had a long chat with Bishen [Bedi] last night and he was very helpful.'

Shane is conscious of those who have gone before him in the game and is quick to acknowledge any help he has received. He admires those who have done well and he respects the traditions of the game. He is also always on the lookout for a tip that will make him a better bowler. He will be well aware that Sachin Tendulkar has had the better of their duel in this series, but he will also know deep down that he has bowled better to Tendulkar than to any other Indian batsman in this series. That will mean much to Shane Warne because he has a lot of pride in his performance. He may be bettered on a particular day but he never submits, one of the many reasons why he is a champion.

By the late Nineties, predicting Ashes defeats for England was simple. This is my excuse for over-confidence in 2005.

[*The Bulletin*, 30 October 1998]

If Mark Taylor led famous mountain-climbing expeditions rather than an elite cricket team, he would have just conquered Everest, the world's tallest peak, and now be preparing to take on Mount Kosciusko, Australia's most elevated piece of ground.

To make the comparison even more realistic it would be fair to say that Taylor tackled Everest in ideal conditions, whilst a challenge has been added to the Kosciusko ascension, by attempting it during a snowstorm. Nevertheless, taking on England in Australia after beating Pakistan at home is not likely to bring Taylor crashing back to earth with a thud.

Taylor inherited a good Australian side and he's improved its performance, distinguishing him as one of the best captains to wear the baggy green cap. In the process he's stamped his authority on the team; if you think of Taylor the first words that come to mind are 'resilient' and 'positive', and those two characteristics were evident in abundance in Australia's defeat of Pakistan. Despite the mountaineering analogy, Taylor is not one to have his head in the clouds and he'll ensure his team doesn't get carried away with what it has achieved and forget the tasks ahead. Australia will be ready for England.

The victory in Pakistan will have done wonders for the Australian team's confidence, but because the senior members have suffered some setbacks in their careers they won't allow this to blossom into over-confidence. Despite Taylor's optimistic view of life, there remains in his team a hint of the pessimism that prevailed during the Allan Border years, which serves to keep the side constantly at the ready. The underlying feeling of insecurity probably emanates from the vice-captain, Steve Waugh, who has inherited the Border 'grind 'em into the turf' outlook, which is not surprising because he suffered through more of the lean years than any other member of the current team.

In addition to building confidence the tour of Pakistan has also seen some significant gains made on the field. The return to full fitness of Glenn McGrath is a huge boost. He is Australia's warhead and his explosive ability, especially early in an innings, often splits open the opposition's batting line-up, making clean-up operations easier for the other bowlers. The fact that this has been acknowledged by Mike Atherton on the eve of the Ashes series has to help Australia's cause. Whilst Stuart MacGill is still inconsistent (a familiar trait among all but the great leg spinners), he has followed up a good Test debut with a creditable series performance. This places him as the next best spinner to Shane Warne and deserving of a spot alongside the blond bamboozler whenever Australia requires two tweakers.

On the batting side, Justin Langer has resurrected his Test career in exactly the manner you would expect – through hard work and determination. I don't believe he should be batting at number three when there's a counter-attacking alternative with Ricky Ponting's skill available, but there's a conservative element in this selection panel that is more comfortable with that style of player in the first drop position. Unfortunately this has retarded the Tasmanian's progress and will continue to do so. Despite that misjudgement, any team with Ponting waiting in the wings must be regarded as strong in batting. This was emphasised in Pakistan, where Darren Lehmann was given an extended opportunity to display his wares at Test level and he unveiled similar skills to those that have been on show at first-class level for many years. With such a strong batting line-up it's hard to imagine many Australian collapses against this England attack.

Despite the carry-on over preparing to face the wiles of Shane Warne, the main reason I don't rate England's chances of regaining the Ashes is the lack of a balanced bowling attack. Alec Stewart has at his command a capable group of seamers, but ideal conditions rarely prevail in Australia. On the other hand, Taylor has a well-balanced combination able to exert pressure on the opposition on most pitches, and sooner or later the England batting line-up will succumb. If Taylor has at his disposal McGrath, Warne and Jason Gillespie for the bulk of the series then I can't see Australia losing a match. More to the point, if none of Australia's 'big three' were available for even a Test, I still couldn't see England winning a match.

And what about the English theory of utilising the expertise of former Australian leg spinner Peter Philpott to unravel the mysteries of Warne? Well, Philpott makes a good point when he says, 'You must attack good leg spinners.' Without an aggressive plan to combat Warne, a batsman will perish quickly and often without trace. However, to attack a good spinner a batsman must have the wherewithal and this requires good footwork, both coming forward and pushing back. Quick and decisive footwork has to be learnt at a young age, not in the late twenties or early thirties. It's all very well for Philpott to show the England batsmen how to bowl leg spin to better understand the art, but it would have been a wiser policy for someone to teach them how to *play* that type of bowling when they were growing up. A perfect example of why the best coaches should be employed at junior level instead of being wasted on international players.

There is no doubt England has improved since the dark days of 1993 when they slid down the slopes on a toboggan guided by Graham Gooch. Under Mike Atherton's leadership they have shown more fight, but they still lack the consistency to beat really good sides over a series. Expect them to be more aggressive with Alec Stewart in charge, but the inconsistency problems haven't been eradicated and they'll surface again during the Ashes series.

Whilst it will look as though it's the batsmen who have cost England the series when they collapse, the bowlers will actually be partly to blame. If they are not capable of restricting Australia to reasonable totals, then eventually the mountain of runs will cause a landslide and the England batsmen will be buried by their opponents' relentless attack. It's a simple ploy, but a very effective one, especially against inferior opposition. It has taken Taylor to the loftiest peaks and there's no reason why it will fail him when he's tackling a mere mountain.

By 1998 England was having some success against other countries, but this was still the perennial question before each Ashes series.

[*The Daily Telegraph* UK, 17 November 1998]

I s England a real contender in the Ashes contest or are they still the pretenders they were first shown to be way back in 1989?

When England clinched a fighting series win over South Africa, it suggested improvement under the aggressive leadership of Alec Stewart. However, everything they've done since, from a comprehensive Test beating by Sri Lanka to a stumbling one-wicket victory over Queensland, points to the same old inconsistent England. To further add to England's growing woes, the two inept batting displays in Cairns were closely scrutinised by Ian Healy, one of the driving forces behind Australia's success dating back to 1989. From what he saw it wouldn't surprise me if Healy's report to Mark Taylor is restricted to simply saying 'SNAFU' – Situation Normal All Fouled Up.

There is no doubt that despite all the problems England has encountered on this tour the Australian players will be wary of their opponents. Nevertheless, they will know deep down that if the screws are applied at the Gabba and England is beaten, then there is potential for the opposition to unravel. The first two pitches in the series are quick with a bit of bounce, ideal for Glenn

McGrath and Jason Gillespie, and the type of surface on which England have had trouble in the recent past. If the two Australian speedsters get on top early and remain dominant then there may not be much of the carcass left for Shane Warne to feed on.

The major advantage for Australia is a psychological one. The bulk of Taylor's team has been involved in administering previous beatings, and many of the current England players were on the receiving end. Another hammering in Brisbane would be enough to set off any inferiority complexes that are lurking beneath the surface and this could then lead to another drubbing at the WACA. England may have come back hard to win the series against South Africa, but this Australian team isn't noted for its on-field charity, and there still remains a bit of the old Allan Border 'grind 'em into the turf' attitude.

The psychological factor shouldn't be underestimated, as the swing to Australia could be sudden and dramatic. England's four major players – Stewart, Mike Atherton, Darren Gough and Angus Fraser – have all experienced a lot of Ashes disappointments, and despite their positive approach and fighting qualities, further reversals will be debilitating. In addition, a failure by the 'core four' to get England off to a good start in the series will have a demoralising effect on some of the less confident individuals in the side, and they could start to act as a handbrake on progress. The Australians have the wherewithal to overcome a sluggish start to the series, but I seriously doubt that this applies to England.

Before a ball is bowled we'll be able to gauge England's mental approach to the first Test. If they opt for seven batsmen it will announce that they are worried about the batting in general and, in particular, the inability to get a decent start. If they pick five bowlers it will send a strong message to Australia that they believe a win is possible. The toss then becomes the next important indicator. If the flick of the florin favours Stewart, any move to send the opposition in could be construed as shielding the top order from McGrath and Gillespie. Consequently, the England captain will need to be clear in his own mind that any such decision is based on a positive rather than negative policy.

For his part Taylor is always comfortable batting first, and this isn't solely dependent on having Warne at his beck and call. McGrath has been every bit as effective in the fourth innings as Warne, and as long as the lanky quick continues in this vein, the ability of Stuart MacGill to turn his leg break will spell danger. It's this variety in attack and the lack of dependence on a nucleus of players that make Australia a stronger and more reliable unit than England. Australia can recover from early setbacks because of the mental strength of Steve Waugh, the determination of Healy and the brilliance of Ricky Ponting. They also have the ability to withstand long periods without a wicket, comfortable in the knowledge that something will soon happen with an imaginative captain, a diverse attack and fieldsmen who rarely allow batsmen a second chance. Actually, Warne's absence will be felt almost as much for his all-round qualities as his wicket-taking potential. Until he returns the slip cordon is weakened and the tail is less productive, positives for England that they need to capitalise on to ensure Australia doesn't receive a huge boost from winning with a weakened combination.

Whilst I can't see England bowling Australia out cheaply twice and winning a Test in this series, they do have the potential to make it a hard, grinding affair. If Stewart's men can keep it close for long enough then the breaks may just come their way and an upset is possible. However, if they wilt early there will be no coming back and Australia could run away with the series. We may well know the answer to 'are they contenders or just pretenders?' before the Gabba Test is concluded.

The cricket corruption saga strikes in Australia.

[*The Daily Telegraph* UK, 10 December 1998]

As the third Ashes Test looms and another betting scandal erupts, this time involving two of Australia's stars, it could be a case of the storm before the lull.

The news that Mark Waugh and Shane Warne both accepted money from a bookmaker is disturbing, but the fact that the Australian Cricket Board (ACB) tried to hide the subsequent fines was downright stupid. Whilst there's no suggestion that the two players were trying to influence the result of a game by accepting money, Waugh and Warne were misguided in becoming involved with underworld figures. At worst their action could have led to a more sinister situation, and once criminal types are owed a favour there is no legal way out.

When Waugh and Warne later accused (the then) Pakistan captain Salim Malik of offering bribes indicates that at least the cricketers had learnt it was best to go public in these cases. Why then did the ACB, in conjunction with the International Cricket Council (ICC), decide to stay quiet and hope the matter would disappear?

It is typical of the 'ostrich approach', which most cricket administrators adopt when a controversy arises, and no doubt the ACB thought it was helping Waugh and Warne, but in reality it has done them no favours. However, its motive becomes more sinister in the light of the Pakistan judicial inquiry. Surely the name of a bookmaker is relevant to the inquiry, and on that basis alone the matter should've been divulged.

The fact that it's only come to light via a leak begs the question: 'What else is the ACB hiding?' If there is more, let's hope that cricket administrators will finally realise the folly of the 'ostrich approach'. In addition to using this issue as a lever to gain global control of the game, the ICC should immediately write into the Code of Conduct that any player or official associating with known gamblers or betting on the game will be banned for life. That way everyone understands the seriousness of the situation.

Having seen how the bribery scandal has torn apart Pakistan in recent matches, it'll be interesting to observe this affair affects the Australian team. There is no internal conflict involved in this situation so it won't hurt Australia as much as it's obviously harmed Pakistan. However, I doubt that Mark Taylor's team will remain unaffected. If it does nothing else it will detract from their preparation for the Adelaide Test as well as being an extra unwanted burden on the mind of Mark Waugh.

Considering the events of the last couple of days the Australians will be glad when the Test starts and the controversy is hopefully pushed to one side. For them the affair will have been the storm, whilst retaining the Ashes could well be the lull that follows.

Another Ashes series, another Australian win. Better get it in whilst I can.

[*The Daily Telegraph* UK, 6 January 1999]

Australia has won their sixth successive Ashes series and now it is time to play 'What happened and where are they going?'

The two-Test margin was fair because Australia was the superior side mentally as well as in batting, spin bowling and fielding. The only area where England matched Australia was in pace bowling, and the quartet of Darren Gough, Dean Headley, Alex Tudor and Allan Mullally should provide the nucleus of a good attack for some time to come. There is no doubt that England are more competitive than they were in 1997 and a good deal of the credit for that must go to those bowlers, although it is no coincidence that the hardest fought Tests were the last two, when Alec Stewart opened the batting.

Stewart must continue to open because he is a fine counter-attacking batsman against pace and he boosts his team considerably, in addition to causing his opponents to do some serious thinking. As a captain Alec sets a good aggressive example with the bat, but he's tactically shallow and the attack would be improved with a more innovative leader. At the end of the series the bowlers would have been entitled to line the batsmen up and ask, 'What happened to your contribution?' The batting failed every examination in the series, whilst the fast bowlers answered all questions, most of them correctly, and they even came up with a few unexpected embellishments. Headley is a bowler who grew in stature before our eyes, proving once again what an amazing effect confidence can have on a player.

Australia's report card shows an unexpected improvement in spin bowling entirely due to the maturity of Stuart MacGill; a steadiness in fast bowling thanks to the consistency of Glenn McGrath; and a pass in batting, despite the failure to answer one question. Australia is still a long way from overcoming the fourth-innings jitters, a situation in which only the Waugh twins seem capable of playing anywhere near their reputation. On the subject of fielding, the disparity in athleticism is a huge hurdle for England to overcome, and the divide is even greater when it comes to mental toughness. On the third evening of the SCG Test a senior Australian bowler mockingly clapped Nasser Hussain (a senior England batsman) off the field after he'd survived a torrid period. Hussain did not confront the Australian in a situation that cried out for the response: 'And I trust, mate, that you'll still be saying well played tomorrow afternoon, when I hit the winning runs.' There are sure signs that the England fast bowlers now believe in themselves, but there is no such life among most of the batsmen.

The final report cards read as follows: England tried hard and made some good gains, but still has a lot of work to do in batting, spin bowling, fielding and mental approach. Six out of ten. The Australian class is well led and others have absorbed the lessons taught by master Warne. They continue to be resilient in bowling and are not put off by absenteeism, but the batsmen have an infuriating habit of failing to knuckle down at final exam time and consequently the mark is a little down – eight out of ten.

Now, looking forward to the next big exam in 2001. From the

first Test in 1997 to the last in 1998–99 England has selected twenty-three players and Australia twenty-one. There are five England players and six from Australia who appear on both their team's lists. To get a better guide on how things might turn out in the next Ashes series, we need to look at who out of that nucleus will still be useful players and, in addition, how many of the remainder are likely to still be contributing.

In England's case Stewart, Hussain and Gough should continue to be valuable contributors, whilst Australia might get one more series out of the Waugh twins and Ian Healy, and Warne and McGrath will still be the heart of the attack. On the score of stars still burning brightly it's reasonably even, but when it comes to players who might graduate to important roles in the future, Australia has a big advantage.

Headley, Tudor, Mullally and Mark Ramprakash should be in the thick of the fight for England and Peter Such is a possibility, whilst Mike Atherton and Graham Thorpe are dubious because of back problems. They'll also be hoping that the Hollioake brothers develop and become regular members of the team. For an Ashes series, England can no longer rely on Graeme Hick, John Crawley or Mark Butcher because of various inadequacies with the bat.

Australia, on the other hand, can look to Michael Slater, MacGill, Damien Fleming, Michael Kasprowicz, Matthew Nicholson, Jason Gillespie and Adam Gilchrist (as Healy's back-up) with some certainty, whilst I wouldn't write off any of Justin Langer, Darren Lehmann, Ricky Ponting, Greg Blewett or Matthew Elliott.

Australia has a good blend of experience and youth, plus depth in most positions and a system that produces mentally tough players and good leaders. Meanwhile, England is still struggling to find the right formula for its first-class cricket,

which has a tendency to produce good individuals but not sufficient enough well-rounded players to mould into a champion
team. Consequently, Australia should make it seven Ashes series
on the trot and retain the newly created Waterford Crystal urn.

Following Mark Taylor's retirement, Steve Waugh took over as Test captain in early 1999. It's always difficult to follow a very successful captain and it didn't help that Waugh's first campaign was in the Caribbean.

[*Tony Cozier* magazine, 4 February 1999]

Mark Taylor's retirement means this Australian side is actually stronger in batting, but they will miss his calm but controlling influence on the field. I think Steve Waugh will be a good solid captain, with more of an Allan Border 'grind 'em into the turf' attitude than the 'aggressive from the outset' style of Taylor. I believe a glorious opportunity was missed when Shane Warne wasn't given the captaincy, as he has the potential to be an outstanding leader in the toughest category of them all – a bowling captain.

Waugh will lead a very good side; not as good as the West Indies in their invincible era, but they deserve to rank as the latest of the great ones in Australian cricket, along with the teams of 1920–21, the 1948 Invincibles, those of the late Fifties and early Sixties and then the early to mid-Seventies. They are a blend of youth and experience, with a couple of fine strike bowlers, two world-class batsmen and a counter-attacking opener, and they field brilliantly, especially in the catching department. They appear to have only the one real weakness: an inability to chase meagre totals successfully in the fourth innings. This problem has plagued them since the Allan Border era, and despite the fact that Mark Taylor took the side he inherited to a higher plane he was unable to eradicate this glitch. It will be interesting to see if Waugh, with his dogged determination, can overcome this flaw.

Taylor was a first-rate captain, proactive and always looking for victory from the outset, but whilst Waugh is tactically astute he is such a single-minded player that he will find it harder to adjust to team requirements. Taylor retires as one of Australia's best skippers, and how Waugh – who inherits a very good side – handles what will eventually be a 'changing of the guard' period will determine how he is judged.

Steve Waugh will have at his disposal two tremendous strike bowlers in Warne and Glenn McGrath. Yes, that's the same Warne who had a shoulder operation and only took two wickets in the final Test against England, whilst tyro leg spinner Stuart MacGill was capturing twelve. Don't be fooled; Warne is still a top-class bowler and he isn't far from being back to his best. What he has lost in physical attributes (mainly his wrong-un, which was always his least dangerous delivery), he's made up for in mental strength. The lay-off from the game has allowed him to hone his extremely active cricket brain and he probably has more patience now than before the operation. Once he starts to get his flipper under control he'll again be a formidable opponent.

McGrath is now a complete fast bowler, having graduated from university after passing his entrance examination last time he was in the Caribbean. The lanky fast bowler regularly makes early breakthroughs with the new ball and he is every bit as dangerous as Warne when bowling in the fourth innings, because of his ability to swing the old ball and deliver telling yorkers. McGrath likes to impose his will on an opponent and on most occasions he has his way. However, he did goad the laid-back Alan Mullally once too often in the recent Ashes series and the tall left-armer should thank him for it – he hasn't looked back from that moment at the MCG.

This pair of spearheads is backed by Damien Fleming, who is much-improved since he reverted to a short run, and MacGill, who probably spins his leg break further than the young Warne. Fleming has added a little pace and is more than simply a swing bowler as he was when his tour of the Caribbean was cut short in 1995. He's had shoulder problems again this season in Australia and this will be of major concern to the selectors, although Adam Dale is an adequate back-up.

MacGill has learnt quickly, and although he is predominantly a side-spinner he is gradually introducing some subtle variations. He has a good wrong-un, which many Englishmen failed to pick, and he has decreased the number of short deliveries that plagued him after a good start on the Pakistan tour. He is a fiery customer, but he is working on keeping cool, although this will only be fully tested if someone with quick footwork like Carl Hooper really takes to him.

With such a well-balanced and potentially potent attack, Australia doesn't need big scores, just adequate ones made quickly. They are well equipped to handle this need with Michael Slater having returned as a wiser but still aggressive batsman, and the Waugh twins a formidable pair. Slater has to prove that he can dominate a top-class attack in the first innings, but he certainly did it against a much-improved England bowling line-up in the second innings on a number of occasions. Nevertheless, when the chips are down (perhaps not the ideal saying for Mark), the Waugh twins are the ones Australia will rely on heavily.

Mark has added a tougher edge to his batting whilst not compromising any of his elegant style, and Steve is still the hard-nosed competitor with the steel-trap mind. If the Australian batting is to be put under the pressure that exposes cracks that split wide open, both the Waughs have to be contained. Slater will be joined at the top of the order by Elliott, who is a good player of pace bowling and a proven big-score batsman. He drives well and plays the horizontal bat shots powerfully, so this combination has the potential for explosive starts like those produced by Gordon Greenidge and Desmond Haynes in their heyday.

The stars apart from Slater are aging and the younger brigade have all faltered, but there is sufficient talent among Elliott, Darren Lehmann, Ricky Ponting and Greg Blewett to provide hope for the future. One or more of that quartet could use the Caribbean as their springboard to a long-term tenure.

There is one other area of strength in this Australian side, and that is the all-round talent of Ian Healy. The effervescent wicket-keeper-batsman still works as hard as anyone in the team and he's lost none of his skill with either the gloves or the bat. His temperament is one of his great attributes and he contributes a lot to the thinking and the attitude of this team. He's very much a part of the hard edge that makes this side so competitive.

If you want to crack this team, you have to find a way to dominate the Waugh twins, Healy, Warne and McGrath. That is no easy task and one that appears way beyond the capabilities of the current West Indies.

The one-day side is a slightly different make-up, but no less talented and tough. Apart from the unlucky Healy, the core is the same and they are complemented by some skilful individuals. Adam Gilchrist is the most exciting and Michael Bevan the most successful of the others, and the team is building towards a strong showing at the World Cup. I'm expecting the Australians to retain the Frank Worrell Trophy and have a morale-boosting win in the limited-overs series as an ideal warm-up for the World Cup challenge. Anything less than a convincing double would rate as a major upset.

The curious case of a one-day master who was a five-day flop.

[*The Daily Telegraph* UK, 29 April 1999]

How can Michael Bevan be ranked number one (on the computer) as a one-day batsman and be excluded from the Australian Test side?

The cynical answer would be: 'They're allowed to bowl bumpers in Test matches.'

The actual reason is more complicated. It's true, Bevan does have trouble with the short-pitched ball and this has affected him mentally and also acts as an immediate spur to opposing captains and fast bowlers the moment he walks through the gate. The complete answer to Bevan's problem is probably, 'Short-pitched bowling and a comfort level.' When Bevan walks in to bat in a Test match he is apprehensive and the bowlers are expectant. When he strides to the wicket in a one-day game, he is expectant and it's the bowlers who are apprehensive.

Bevan's remarkable success in the one-day arena stems from a profound knowledge of his own game, faith in his ability, wonderful hand–eye co-ordination and the athleticism of a high-grade sprinter. Remarkably, he complements all those assets with a well-controlled temperament, and yet in the Test arena he has a tendency to panic when facing fast bowling. There must have been some budding psychologists among his early team-mates, who nicknamed him 'Schizo Bev'.

There are two Michael Bevans. The one who for most of his Test career looked like a rabbit caught in the headlights when he batted against pace bowlers, and who by the time he lost his place in the side was even dismissed by mediocre spin bowling. Then there's 'The Finisher': the batsman who is in total command from the moment he walks to the wicket in a one-day game.

That's the Bevan who terminated a game against the West Indies with a cool-headed boundary off the last ball and continues to successfully guide his partners through the minefield that is the last few overs of a one-day innings. Bevan has a couple of spots picked out where he aims his boundaries (through wide mid-on is a favourite) and if the delivery is not in his zone he settles for something less, but rarely a dot ball. He has an uncanny knack of hitting a boundary just when it is needed, and heaven help a fielder who is not quick to the ball, because he's the best player at picking up extra runs since the Pakistani pair Asif Iqbal and Javed Miandad regularly ran fieldsmen ragged. It is this pace which allows him to control the strike late in the game.

And I've never seen Bevan yorked. Never mind actually being dismissed by a ball in the block hole, he avoids them as though they are a deadly virus and often manages to whack attempted yorkers to the boundary. This he's able to do because of quick footwork, but he doesn't move around much before the bowler actually delivers the ball: once he sees the line and length he is decisive and moves like a panther.

All this from a guy whose feet betray him when he's wearing white, from a player whose career as a Test batsman was prolonged by his ability to take wickets as a left-arm Chinaman-bowler. He is a batsman whose one-day average is more than double his Test equivalent, in a game where the trend among top players is in the opposite direction. Here's a player who regularly wins one-day games off his own bat, and yet in the one Test where he had a big hand in the result it included a ten-wicket haul. In that match against the West Indies he had an opportunity to post his first Test century, but his timing was so astray that he was unable to reach the boundary or control the strike and was eventually stranded on eighty-five not out.

He has amassed an amazing number of not-outs in one-day cricket, many of them by virtue of guiding his team to victory. I can only recall one occasion where he's misjudged the chase and been caught a few runs short with wickets in hand. 'The Finisher' has terminated many a one-day match and Australia will be relying on him for repeat performances during this World Cup. Incredible, when you think all this responsibility falls on a batsman whose Test career may well be finished.

When Terry Jenner was sentenced to six-and-a-half years in gaol on 22 September 1998, I wrote in the *Sydney Sun* that he would make a good coach. I didn't realise how good, and it's to Terry's credit that he has become known universally as the 'Spin Doctor' following his long association with Shane Warne.

———

[Foreword in *Over the Top*, published by Information Australia, 30 April 1999]

There are very few guys who walk away from gaol and say, 'I'm a better man for having been inside.' Terry Jenner is one.

Maybe one of the reasons for TJ 'prospering' in gaol is because of the way he accepted his punishment. When the gaol term was published in the Sydney papers a QC who is a member of the tennis club where I play told me, 'The sentence given to your mate Jenner is way too harsh. You should let him know that an appeal would almost certainly get it reduced.'

I immediately got in touch with TJ and passed on the comment. He responded by saying he knew that it was harsh, but he didn't want to get his hopes up and have them dashed again so he wasn't going to appeal. He went on to explain that he needed to be put away and he'd just do his time and then get on with life. It was this acceptance of his punishment as a necessary part of his rehabilitation that probably helped TJ to get through a tough period in his life and come out a better man. Having spoken to him since, he says, 'A great weight was lifted off my shoulders when I was actually caught. It put an end to the double life I'd been leading and all the lies I had to tell to cover my tracks.'

I can understand how that would've eaten away at TJ. When he was sentenced I wrote a column which said in part, 'I don't consider Terry Jenner to be a criminal. Never have, never will. In fact, I've always classed TJ as a very honest cricketer, so honest at times he made life difficult for a captain.'

There was never anything behind the back with TJ. If he had a problem that related to my captaincy I'd know about it, usually less than five minutes after stumps. The good thing was once we'd discussed the problem, the matter was closed, and it didn't impact on what occurred the next day. I can still hear the sound of that beer bottle thumping down on the wooden table in the middle of the Adelaide Oval dressing room. It was a very definite signal that TJ had a problem and he wanted to talk it out over a beer. The sound still occasionally wakes me in the middle of the night – probably in the way TJ shoots bolt upright to the screech of metal doors clanging shut.

Why did I support TJ when he was going through a rough time? Because of the belief that he wasn't a crook and didn't deserve to go to gaol, especially when legitimate criminals like Alan Bond and Christopher Skase were roaming free. This offended my sense of fair play. Also, because I felt he needed help rather than incarceration. And finally, I guess, because once you are captain, you're their skipper for all time.

It was my job to be there to help and to listen when a player had a problem, and in return I expected them to play hard for me on the field. 'If you expect one hundred per cent you have to give one hundred per cent' was one of my rules as captain. TJ had always tried for me when I was captain of South Australia and Australia and he made some monumental contributions. We'd played in three Shield-winning sides together (two under my captaincy) and he took more than 250 wickets for SA. He took four wickets in the first innings of the Test we won in Trinidad and five in a drawn game at the same ground. He made a match-turning seventy-four on a damp wicket at the Adelaide Oval in partnership with Doug Walters against England in 1974–75. Those were some of his exploits on the field. As a senior player TJ didn't shirk responsibility, and when I was having a running battle with the South Australian Cricket Association in 1975–76 it was Terry who organised a meeting of the players which resulted in a show of support for the captain. These things are not easily forgotten. Should never be forgotten.

Off the field TJ could be excellent company: humorous, observant, full of ideas and always able to express himself – some of the reasons why I wrote in 1988, 'He'd make a damn good coach.' If he was at odds with the world it was wise to find a different pub and let the mood pass. In short, I'd had a lot of good times with TJ and a few disappointments along the way and we'd survived it all, so his period in gaol was no time to walk away.

There were a couple of things that worried me when I went to visit TJ at Mobilong. The first was the business of sex in gaol and the second was suicide. TJ answered the first question with typical humour: 'Don't worry, mate, I'm too old. They want the young good-looking guys.' The second he handled with thought and his usual candour. 'Mate, there are twenty questions they ask you on a form and I've always written "yes" to the first nineteen and "no" to the last one.' That was the answer I wanted to hear.

I knew TJ was going to survive gaol when I had a letter from him that responded to my line 'Don't lose your sense of humour.' He told a lovely story about bowling to David 'Cracka' Hourn of

New South Wales. It wasn't just the hilarious punch-line, but also the way he was able to weave the story like a good tapestry artist that gave me faith in his future. Those who have heard TJ as an excellent after-dinner speaker in recent years will know exactly what I mean.

TJ didn't lose his sense of humour in gaol, but he did find his way. He is a better man, as he says, and importantly he is helping other people to improve themselves. A number of times since TJ has been out of gaol, I've heard worried people tell me, 'TJ's back on the punt.' The first couple of times I broached the subject with him, and he gave a plausible explanation of how the mistake could have occurred. The last few years I've stopped even asking.

I'm glad TJ has written a book, as he has a lot to offer on a subject (addiction to gambling) about which very little is known. He also has a lot to offer on another subject about which little is known – leg spin bowling. I'm sure he'll continue to help people in both categories, which will follow a trend in TJ's life. Terry Jenner has helped a hell of a lot more people than he's hindered.

Shane Warne turned the 1996 World Cup semi-final with a devastating spell of leg spin bowling. Here he was again in 1999 purveying his special brand of magic in another World Cup semi-final.

[*The Daily Telegraph* UK, 17 June 1999]

Shane Warne proved at Edgbaston that form is temporary but class is forever. He produced an amazing spell when Australia appeared to be dead and buried, not only taking wickets but inspiring his team-mates to produce a super-human effort which saw them through to the final at Lord's to meet Pakistan.

It was like old times when he curved one through the air and then spun it sharply past Herschelle Gibbs' bat to hit the top of off-stump. It brought back memories of 'The' Mike Gatting ball at Old Trafford in 1993, and Warne's shouts of 'come on' as he pumped his fist, rallied the troops and made them believe a place at Lord's was still within their capabilities. Not since the days of Dennis Lillee have I seen an Australian bowler inspire his team from a seemingly hopeless situation the way Warne did at Edgbaston. It was almost a replica of his effort at Chandigarh in the 1996 World Cup semi-final, when he demolished the West Indies' batting in taking four crucial wickets to push his team into the final at Lahore.

Warne is not only a top-class bowler, he's also a smart cricketer and an unselfish team man. His unbridled enthusiasm after taking his first three wickets inspired his team-mates to the point where they began to believe victory was possible, but he then had to calm himself so that his mind was totally focused before bowling the next delivery. He was dominant in his first spell as he wove a web around the leaden-footed South African batsmen, and despite taking some stick in the last couple of overs he still had one more trick up his sleeve. In his final over, Warne beat a determined Jacques Kallis through the air and caused him to loft a simple catch to Steve Waugh, and this brought about another Australian rally. In the end the Australians held their nerve in the face of another Lance Klusener onslaught and it was enough to take them into the final.

It was ironic that South Africa was brought undone by spin bowling, an art they have shunned in order to stick with a regimented policy of building up pressure via accurate seam bowling. That will amuse Warne, and he'll be hoping his semi-final effort isn't in vain, as it was in the 1996 World Cup.

Steve Waugh always enjoyed the grand stage provided by the World Cup. In the 1999 tournament he grabbed his first major trophy as skipper.

[*The Bulletin*, 20 June 1999]

Steve Waugh plays his cricket with a lot of pride and he is now also a very proud skipper, having added a World Cup win as captain to his 1987 Cup-winning medal. Steve is the only player to have been in both of Australia's World Cup wins. The fact that he's still around twelve years after playing a major role in the 1987 victory is testimony to his resilience, but to still be playing effectively is an indication of his skill. Steve is now in the third stage of his career and, remarkably, he's turned back the clock, somehow stopped the aging process of a cricketer and returned to the habits of his youth. As a brash youngster Steve came into the game blazing shots in all directions, then after being dropped from the Australian side he returned as a more cautious player, accumulating runs like an automaton and eliminating all risks. On taking over the captaincy of the limited-overs side, he was suddenly lofting bowlers over mid-wicket with all the contempt of a young player who has an eagle eye and doesn't realise things can go wrong.

Unlike his batting, which was full of aggression and well-timed counter-attacks throughout the World Cup, Steve Waugh's captaincy gained in stature as the tournament became more competitive. Early on Waugh was steady rather than startling, but things turned for the better the moment he gave Glenn McGrath the new ball, instead of wasting his talent for removing top-order batsmen by relegating him to first change. This allowed McGrath to do what he does best – lead the charge rather than follow – and he responded by getting valuable wickets like Brian Lara and Sachin Tendulkar at crucial times. When a bowler like McGrath performs those feats it inspires the other players and they start to believe in themselves.

Waugh also showed faith in his other inspirational bowler, Shane Warne, at a crucial moment in the tournament. Warne took a pounding from Neil Johnson in the early overs of the Zimbabwe innings, but Waugh called on Warne in the semi-final when South Africa appeared to be cruising to victory, and the blond bamboozler responded by taking three wickets, causing the opposition to panic. A pumped-up Warne not only took wickets, but he was also quick to urge on his team-mates, and once again a Waugh move had ensured the team believed that victory was possible.

Backing his players is one of Steve Waugh's important traits as a skipper, and another is his unnerving ability to lead from the front with the bat when his team is in trouble. There was no better example than his magnificent hundred at Headingley, where he applied the Lazarus touch to Australia's hopes of reaching the semi-finals when South Africa appeared to have the match won. Timing has always been a feature of Steve's batting and it is only equalled by his ability to judge perfectly the moment to counter-attack when an opponent is in control. Like a belligerent boxer, Steve rose from the canvas and threw a big punch at Headingley, and by the time Hansie Cronje had regathered his senses, the ten count had been applied. This was a classic case of the meticulous planning which has always been a part of the Waugh game, and once again he had read his opponent well and outmanoeuvred him perfectly.

As a player, the quietly patriotic Steve Waugh was mostly undemonstrative, leaving all the leaping around and backslapping to more boisterous players like Merv Hughes and Shane Warne. A quiet pat on the back and a word of encouragement was all Waugh felt was necessary, and he applies the same principles to captaincy: a gesture here, a word there is about all the emotion the skipper exudes. This is a good habit, as a captain doesn't want to show any outward sign of concern to his own team, nor, just as importantly, send any signals to the opposition. Waugh will never captain with the flair of Warne, but because of his calm approach and meticulous planning he won't make many mistakes.

The fact that he wasn't even required to bat in the final would've given him great satisfaction, but it didn't mean he had little influence on the game. Apart from leading his troops and applying more and more pressure through field placings and bowling changes as Pakistan slipped further into the mire, Steve also held a smart catch at a crucial time. Glenn McGrath had just uncharacteristically grassed a sitter offered by Abdul Razzaq and the youngster was starting to look quite comfortable when Waugh dived and grabbed a hot chance at cover to ensure the Australians didn't pay a heavy price for that mistake.

Timing is the hallmark of Steve Waugh's cricket. He has it in spades as a batsman and he's acquired it as a captain. It's no coincidence that as his leadership improved through the tournament, so did his team's performance. The Australian team saved its best for the most important occasion, just as a proud captain has done so many times.

When three South African players were accused in early 2000 of having accepted bribes to under-perform it was a major surprise. I had enjoyed Hansie Cronje's company a few times, including the series in India where he enticed Herschelle Gibbs and Henry Williams into his web of entrapment. This was his greatest crime as far as I'm concerned: a captain is supposed to help young players up the ladder, not lead them up the garden path.

[*The Bulletin*, 15 April 2000]

International cricket has just suffered a body-blow to its integrity that far exceeds the damage done when Bodyline threatened to terminate diplomatic relations between Australia and England in 1932–33. However, amid all the suffering, the administrators have accidentally bumped against a lifeline that could help save the game from foundering on the rocks of greed, if only someone has the good sense and strength of will to grab hold of the buoy and swim with the tide.

When Hansie Cronje, one of the most respected players in cricket, admitted to 'not being honest' in his denial following charges by the New Delhi (India) police of 'cheating, fraud and criminal conspiracy related to match-fixing and betting', a pall of gloom fell over the game. At first it was believed that Cronje had been snared in a trap initiated by an International Cricket

Council – sanctioned undercover operation. This news was too good to be true; to believe that officials who had traditionally operated at the speed of a slow-moving glacier could suddenly attain Internet velocity. Eventually it was revealed that the New Delhi police had accidentally come across the evidence whilst conducting a low-key extortion investigation. Never mind the method, the resulting evidence is what counts.

This is the first time that cricket, which has been dogged by rumours of match-fixing for the better part of a decade, has actually had anything that remotely resembled hard evidence rather than hearsay, innuendo and insinuation. Why not spread the net of criminal investigative minds and, if they produce further evidence, implement judicial inquiries?

All we've heard since Shane Warne, Mark Waugh and Tim May blew the whistle on Pakistan's Salim Malik is a call for judicial inquiries. This has resulted in Pakistan, India and Australia all complying, and yet not one player has been charged, despite a lot of threats and accusations. Hard evidence is what is required to eradicate the cheats from the game and make it too dangerous for the leeches to greedily enhance their fortunes by operating on cricket matches. The knowledge that competent criminal investigators are at work combing bank accounts, grilling suspects and doing whatever else is needed to unearth evidence in order to lay charges is one way of helping to cut out the advanced cancer that threatens to become terminal. That, and the adoption of some firmly worded clauses in the contracts of all players and officials, as well as in the ICC Code of Conduct rules. Implementing such measures will indicate clearly the options to any cricketer or official contemplating involvement in any form of match-fixing or forecasting: if they are found guilty it'll result in a life ban. Those two potent and complementary actions are necessary to send a strong message to all players and officials as well as to the cowardly leeches who aren't even prepared to gamble their tainted cash without having the odds stacked in their favour.

It may well turn out that Cronje is the player who bears the brunt of the first wave of indignation, but the fact that an un-related trap appears to have snared the unlikeliest of victims can only be attributed to 'God moving in mysterious ways'.

The officials must shoulder a good deal of the blame for the precarious situation in which cricket finds itself. Not only have they not been forceful enough in writing the rules and trying to track down offenders, but they've also done little to educate and prepare players for the many pitfalls they encounter whilst playing a high-profile game. In most cases this is because the administration is operating in the twenty-first century with 1960s credentials. It is also asking a lot of sportsmen to behave in an impeccable fashion when many around them, in some cases the highest levels of government, are reportedly involved in their own illegal capers.

Unfortunately the early signs following the euphoria of the alleged capture of hard evidence aren't promising. In South Africa, officials have gone from disgusted indignation (that their favourite son could be challenged) followed by a short period of humbling backdowns to counter-attack mode, pointing the finger of blame elsewhere. According to United Cricket Board (UCB) chief, Dr Ali Bacher, 'The problem seems to arise, emerge in the [Indian] subcontinent, that's where the origin is by all accounts.'

In that same interview Bacher also appeared to be trying to justify Cronje's actions when he said, 'During the tour of India he was harassed continually by bookmakers.' On the face of the evidence so far, it would appear, Dr Bacher, that there was a logical reason for such constant contact.

The fact that Dr Bacher has traversed these feelings in a short space of time and then come out with guns blazing and pointed in the direction of the subcontinent only confirms that politicking and prejudice are still high-priority credentials at the ICC.

The ICC has been rendered powerless for so long because too many of its number are more involved in constructing a personal power base and indulging in 'one-upmanship' than with administering in the 'best interests of the game'. If, in this hour of crisis and need, this is the best Dr Bacher, one of the more powerful officials on the ICC, can come up with, then it is a strong indication that the motor running cricket is spluttering and in need of a complete overhaul.

Surely the fact that Cronje, one of the standard-bearers for a game that is in trouble, has shown that he is susceptible must ring an alarm bell that sounds like a 1940s London air-raid siren to those holed up in the ICC bunker. If Cronje's plight is not enough, then the fact that the leeches have progressed from trying to fix the results of matches to manipulating what individuals do (or don't do) on the field should be worrying enough to prompt immediate and decisive action.

I worked on the series of matches that are being questioned by the New Delhi police and I can't say I noticed anything suspicious. This could be because I see the game through rose-coloured glasses, but I'm more inclined to think it is because manipulation of things like individual scores or bowling changes is difficult to detect and nigh on impossible to prove. This should be of the gravest concern to the officials and is even more reason why hard evidence, like that which is alleged to be in the hands of the Indian police, should be applauded, not ridiculed.

The administrators may believe that 'a fool and his money are soon parted', and they have compelling evidence on their side when, despite all the publicity about match-fixing and score-rigging, people still bet on cricket. However, it is unreasonable to expect people to continue to part with their hard-earned cash at the turnstiles when there's a chance the result is already determined, or the performance of some individuals may be diminished. I certainly wouldn't want to knowingly watch or work on such matches and yet I would love to have witnessed the Bodyline series, because it was a tough contest played according to the laws at the time.

The game is in big trouble. It has been in that predicament for a while and something drastic needs to be done. Cricket will continue to suffer in the short term and I have no doubt there will be more revelations in the near future that will rock the foundations even further. It is a sad indictment on the game's administration that things have reached this desperate stage and that it's only been uncovered by a freak occurrence. If, having been handed this golden opportunity, the administrators continue to bicker and procrastinate whilst the game withers, they will be as guilty as any player convicted of match-fixing.

In mid-2000, the Australian Cricket Board (ACB) set a danger- ous precedent and it became obvious that Shane Warne would never captain his country in a Test match, more's the pity.

———

[total-cricket.com, 9 August 2000]

The ACB's decision to demote Shane Warne from a position of authority has set a dangerous precedent. The standard for Australian cricketers aspiring to a position of leadership has now been set, and it includes not only off-field activities as they pertain to representing your country but also private matters. They don't set the bar that high for politicians, otherwise Bill Clinton wouldn't still be president of the USA.

The irony of the whole matter is that the ACB 'baulked' with the bar at an acceptable height when they appointed Warne vice-captain even though he was guilty of taking money from a 'bookie' for information on cricket. However, in that case the ACB was also culpable, having covered it up for four years, and so it probably felt that if it ignored Warne's credentials then it would be hypocritical if some board members weren't sacked for failing to do their duty. Relieved of the feeling of guilt and possessing a long history of buckling at the knees at the thought of having to answer tough questions, the ACB overturned the selectors' choice (Warne) and appointed Adam Gilchrist as vice-captain. If the ACB continues to maintain that stance then some very good candidates aren't ever going to be considered for the captaincy, because the Australian larrikin nature includes some of the best qualities for leadership.

In addition to this decision leading to misguided appointments, the ACB members also lack the personal experience of what's required to lead a team at international level, and that's why it's best if the selectors (generally ex-internationals) make the choice. In this case the ACB was fortunate in having some good alternatives, as most other countries can only dream of sacking a player with Warne's leadership capabilities. The fact that the ACB plumped for Gilchrist rather than Ricky Ponting is a further indication that the bar is being set at record levels, because the right-hander also has a couple of black marks against his name for off-field misdemeanours.

I'm sure in the past a player has missed out on the Australian captaincy because of 'matters other than cricket ability'. Keith Miller is one player that comes to mind immediately, but it was done unofficially then, and now the standard has been made public. The ACB is setting the bar dangerously high, because not too many players from any era would avoid the prying eye of today's media on the board's current criteria.

The biggest danger is that it's always the high-profile players who are most at risk of being hounded by the media, and more often than not the choice of leader comes from that group. Sadly, it appears that from now on anyone convicted of an indiscretion by the media is for the high jump, but that's not the players' specialty: in case the ACB hadn't noticed it is supposed to be cricket.

When Ian Healy played his last Test in late 1999 many people wondered if his position could be filled adequately. Adam Gilchrist soon answered that question with an amazing entry into Test cricket. There haven't been too many better.

[*The Bulletin*, 4 November 2000]

What is a Gilchrist? A cricket fan might answer Adam, a left-hand-batting wicket-keeper, but his predecessor Ian Healy, understanding the difficulties associated with the position, might have a totally different definition.

Two Test matches after Adam Gilchrist had replaced Healy as the Australian glove man he was in the process of playing a brilliant match-winning innings of 149 not out against Pakistan, following an equally impressive eighty-one on debut, when the former keeper said on commentary, 'It's nice to know you're missed.'

Just over twelve months on from his Gabba Test debut Gilchrist will walk out onto the same ground as not only the incumbent wicket-keeper, but probably also the current Australian vice-captain. It took Healy more than six years of hard slog to become vice-captain of Australia and he (along with all but two of the other keepers who've ever worn the baggy green cap) never led his team in a Test match. Healy played 119 Tests and was never appointed captain, and yet people are talking about Gilchrist as Steve Waugh's likely successor and he's about to reach double figures in games. It wouldn't surprise me if Healy believes the left-handed Gilchrist is actually descended from one J. Christ, a carpenter of great repute. If that is Healy's belief he will have plenty of followers.

After only nine Tests Gilchrist has already accumulated a century and has the Australian record for the most dismissals (ten) in a match. Rod Marsh became the first Australian keeper to score a Test century in 1972–73, almost a hundred years after Jack Blackham (the Prince of keepers) donned the gloves in the initial international in 1876–77.

In addition to his achieving much on the field, the administrators thought so highly of Gilchrist's leadership skills they appointed him vice-captain after Shane Warne's demotion. It's an incredible rise to prominence for a man who couldn't retain the number-three spot in a depleted New South Wales batting line-up and later moved to Western Australia because he foresaw no way past Phil Emery as the Blues' keeper.

Gilchrist should be a believer in the adage 'go West, young man', because from the moment he moved to Perth his star began to rise. He quickly learnt to ignore criticism, as he was booed onto the WACA ground simply because he'd replaced local hero Tim Zoehrer. That experience stood him in good stead for his Test debut, when he ousted Healy at the Gabba. However, he soon won over the fans in the West and by the end of his second season for WA (1995–96) he'd acquired plenty more admirers with an incredible free-stroking century in the Shield final at the Adelaide Oval. It wasn't long before this reputation as a clean striker saw him replace Healy in the one-day side, but it was a move to the top of the order, which resulted in a century against South Africa in a final, that really made people sit up and take notice of this glove man who could bat.

He began to put more pressure on Healy's Test position with regular one-day centuries, but the gritty Queenslander answered each challenge with runs of his own. However, as soon as Healy stopped making runs the selectors acted quickly and Gilchrist hasn't looked back since that Gabba debut.

Of all his brilliant achievements, probably the one that has most surprised onlookers is the way he's handled standing up to Warne. Healy built a large part of his enviable reputation on his ability to 'read' and handle the blond bamboozler, and by the end of his career it had grown to the level of being psychic, unless there's a subtle, as yet unrevealed code in the saying 'Bahwling, Warney'. Despite the high standard set by Healy, Gilchrist hasn't drawn criticism for his keeping, and so assured is he with the gloves that not only is he being touted as a future captain, but there's also been no discussion on who might be the next long-term keeper.

Gilchrist's smooth transition as a Test keeper tends to confirm the opinion of Marsh, another great Australian left-handed batting keeper, who says, 'If you don't get better as the incumbent then you're an idiot.' Rodney's blunt assessment arises from his logical conclusion that if you're doing the job or practising almost every day and thinking about what you're doing then you must improve.

Gilchrist's handling of the media has been almost as smooth as his glove work. First he had to deal with the questions about taking over from Healy, and then followed the grilling when he replaced Warne as vice-captain. Now there's the speculation about whether he'll break the barrier that has seen only two Australian keepers become Test captain, the aforementioned Jack Blackham (eight matches) and Barry Jarman (one match, as a stand-in for Bill Lawry). For those who suggested Gilchrist shouldn't become captain he had a logical answer in saying he wouldn't give any guarantees he'd be a successful skipper, but not to rule him out of the job just because he's a wicket-keeper.

Along the way Gilchrist has impressed a lot of people with his credentials as a leader. He's led WA as well as Australia A, and Marsh, a shrewd cricket judge, appointed him captain of an academy touring side. In each case Gilchrist handled the job competently, and if he is given the Australian role he only has to apply the same principles, because after all he's captaining ten other guys, the same as when he led the NSW primary-schools team. Just because every move you make at international level is closely scrutinised doesn't mean the task is a great deal different from leading WA – it's basically still a matter of earning your team-mates' respect and having faith in your decisions. Pressure can come from within if you start trying to meet others' standards rather than sticking to your own.

A lot of humbug is talked about captaincy; after all, it is not nuclear science or brain surgery. With more money in cricket and hence more professional positions, there's a tendency to complicate the modern game. Sure, games are always evolving, but every now and again it doesn't hurt to recall the words of Richie Benaud, who once told me, 'Cricket is a simple game, and the simpler you keep it the better off you'll be.'

Gilchrist has a simple batting philosophy: if the ball is up he drives it and if it's short he either hooks, cuts or pulls it. If it's on a good length he stops it. If he applies the same commonsense and logic to the task of captaincy there's absolutely no reason why he can't lead Australia, keep wickets and continue to make runs in a hurry. It would be unwise to bet against Gilchrist getting the captaincy: he's been a leader throughout his formative years and he's matured quickly since being selected in the Test team. In fact he's achieved so much in such a short time that his next trick may well be to walk on water.

Glenn McGrath has made 'targeting' an opponent an art form, but he reached his zenith at the WACA ground in late 2000. To cap off a memorable match, McGrath was also part of the team that beat the West Indies and created history by winning their twelfth Test in a row. The following match reports tell the intriguing story.

[total-cricket.com, 1 December 2000]

The amazingly consistent Glenn McGrath continued to mesmerise Brian Lara and a number of his compatriots as Steve Waugh took advantage of the West Indies' fragility with the bat by sending them in after winning the toss.

McGrath is a top-class fast bowler: accurate, hostile and thoughtful – the perfect combination for longevity in the hardest job in cricket. McGrath reached the zenith of his career so far when he took his three-hundredth wicket in Test cricket and followed it with another, with the next ball to give him a hat-trick. To cap a marvellous achievement his prized victim (the three-hundredth) was none other than Brian Lara, a first-ball duck, the thirteenth time he's snared the gifted left-hander. McGrath is a fine bowler, but he has a career as a commentator awaiting him when he retires, because he predicted earlier in the week that Sherwin Campbell would be number 299 and Lara the big prize.

Lara is in a mental mess and he needs to get his head sorted out quickly, otherwise he'll soon be in as big a tangle as most of the other batsmen from the West Indies. The only two who seriously challenged McGrath and his cohorts were Wavell Hinds and Ridley Jacobs. Both came out intent on playing sensible cricket: they tried to score regularly and hit the loose balls, exactly what is required to counter excellent bowling. Hinds did a good job of keeping his head whilst all around were crashing and he regularly drove the ball through the off-side, hitting seven boundaries in a good half-century. He and Jacobs added seventy-five, after the West Indies had slumped to 5 for 22, to avoid yet another monumental collapse. Left with a frail tail, Jacobs wisely attacked the bowling, cutting and pulling Stuart MacGill's short deliveries and driving the faster bowlers. Jacobs received surprisingly stout if not that skilful support from Mervyn Dillon and suddenly a score in the region of the West Indies' match total in the first Test became a reality.

The Australian fielding assisted the Windies' cause with four chances being grassed. Ricky Ponting was the main offender, with two dropped and a skier he completely misjudged in the swirling breeze. Despite the good fortune the West Indies fell just short of two hundred and unfortunately Jacobs was stranded only four short of an initial Test century. A dejected Courtney Walsh was the last man out, edging an away-swinger from Jason Gillespie to give the spindly pace man a confidence-boosting three wickets on his return to Test cricket after breaking a leg.

Gillespie was soon back out in the middle as a nightwatchman with the West Indies hitting back in removing Michael Slater and Justin Langer in quick succession. However, Matthew Hayden stood firm, driving well through the off-side and hitting some spanking pull shots as Marlon Black pitched too short. The West Indies' pace bowlers will need to find the right length quickly on the second day and get the batsmen onto the front foot at the WACA, otherwise Australia will win their record-breaking twelfth consecutive Test on the back of McGrath's monumental performance.

[total-cricket.com, 2 December 2000]

Mark Waugh led an Australian charge with a brilliant century as the West Indies disintegrated to the point where the tail-enders made a mockery of their short-pitched bowling and shoddy fielding. Mark Waugh posted his eighteenth Test century as the hapless Windies allowed Steve Waugh the luxury of declaring exactly two hundred runs ahead.

It was no surprise that the West Indies wilted as their fielding practice is appalling. The fast bowlers are butter-fingered and nowhere near as athletic as their predecessors, and incredibly no one was doing anything to correct the mistakes being made during the warm-up: this was practice without a purpose. It was no surprise then when Matthew Hayden top-edged an attempted hook shot and Marlon Black dropped it, the ball barely touching his fingers as it continued on its path to the boundary. Hayden didn't prosper from the let-off as Black bowled him just as his form was suggesting a second Test century. The nightwatchman, Jason Gillespie, fell shortly afterwards, then the Waugh twins began their partnership in aggressive fashion and the danger signals started flashing for the Windies.

Both Steve and Mark came out after lunch looking to punish the bowling, but Courtney Walsh found the edge of the captain's bat and then Black moved one off the seam to skittle Ricky Ponting. The Australian lead was only twelve when Adam

Gilchrist joined Mark Waugh, but the initiative was soon wrested from the West Indies with a blistering partnership that saw the fifty posted at the rate of nearly a run a ball. Gilchrist hammered boundary after boundary in the region from back-ward point to cover as Black pitched too short, whilst Waugh glided the ball through the on-side and smashed a couple of cuts to the fence. This partnership was a good example of how Gilchrist can change the game quickly with his brisk scoring, and when he has a partner like Mark Waugh playing confidently the combination is lethal.

To compound the Windies' woes, Jimmy Adams failed to take the new ball straight after tea when it was available and opted for his own gentle finger spin. The pair pounced on this oppor-tunity until the new ball was belatedly taken and Gilchrist was dropped by Black at mid-wicket as he pulled a short one from Nixon McLean. This allowed the keeper-batsman to pass fifty, but McLean then showed his fast-bowling team-mate how to catch in the outfield when Gilchrist guided a short one over the heads of the slips and into third man's hands. Mark Waugh was then brilliantly caught by Adams in the covers, but what followed was like comedy capers as the bowlers continued to pitch short. Brett Lee and Stuart MacGill sprayed shots in all directions and ran for everything they hit.

The West Indies were demoralised as they slouched off the field, and to continue his nightmare tour Sherwin Campbell was soon out as he drove at a full delivery from Lee. The final ignominy came with three balls remaining, when Glenn McGrath accounted for nightwatchman Mervyn Dillon. This Test appears headed for another third-day finish.

[total-cricket.com, 3 December 2000]

The West Indies capitulated at the WACA ground to present Australia with their record-breaking twelfth successive Test victory. If Clive Lloyd hadn't been so conservative back in 1984 Australia would've been chasing thirteen victories for the record, but, that aside, the former West Indies captain must have been appalled that his team's record wasn't defended with greater determination.

The Australians steamrolled their opponents, with Glenn McGrath defying all cricket laws and nominating his victims before taking his three-hundredth wicket, and this set the tone for the match. There is no denying the strength of this Australian attack, but they have been up against a side in this series that has compounded its ineptitude by failing to plan its operation. A good example of this lack of thought came with the second-innings batting order. Ridley Jacobs, who has been the in-form player in this match along with Wavell Hinds, was relegated to number eight because of the nightwatchman, whereas he should've been promoted on the strength of his defiant first innings to number five, ahead of Jimmy Adams.

At the top of the order, Darren Ganga is quite a good defensive player, but he struggles to force the issue against bowling of high standard and consequently he has survived for a while in this series, but never prospered. He made his second twenty in the series before Jason Gillespie found the edge and Matthew Hayden took a brilliant catch at third slip. Gillespie had just replaced Glenn McGrath before collecting that wicket, but the senior pace man was quickly reintroduced at the other end with the advent of Brian Lara. This time McGrath failed to get his man, but on one occasion Lara appeared to avoid facing the lanky quickie by running a slow single and the fast bowler was quick to notice this reluctance.

However, the other half of the Mac attack, Stuart MacGill, claimed the prize scalp of Lara, bowled attempting to pull a ball that spun and hurried past the flailing bat. Right on lunch, Hinds' commendable resistance ended as it had started, with an aggressive shot. He was bowled attempting an off-drive to the leg spinner, a shot that had brought him plenty of runs in the match. The West Indies' batsmen were loath to leave their crease to disrupt MacGill's length, and consequently he was able to exploit the footmarks outside the left-hander's off-stump.

Jacobs once again provided assertive resistance, and with the solid support of Jimmy Adams the West Indies looked likely to at least force Australia to bat again, until they had a horrible running mix-up and the keeper was run out. That abysmal piece of out-cricket exposed the tail and Brett Lee produced two yorkers and a well-directed delivery to finish off the match and clinch the record-breaking victory. The Australian side gathered in a group to celebrate on the field and were later congratulated in the dressing room by Sir Vivian Richards, a key member of the West Indies side that had previously set the record. This was role reversal at its best, because Australia were the downtrodden back in 1984 and now they are the undisputed world champions.

In January 2001 Australia was close to completing a consecutive Test wins streak that began in Harare (1999) and finally ended in Kolkata (2001). It's a streak that will be hard to beat, and I recorded my thoughts on Steve Waugh's captaincy, as well as making some batting comparisons with his brother.

[*The Sunday Telegraph* UK, 6 January 2001]

A good captain should stamp his personality on the team, and Steve Waugh has certainly done that with the current Australian side. It has become statistically the best side of all time in accumulating fifteen straight Test wins in a relentlessly ruthless fashion.

That sums up Steve Waugh: he's relentlessly ruthless and he's also extremely aware of Test records and the traditions of the game. By focusing his mind and harnessing his skills like not many others have in cricket, Waugh has ensured that when he retires his name will be indelibly imprinted on the rich history of the game. The big difference in this Australian side from the one Mark Taylor so successfully led is that there's no let-up in standard even when a series has been won: they are relentless in their ruthless pursuit of Test match victories.

Is Steve Waugh currently the best batsman in the world? If you want someone to save a team in trouble and if you believe batting is an exercise in the statistical accumulation of runs then Steve is your man. My preference is to watch someone with artistry and flair in his batsmanship, and consequently I rate Steve as the second-best batsman in the Waugh family. Put the twin brothers together and it's a sound foundation for a very strong batting line-up.

Is Steve Waugh a great captain? That's hard to judge. Through no fault of his own Steve has captained Australia in a period when much of the opposition has been weak and his side hasn't been fully tested. However, you can do no more than beat those that come before you and that he has done with ruthless efficiency. The turning point in his captaincy came at the World Cup when Australia reached the Super Six stage with no points in credit. Up until then Waugh had captained the side in a conservative fashion, and that is not the style best suited to Australian cricketers. Forced by the system to be more aggressive he responded appropriately, and everything from that moment has been onward and upward.

At the same time he discarded his personal battle with his predecessor's reputation, stopped trying to justify his captaincy when compared with Taylor's and became his own man. This was undoubtedly his best move, and not a surprising one from a person who thinks deeply about his cricket. Waugh also has a couple of other good traits as captain: he gives nothing away in his expression, and showed in the heart-stopping World Cup semi-final with South Africa that he has nerves of steel, which both result in a clear mind when trouble is at hand.

The big test for Steve Waugh's captaincy will come when the Australian team is put under the hammer by a side that realistically has the ability to beat them, and that could well happen in India. That's when anger takes over and the thinking becomes blurred. On the odd occasion when a team has pressured Australia the bullyboy tendencies have come to the fore, but so far it hasn't been costly because of the oppositions' inability to keep the upper hand.

Maintaining supremacy is no problem for Waugh: once he has his foot on an opponent's throat it stays firmly planted until victory is claimed. At the MCG, with Australia holding a three–nil lead in the series and an advantage of 360 runs in the game, Waugh still pushed the field deep to allow nineteen-year-old Marlon Samuels a single so that his bowlers could have a crack at perennial number eleven Courtney Walsh. Number-one rule in Steve Waugh's playbook must surely be 'leave nothing to chance'.

Strangely for a man so focused on winning and ensuring there are no loose ends, in his tenancy as captain Waugh has allowed his coach to have a considerable say in the running of the team. This is a distinct change from the Taylor era, where he made it patently clear he was in charge and his assistants were there purely to do his bidding. There's also an apparent difference in style on the field: where Taylor had flair and was likely to take risks, Waugh is clinical and thorough. Nevertheless, Waugh occasionally surprises with a generous declaration like the one he set India at the MCG in 1999–2000 and, whilst his captaincy style is more like Allan Border's, a cricketer he admires, that world-record-holding batsman would never have offered India the opportunity to score 376 with ample time to win.

Surprises are part of the Waugh make-up. Twin brother Mark is a gambler off the field and a free spirit when wielding the willow, whilst Steve is generally cautious on and off the field. On days off Mark will head for a racetrack, a trotting track or even the greyhound racing, whereas Steve is more likely to be found giving comfort to children at a leper home in India, or photographing one of the great sights of the world. Mark was fined for giving information to an Indian bookmaker and yet Steve is as unlikely to give away information to a stranger as former Liverpool football manager Bill Shankly, who, when asked by a reporter to name his team for a European Cup semi-final, replied, 'I'm not giving away secrets like that to Milan. If I had my way I wouldn't even tell them the time of the kick-off.'

However, there's been nothing out of character during Australia's record-breaking run. When the team has been in trouble Steve has made runs; the rest of the time he's hardly been noticed out on the field, just a gesture here and quiet word there and things have run along according to plan. Not surprising for a man who likes winning, takes pride in records and plans each campaign with military precision.

Incidentally, cricket never was a gentleman's game. In the early eighteenth century players were prosecuted for playing on the Sabbath and by the 1730s stake-money of a thousand pounds a side was not uncommon. This meant that gambling was also a lucrative (for some) sideline at cricket matches. In 1737 there was even a death, when a man died after being hit by a stone.

———

[total-cricket.com, 22 January 2001]

'Stand your ground, son,' might be good advice for a boxer but it's becoming a bad habit on the cricket field and will lead to trouble.

Australia, already leading the league in most playing categories, is now well in front when it comes to batsmen staying at the crease if there's even the slightest doubt about the legitimacy of a catch. This lamentable situation has been created by administrators giving far too little thought to suggestions that sound like a good idea at the time. The idea of referring 'doubtful' catches to the third umpire so he can adjudicate from videotape replays is an indictment on the law-makers' cricketing nous and knowledge of television coverage. Far too often these decisions are influenced by 'inconclusive evidence' and in this situation the third umpire then has no option but to rule 'not out'. Hence there's a preponderance of batsmen standing their ground. This is going to lead to animosity between players as honesty among cricketers suffers the same fate as the penny-farthing bike and the Tasmanian tiger.

It's time to put an end to all this madness. It might be all right to include videotape in the same sentence as sex and lies but it is totally misplaced rubbing shoulders with most cricket decisions. I will grudgingly grant a place for run-outs, stumpings and hit-wicket appeals to be decided by a third umpire, but that's where it should end. The fact that cricket administrators are running a trial in South Africa to see if it's feasible to refer lbw decisions to the third umpire is an indication that they either don't understand what they see (on a cricket field or a television set) or they are mad with power, or a combination of both.

To see Ricky Ponting standing his ground after Stuart Carlisle had gleefully claimed a catch at short cover, only ten metres from the prying eyes of umpire Peter Parker, was to witness a game heading down a path only slightly less treacherous than the match-fixing minefield. Not surprisingly, when this decision was referred to videotape the evidence was inconclusive (surprise, surprise, most cameramen don't react quite as quickly as inter-national fielders, otherwise they'd be on the other side of the viewfinder) and Ponting was reprieved. The bowler, Mluleki Nkala, was upset, the fieldsman incensed (his integrity had been called into question), but fortunately their anger abated quickly.

If Ponting had been in Carlisle's position I doubt he would have reacted so graciously, judging from the ridiculous way he carried on in the Adelaide Test after Daren Ganga was given not out following a caught-behind appeal. If he'd 'buzzed' a Zimbab-wean batsman (say Heath Streak) with a throw from short cover the way he fired one past Ganga's ear it could easily have led to an ugly incident. On second thoughts, a serious threat from Streak to exercise his ample muscle power might be just what the talented but fiery Ponting needs to settle his trouble-some temper.

Having seen bountiful evidence that trial-by-videotape isn't a realistic option in most cricket decisions, the administrators should be encouraging umpires to take more responsibility for decisions and players to have trust in their fellow competitors. Instead they are looking to increase the use of videotape, which will only breed a poorer standard of umpiring and less honour among players. When (notice I didn't say 'if') this leads to a situation where cricket becomes the undercard for 'Saturday night at the fights' those same administrators will be the first to throw their arms up in horror and say, 'And cricket used to be a gentle-man's game.'

The first Test in Mumbai was not Michael Slater's finest hour.

[total-cricket.com, 1 March 2001]

The Indian team will think that God is an Australian follow-ing the unlucky mode of Sachin Tendulkar's second-innings dismissal. Just as India appeared to be working their way back into the game, Tendulkar fell via a ricochet, the rest of the batsmen were unable to dodge the bullets that followed, and Australia went on to claim their sixteenth consecutive win in comprehensive style.

However, the win wasn't completed with total cool and calmness as Michael Slater lost control when a decision referred to the third umpire went against Australia. He believed he'd caught Rahul Dravid when he pulled a long-hop from Damien Fleming towards square-leg. It was a close thing, although I thought the ball touched the ground before Slater had it under control and the third umpire quite correctly ruled in favour of the batsman. Slater then tempted fate by remonstrating with umpire Venkataraghavan (who had referred the decision) and expressed his disgust with Dravid for disputing his honesty. This carry-on was a bit rich, because Australia had benefited from similar situations during the season at home without one opponent disputing their integrity.

The Indian pair survived this period of intensity as Tendulkar played with great concentration and determination whilst still despatching anything astray. Tendulkar showed that a class player can handle a very good attack under difficult conditions. He will believe that Dame Fortune took a few days off during this Test as he only made one mistake in the first innings and his only mistake in the second dig was to crunch a pull shot into the shoulder of Justin Langer and then watch in dismay as the ball ballooned to Ricky Ponting. This was a desperately unlucky break for India, but Ponting made the most of the situation by sprinting metres and then throwing himself sideways to take a brilliant catch centimetres from the ground. Good teams make their own luck.

This was the perfect situation for the remaining Indian batsmen to show they could assist Tendulkar in winning a game, but they let themselves down badly. Sourav Ganguly's perform-ance was reprehensible; there was a single in the shot that went well to Slater's left and when he hesitated and then loafed he had the hide to blame his partner for his run-out. It was a classic case of one team wanting victory badly and the other side being unsure of their ability to win: Slater was desperate, Ganguly was casual.

In the end it was Australia versus Tendulkar, just as it was so often in the recent series Down Under. It must be made clear to the other batsmen that they have to contribute or else others will be found who can help the little maestro. I would start the ball rolling by letting the captain know that he has to shed his arrogant attitude towards his team-mates, because on form his batting position is vulnerable. The secret is to find some batsmen who treat the Australian bowlers as mere human beings rather than gods.

In March 2001 the Australian Test team was rampant; sixteen victories on the trot and still counting. The build-up to the Kolkata match was the prelude to ten amazing days of Test cricket. India's comeback was one to rival Lazarus', triple by-pass and all.

[total-cricket.com, 9 March 2001]

If Sourav Ganguly has had a manicure lately it was a poor decision, because he's hanging by his fingernails and the Australians will have no compunction about sending him crashing into the abyss.

Ganguly has made a number of poor decisions lately (not all of them on the field); however, it is his arrogance towards his fellow players that is the biggest threat to his tenuous hold on the captaincy. That and his inability to make big scores in Test matches against teams with a strong attack. He is without a century against Australia, Pakistan, South Africa or the West Indies, having not yet fed off the carcass that remains of their formerly robust Caribbean pace attack. If Ganguly can't change that trend in this series (the signs weren't promising in Mumbai) and in the process treat his players with more respect, then not only is the Gavaskar–Border Trophy lost but his leadership is also in peril.

Apart from scoring runs heavily, the thing Ganguly needs to do is restore order to the chaos that masqueraded as a batting line-up in the first Test. If Rahul Dravid can't dominate a good attack occasionally then he has no place at number three and his admirable stubbornness would be best employed blunting the new ball. The only player who has shown any sign of dominating this Australian attack on a regular basis is Sachin Tendulkar and he must bat at three. He is far better off coming in at the fall of one cheap wicket than two, and a substantial innings from him in that situation will have the dual effect of boosting his own batsmen's confidence as well as blunting that of the Australian bowlers.

The trio of Glenn McGrath, Shane Warne and Jason Gillespie is Australia's greatest attribute, because it is extremely hard to conquer. The batting, on the other hand, is outwardly strong, but it does have some minor cracks and if the right amount of pressure is applied it can be broken just like a poorly soldered joint. The Australians can be thankful that through the extreme generosity of referee Cammie Smith the batting wasn't weakened for the second Test by the enforced absence of Michael Slater. Slater may have been remorseful and dutifully apologised to all on the receiving end of his tantrum in Mumbai, but if the authorities are hopeful of avoiding fisticuffs on the field then they have to start providing examples of what is not acceptable behaviour.

Ganguly's team missed a big opportunity to go one up in Mumbai and in the process keep the Australians wondering if they really were bereft of the nerve and skill to win in India. Having failed to push home the advantage at 5 for 99 in the first innings the Indian attack has been drastically remodelled for Kolkata thanks to a combination of forced changes and hasty omissions. At least the injuries to two pace bowlers should lead to the inclusion of Zaheer Khan, because he is a young bowler with the temperament and skill to succeed against Australia given reasonable conditions.

Unfortunately for the aggressive left-armer and his fellow bowlers the Australians now know they have what it takes to win in India and a series victory is well within their grasp. Having won on a pitch that provided substantial assistance to the spinners will have further boosted the Australians' already high confidence level, and the success enjoyed by McGrath and Gillespie will have added more fuel to the argument that good pace bowlers can play a big part in winning a series in India.

Trying to stop the Australian juggernaut now is going to be like halting a herd of charging buffalo: it will take skill, courage and a good deal of innovative thinking. A big innings from Ganguly and some inspiring leadership would be a good way to halt the stampede before it pushes him and a few others off the cliff edge.

A Sardarji is the Indian nickname for a Sikh. They stand out with their colourful turbans and are renowned for their fighting spirit. Harbhajan Singh embodied this attribute as he single-handedly dragged India back into a series they appeared to have no chance of winning prior to his heroics. The following match reports tell the story of one of the most amazing come-backs in Test match history.

———

[total-cricket.com, 11 March 2001]

Harbhajan Singh produced India's first hat-trick and in doing so not only bowled his side back into the Eden Gardens Test match, but also restored some pride to its cricket. The spinning Sardarji bowled with deceptive flight and much thought as he brought the Australian middle order to its knees on a day when the Indians showed a lot of spirit to fight back after Matthew Hayden had threatened to single-handedly push them over the edge.

Hayden has been a prolific run-scorer at first-class level (forty-six centuries) but he had struggled to assert a similar authority over Test-match bowlers until this tour of India. His confidence grew at the rate of grass in the monsoon season during the Mumbai Test and he added some fertiliser in Kolkata with a handsome innings on a good batting pitch. This was reminiscent of the way Hayden bludgeoned first-class attacks in Australia, with firm drives through the off-side and the added dimension of strong on-side driving every time a bowler strayed onto the pads. His growing confidence was evident in his footwork against the well-flighted left-arm spin of Venkatapathy Raju. He regularly skipped well down the pitch and lofted the ball into the outfield and over the rope, and when he was short of the ball he pushed out firmly and took the single. However, three shy of his century he was deceived by Harbhajan and holed out at mid-wicket. Erapalli Prasanna would have been proud of the bowler as he issued 'an invitation to loft into the outfield' (as distinct from one to hit the ball into the stands), and this began a good period for India. Sourav Ganguly had encouraged his bowlers to peg away with a plan in mind and Zaheer Khan and Harbhajan performed better than their experienced team-mates under tough conditions; an encouraging sign for India. Zaheer should have had Hayden caught in the slips at sixty-seven, but undeterred he accounted for Justin Langer by concentrating on off-stump and eventually finding the edge.

This was straight after tea and then a rejuvenated Harbhajan spun a web around the Australian batsmen, mixing his quicker one with some clever flight. It appears that having done a lot of remedial work on his action, Harbhajan has also given a lot of thought to the way he has to bowl to get Test-match batsmen out. Today he encouraged the right-handers to drive through the off-side, a must to be a successful off spinner, and he produced two top-class quicker balls to account for batsmen of class in Mark Waugh and Ricky Ponting. He should be forever grateful to Sadogapan Ramesh for the unbelievable catch that gained him his hat-trick: even the most hopeful bowler doesn't expect a bat-pad fieldsman to move quickly to his right and snare a ball that's progress hasn't been slowed by the pad.

Following an ordinary match in Mumbai, Ganguly was inspirational in front of his home crowd, and he played a significant role in India's moving quickly from the outhouse to the penthouse. His captaincy was thoughtfully aggressive and he never buckled under the Australians despite their quick rate of progress fuelled by a plethora of boundaries on a lightning-fast outfield. He even contributed with the ball in a spirited bowling performance that included bouncing the faster bowlers. Having retrieved the situation with aggression in the field, the Indian team need the same sort of application and intent with the willow, and it won't hurt if the captain provides a substantial score in the middle order. If the Indian batsmen do play well this should be a fascinating Test match.

[total-cricket.com, 12 March 2001]

An Australian band called Skyhooks sang about 'Horror movies right there on TV, horror movies shockin' me right out of my brain.' Well that's what Indian fans saw on day two as Steve Waugh led an Australian charge that all but buried India's hopes in the series. Waugh was magnificent, cast in his typical role of leader of the rear-guard action, but he must have been pleasantly surprised by India's amazingly conservative tactics.

If a captain doesn't attack from the opening delivery it's extremely hard to go on the offensive once a batsman is set. That is an adage that Sourav Ganguly will be more aware of after the first session of play on the second day, having sat back against Steve Waugh and watched in horror as the Australians took everything offered by the Indians to compile an imposing total. Allowing a front-line batsman easy singles in order to get at the tail-ender is a tactic I've seen employed a lot but never with much success. It was an undeniable flop at Eden Gardens, because

Waugh and Jason Gillespie produced a record ninth-wicket partnership for Australia against India. It appeared that Ganguly went out with plan A in mind and had no fallback position, and this mistake was compounded by a poor umpiring decision that reprieved Gillespie when he was caught behind on eleven.

At the other end Waugh concentrated in his usual relentless fashion, and every time the bowlers erred he administered the appropriate punishment. Waugh is quite content to allow the tailenders plenty of strike, believing that this instils confidence, and it wasn't misplaced as Gillespie – a player renowned for solid defence – produced some delightful drives, including the toughest shot of all, the cover drive from an off spinner. Never one to allow the opposition a moment's peace, Waugh hit a six to take him to ninety-nine, and the single that followed brought a rare show of emotion from the Australian captain. A man who has closely followed the history of the game, Steve would be acutely aware of Eden Gardens' reputation, and it would mean a lot to Waugh to score his first Test hundred in India at this wonderful coliseum of cricket. His century was an amazing feat of perseverance as he was only on twenty when the eighth wicket fell: a tribute to Waugh's calculated approach and damnation of Ganguly's muddled thinking.

Having conceded the mental upper-hand in the field the Indian team was unable to regain the advantage when they batted. The only variation on a common theme was that Gillespie followed up his batting success by getting the early breakthrough, but Glenn McGrath compensated by quickly claiming Sachin Tendulkar's prized scalp. On this occasion McGrath out-thought Tendulkar, feeding him a steady diet of inswingers rather than his usual line of attack outside off-stump, and this was an indication that he might be starting to assert control over the little maestro.

There was no doubt who was in charge after Tendulkar's

departure: India scored eighty runs and lost five wickets in that period and yet only ran four singles. If you want to play into the Australian bowlers' hands that is the perfect blueprint. There was no attempt to rotate the strike and it was a matter of every man for himself as most batsmen slugged away for the boundaries whilst Rahul Dravid headed up his usual dead-end street and came to a complete halt. Forced to hit boundaries as he was left with the tail, V. V. S. Laxman displayed good footwork in dealing with Shane Warne, but this defiant attitude had been far too long in coming.

There is only one way to play a good team and that is to try to force them into an error – waiting for them to make a mistake doesn't work. If India continues to play Australia in this manner it will be appropriate for Skyhooks to re-release their hit, and it would be a suitable theme song for a new movie: *Dumb and Dumber Part Two*.

[total-cricket.com, 13 March 2001]

On a day when Laxman was Very Very Sure (V. V. S.), he took on the Australian attack and came out a conclusive winner. India scored 297 runs in the day and Laxman plundered twenty-five boundaries in amassing 142 of them to give India some hope of extending the Australians in the second innings.

Relentless and skilful is the way to describe the Australian attack. They have three very good bowlers in Glenn McGrath, Shane Warne and Jason Gillespie, and a solid back-up in the tireless Michael Kasprowicz, and they constantly examine the batsmen's technique and temperament. In collaboration with skipper Steve Waugh they never allow the game to drift, or let a batsman settle into his preferred rhythm, and consequently they are always changing line, length or their plan if the opposition displays any signs of getting on top. In addition, they don't tire easily and they have the backing of a fit, athletic and skilled fielding unit, so any runs made against Australia are hard-earned.

That makes Laxman's effort all the more meritorious, because not only did he score heavily but he also dominated this fine attack for long periods. In particular he played Shane Warne better than anyone else I've seen, skipping down the pitch confidently to drive through the on-side despite the leg spinner extracting slow turn. Anybody wanting to know how to blunt Warne's exceptional skill only has to peruse a videotape of this fine knock and note the way Laxman revelled in the leg-side attack rather than being bamboozled by it, as happens to so many players. Laxman showed the benefit of a mountain of first-class runs coming into the series and the move to promote him to number three came at the perfect time, with his confidence up.

His batting helped the other players around him and he looked set for a long partnership with S. S. Das until the little man was careless with where he planted his big feet. Being a back-foot player, he might benefit from standing with both feet outside the crease to give himself more room to move. Laxman also guided Sourav Ganguly through a tense period at the start of his innings, when he was uncertain against the pace bowlers. Laxman took command of the quickies and soon Ganguly was on more familiar ground with the spinners bowling in tandem, and that partnership had the Indian batting on top for the first time in the series. However, Ganguly allowed himself to get involved in a verbal joust with McGrath and he was out soon afterwards: if responding to a bait helps a batsman then it is fine to continue but it seems to affect the Indian skipper adversely and he'd be better off refraining from the temptation.

Ganguly could also learn a lesson from Steve Waugh's captaincy. At the start of the day Waugh surprisingly pushed the fieldsmen back to allow Laxman a single in order to attack the tail-enders, but when he watched as one of the right-hander's drives whistled past him to the rope he quickly changed his tactics. The adage is never change a successful plan but always scrap an unsuccessful one, and Waugh adhered to the dictum, whereas Ganguly didn't on day two.

The Australians will need to regroup as Warne looked a little weary, more mentally than physically, and this was a result of having to work extremely hard when bowling to Laxman. Laxman's innings did a lot of good things for India – it gave them a number three that could dominate the opposition and it took some of the heat off Sachin Tendulkar – but most importantly it showed his team-mates that the Australian attack isn't super-human. If he can continue to play in that manner and coax a big score out of Rahul Dravid then India might just have the chance of producing a Very Very Surprising miracle.

[total-cricket.com, 14 March 2001]

In surpassing the highest Test score by an Indian, V. V. S. Laxman became only the second from his country to score a double century against Australia, and is now the proud owner of the fourth-highest score against the baggy green caps. In doing so he passed a lot of famous names. His innings was of such high quality that he deserves the honour of being in that company, and in achieving such fame he also lifted India to a position of security.

On an amazing day for India, Laxman and a determined Rahul Dravid survived the whole day, and pummelled the Australians into the Eden Gardens' turf. There's an interesting similarity between Laxman's knock and the previous best, by Sunil Gavaskar: both players made their scores against the best attack of the time. Gavaskar made his against a West Indies attack that contained three champion bowlers, and Laxman did likewise in dominating Glenn McGrath, Shane Warne and Jason Gillespie.

Apart from his exquisite stroke play and faultless concentration there were many other attributes in Laxman's marathon innings. A chanceless double century is something special, but when it comes in circumstances where the team is down and out it becomes exceptional. I had the pleasure of witnessing Brian Lara's brilliant double century (277) at the SCG, where he excelled in piercing the field rather than clearing it, and Laxman's innings featured forty fours and no sixes, a tribute to his timing and placement. This innings was every bit as good as Lara's.

Laxman found a solid ally and a man who was prepared to learn from his junior partner in Dravid. Where Dravid had been Warne's bunny in the past, this time he copied Laxman's habit of dancing down the pitch to combat the spin and drift, and it wasn't long before the leg spinner was struggling to cope with two confident drivers. If Laxman's innings was one of a defiant spirit, Dravid's was a knock of character, showing that he may have been replaced at the top of the order but he isn't about to be forgotten. This irrepressible partnership not only denied the Australians but it also put India into a position of great strength, and if it hadn't been for fatigue Sourav Ganguly may have been able to produce a cheeky declaration late in the evening in order to further test the opposition.

However, so weary were both sides in the last session that it was like two heavyweight boxers who had thrown a flurry of punches in the early rounds and were now too tired to lift their arms in the late going.

Laxman can take further credit for the fact that few of the runs were gained easily as the Australians chased every ball in the field and constantly kept changing bowlers, field placings and tactics in an effort to unsettle the batsmen. Gillespie epitomised the Australian effort, producing a fast and furious spell before tea where he beat the bat a few times and sent a ball thudding into Dravid's protector. The Australians were bloodied but not beaten.

Now Ganguly has the pleasant task of deciding when to set Steve Waugh's team a chase. I suspect that the thought of India's first Test triple-century (to go with the initial hat-trick) will delay the declaration to the point where it's impossible to force victory. From the Australian point of view they would dearly love to extend the record-breaking winning sequence but will not set off on a chase that will put in peril their prime object of winning the series. This could mean a disappointing finish to a Test that has provided much entertainment, but if a draw is the result spare a thought for Adam Gilchrist. He'll be the most confused man in the ground, never having previously played in a Test with any other result than an Australian victory.

Kolkata is called the City of Joy. Always a vibrant city, there was an abundance of joy there on 15 March 2001, when India claimed a remarkable victory and halted Australia's streak of consecutive Test wins.

[total-cricket.com, 15 March 2001]

The Indian team should be celebrating with Hot Chocolate: not the drink but the music of the band who sang, 'I believe in miracles?' because that's what it took to become the third team in history to win a Test after being asked to follow on. Actually it took two miracles to bring India victory: the batting of V. V. S. Laxman and the bowling of Harbhajan Singh, and they were the heroes who provided the City of Joy with something special to celebrate.

At first it appeared that Sourav Ganguly had delayed his declaration a little too long, but in the end it was perfectly timed, as the Australian batting line-up's fragility against good spin bowling was laid bare. Harbhajan made the initial inroads by getting the ball to bounce and turn, and by operating on an off-stump line to the right-handed Michael Slater. Harbhajan has always had the skill to get top-class players out, and now that he has added know-how he's a formidable opponent. His name will be added to those of Jim Laker and Jasu 'Josh' Patel as off spinners who have decimated Australian batting line-ups.

Throughout the match Venkatapathy Raju looked nervous and consequently just lobbed the ball up to the batsmen with very little 'fizz' on it. Nevertheless, he produced his two best overs to get Mark Waugh, a big wicket for India, as he's the Australian player with the sharpest footwork. The Indians must have been encouraged at tea by the fact that they needed seven wickets to win, the same number as they took in the final session on the first day. They also needed to break the Steve Waugh–Matthew Hayden liaison quickly, and that Harbhajan did by forcing the right-hander into error around leg stump. The Indian cricketers can indeed count themselves fortunate that they dropped both these players and still went on to win the match: they can't continue to make those errors and win. That is one area to work on for Chennai, and the other point they'll need to discuss is the matter of Harbhajan bowling more overs from around the wicket to Hayden.

Having got rid of one danger in Steve Waugh it fell to Sachin Tendulkar to remove the other in Hayden. However, before he got the opener he dismissed the dangerous Adam Gilchrist with his part-time leg spin to make his contribution to a famous victory one with the ball and not the bat. This is not surprising as Tendulkar always wants to be in the action, and the fact that his part-time leg breaks so troubled the Australians must give the selectors food for thought for the final encounter. When Tendulkar got two important wickets lbw and that Indian umpire S. K. Bansal gave five for the innings will be looked upon with cynicism in some parts, but in truth if he hadn't given all of them out he would have been affording the batsmen unfair immunity in using their pad. Umpire Bansal may be India's lucky charm (in all six matches he's officiated India has won), but this was a victory gained by the skill of the players.

By winning a match from a lost cause India not only broke the

Australian winning sequence and levelled the series, but they also gave their opponents something to chew over for the next Test. What bowling line-up will the Australians choose? What can they do to boost the middle order, which has crumbled three times? What can they do to combat the marvellous form of Laxman? And perhaps uppermost in their minds will be the thought of what sort of pitch they'll find in Chennai.

The Australians have to regroup quickly, and Steve Waugh, a man who has suffered plenty of reverses in his early playing days, will be quick to point the way ahead. India have to celebrate their moment of pleasure in the City of Joy and then start planning for a hot time in Chennai. The heat will be on in the third Test and it won't all be from the temperature.

Anyone who suggested that Shane Warne might be omitted from Australia's most crucial Test in six years (since the Caribbean, 1995) was either delusional or an amateur motivator with limited powers of perception.

———

[total-cricket.com, 17 March 2001]

I'm not sure whether John Buchanan was trying to wind up Shane Warne or lull the Indians into a false sense of security by suggesting the record-holding leg spinner could be missing from the third Test, but he's succeeded in getting the blond bamboozler angry. Now it's a matter of whether Warne can get even for the mauling he received in Kolkata.

One look at the pitch and a glance at the temperature gauge would have told the Australian selectors all they need to know about the balance of the attack: two quicks and two spinners are a must in Chennai. The pitch is hard and is likely to bounce and take turn (perhaps prodigious on the final couple of days), and Warne will be partnered by off spinner Colin Miller. This could well mean the decider boils down to a contest between the two batting sides to ascertain who is best at playing good spin bowling in conditions that are conducive to it. With the advent of V. V. S. Laxman's ascension to a top-class Test player the advantage probably rests with India going into the match. This slight advantage could be stretched a little further if Sourav Ganguly can win the toss and India bat first against an Australian attack that has been put through the wringer after the follow-on was enforced in the second Test.

Laxman's arrival as a top-class strokemaker brings India plenty of pluses, but the greatest must be the relief it provides Sachin Tendulkar. Not that the little maestro needs much help, but it was becoming an unbearable load for him to carry the dual stroke-making and high-scoring role against the Australian attack and he'll appreciate that the innings could well have gained some momentum by the time he arrives at the crease. In the last contest between these two teams in Chennai (1998) the match was poised like an evenly weighted seesaw until Tendulkar launched a successful attack on Warne halfway through the fourth day. A repeat of the tension in that game and the two teams will be worn to a frazzle by the end of the match.

This decider is going to be a great test of skill, physical conditioning and mental strength. The heat and humidity will perhaps favour India a little and they may well take three spinners into the game with Tendulkar also lurking as a partnership-breaker if required. It is interesting that team manager Steve Bernard, when referring to the 1998 match, said, 'The [Australian] team was physically worn out by the fourth day.' This team is a stronger combination with Glenn McGrath in the line-up, and Jason Gillespie's presence means it is a far better pace attack, but they will need support from the spinners in the hot conditions. The fresh mind of Miller, as much as his underworked physical state, will be of great benefit to Australia, because he wasn't subjected to the pounding from Laxman and, to a lesser extent, Rahul Dravid in Kolkata. That could count for something in a close encounter.

Fuelled by the added atmosphere of the 1986–87 tied Test replay, the air of expectancy in Chennai is great, and there is every chance this could be another memorable encounter. The psychological momentum is with India going in to the match, but the result could well hinge on the ability of three important players to bounce back from setbacks in Kolkata. India won't want another match with Tendulkar not contributing much with the bat, and Australia will expect more from the willow of Adam Gilchrist and from Warne with the ball. This makes Buchanan's surprisingly stringent criticism of Warne a huge gamble, which could either prove to be a blessing or a blunder.

The name of the city of Madras was changed to Chennai in 1996. As Madras it was the scene of the second tied Test in history (after Brisbane, 1960–61) when, in 1986–87, Australia and India finished dead level after five absorbing days of cricket. History very nearly repeated itself almost fifteen years later, as the following match reports convey.

———

[total-cricket.com, 18 March 2001]

Australia took charge of the decider in Chennai in the way they know best: by batting aggressively. Matthew Hayden sounded the bugle and rode at the head of the column, batting in brilliant fashion and dominating the attack, in a manner he's done so often in first-class cricket and is starting to emulate in the Test arena, to score his second century of the series.

Hayden is a hard worker, having spent some time before coming on this tour batting in a specially prepared net in Brisbane. The pitch he ordered was slow and low-bouncing, and the area where he has literally made most strides is in advancing down the pitch to the spinners. He utilised this skill to full effect in the opening session, hitting an amazing four sixes as Australia came out with all guns blazing in an attempt to show who was boss. This appeared to be a deliberate strategy probably designed to help erase from their minds the calamitous collapses in the previous Test and also implant in the minds of the Indian players

319

the belief that there was no residual scarring from the loss in Kolkata.

The strategy worked brilliantly as the first session brought 140 runs for the loss of the out-of-form Michael Slater and Justin Langer. In an effort to stop the flood of runs Sourav Ganguly turned quickly to his Kolkata match-winner, Harbhajan Singh, but the pitch in Chennai is nowhere near as receptive although it did bounce quite a bit. Harbhajan wasn't spared as the left-handers went after him with glints in their eyes and flashing blades in their hands, both players being prepared to loft over the field. Soon the scorebook contained more sixes than my golf card. In fact the run rate wasn't slowed appreciably until Steve Waugh came to the crease intent on accumulating a big first-innings total.

Steve was quickly onto the field when his brother was dismissed attempting to loft leg spinner Sairaj Bahutule, and he made it obvious he was determined to play a significant innings. Where Mark had played flowing shots and then a careless one to lose his wicket just when a century beckoned, Steve was all concentration and solid defence and only on odd occasions could he be tempted into an expansive shot. He was particularly careful when playing the part-time leg spin of Sachin Tendulkar, whom he wasn't reading, and I was a little surprised when Ganguly took Tendulkar off, as he was turning the ball sharply. The two leg spinners worked well in tandem, as Bahutule gained inspiration from Tendulkar, and this pair could be worth another try on day two.

It was a good toss to win and Waugh had no hesitation in batting. His determination to make a big score was only matched by his decisiveness in answering the question of whether the Australians contemplated dropping Shane Warne. 'No,' was his firm answer. With a big score on the cards and two spinners in the team Australia has the chance to win this match, especially if the scoring rate is maintained, as that will leave the bowlers plenty of time to try to prise out the twenty wickets. If the pitch plays as most expect it to, turning sharply on the last couple of days, it will provide Warne with the perfect opportunity to show the world why Waugh wanted him in the line-up.

[total-cricket.com, 19 March 2001]

India staged a rally in the mould of the Kolkata comeback, and two of the leading characters were the heroes of that amazing second Test victory. Firstly, Harbhajan Singh once again displayed his ability to take wickets in clumps, and then V. V. S. Laxman showed how to hit boundaries in batches, and the Australians found themselves caught in the crossfire.

Resilience has been the watchword for India in the last two Tests; in both games they've bounced back from a parlous position by claiming seven wickets in a session. The wicket that started the slide on this occasion came in the most unlikely fashion and involved the player you would least expect to make a mental error, Steve Waugh. The Australian captain appeared so concerned about the response to an lbw appeal that he forgot to follow the ball, and when it spun back like a striking cobra he pushed it away from the stumps with his hand. This was one occasion when the bowler deserved the wicket: Harbhajan Singh didn't get the credit for that victim but he would have had the thanks of his team-mates when he ran through the rest of the line-up.

One of Harbhajan's great traits is his ability to string a few wickets together in a short period, and following Waugh's dismissal he claimed six victims in sixty-two balls, an acceptable strike rate for one wicket, never mind half-a-dozen. The Australians once again experienced a middle-order collapse, and the problem seems to stem from the batsmen not having the defensive technique to survive under these conditions, and so the response is often one caused by panic – not a good way to bat in India. Ricky Ponting ignored the adage that it's better to be stumped by a large margin than a near thing, and his third duck meant that he now has more catches than runs in the series and he's fortunate it's not a five-Test series.

Even another calamitous collapse couldn't derail Matthew Hayden's thought processes and he proceeded calmly to a double century by mixing solid defence with well-chosen aggression. He could easily have been the second Australian (after Bill Brown) to score a double century and carry his bat, but for his unselfish quest for vital runs, and he became Harbhajan's seventh victim, caught on the boundary. He has shown excellent technique in handling Indian conditions, but, unlike Laxman's team-mates, Hayden's fellow batsmen haven't been able to copy his example.

Suddenly, India was chasing less than four hundred where it could have been a much larger total, and there was an air of confidence about the opening partnership. S. S. Das had the tinge of luck that has been missing from his play in the series and he was away to a fast start, and along with Sadogapan Ramesh provided a solid century platform for the innings. Das played well except for a patch late in the day when Jason Gillespie bowled brilliantly and troubled him, but nothing could stop Laxman as he took up where he left off in Kolkata. Shane Warne probed early looking for a chink via the skidding delivery, and he nearly got a couple through, but it doesn't take Laxman long to hit his stride and soon he was driving and cutting with authority and again scoring through a proliferation of boundaries.

The Indians were able to thwart a worthy challenge from Gillespie and Warne and now they are in a position where, if Sachin Tendulkar makes a sizeable contribution, they could hold a handsome lead. Runs have come so quickly in this match that a result can still be attained, and if the Indians hold a good lead on the first innings Steve Waugh will be worried that Australia's habit of collapsing could result in a loss in a series that less than a week ago appeared to be firmly in their grasp.

[total-cricket.com, 20 March 2001]

The last time these two teams met in Chennai it was a cracking contest for three-and-a-half days before India got the upper hand, thanks to a brilliant century from Sachin Tendulkar. On this occasion we've had three absorbing days' play with India just a nose in front, once again thanks to a Tendulkar century, only this time the runs were hard-earned.

This Test series has reached a high standard after a scrappy start, and in the last five days of exhilarating cricket nothing has been tougher than the opening session on the third day in Chennai. The Australians, led by the tireless Glenn McGrath, stifled the scoring and removed S. S. Das and then the dangerous V. V. S. Laxman with some fine swing bowling. This was another fascinating aspect to an entertaining series: India is doing the damage with spin bowling whilst Australia is relying heavily on their two premier pacemen to make inroads. The success of McGrath and the fine bowling (without luck) of Jason Gillespie meant that Shane Warne was kept out of the attack and, incredibly, he didn't appear at the crease in the first session. I could have understood this move if Colin Miller was used purely as a medium pacer to take advantage of the old ball swinging, but when Steve Waugh opted to bowl off spin to Sourav Ganguly, he should have had his best spinner operating.

To add to Australia's woes the field placing for the off spinner was weird, with five men on the off-side despite the fact that the ball was turning towards the leg. In addition to not bowling Warne before lunch, Waugh didn't give him first use of the harder ball after he'd taken the second new cherry, which was difficult to fathom as he'd toiled with the softer version for so long. Having worked so hard for success in the first session against a determined Tendulkar, the middle session proved a fruitless exercise for the Australian bowlers as the maestro and a much more confident Rahul Dravid capitalised on a tiring attack.

Tendulkar maintained his love affair with the Chidambaram Stadium pitch, scoring his fourth Test century at the ground and continuing a remarkable sequence of at least one hundred in ten out of his last eleven series. He displayed his class on this occasion by concentrating fiercely and hitting only ten fours in his century, although it did include two sixes, the second bringing up the three figures, which the little man celebrated with a grin of satisfaction. Dravid gave Tendulkar fine support, although he allowed himself to be tied down by Warne when he was bowling around the wicket. Dravid appears to have a plan of not looking to play any offensive shots off the front foot and waiting for something short, and the leg spinner doesn't often oblige.

Warne toiled manfully and Gillespie was finally rewarded for his monumental effort and fine fast bowling with the wickets of Dravid and Tendulkar. These wickets brought Australia back into the game, and when the tail surrendered meekly India had squandered an opportunity to put their opponents on the mat. It is up to Sairaj Bahutule to play his natural hitting game to try to stretch the lead past one hundred, and then some of the Australian batsmen will have their defensive techniques tested against the ball that is turning. In this match we may have to wait until the fifth day to get a clear idea of which way this tussle is going to fall.

Off spinner Erapalli Prasanna (the best opposition spinner I played against), left-arm orthodox bowler Bishen Bedi and fast leg spinner Bhagwat Chandrasekhar were a talented triumvirate in the late Sixties and early Seventies. They were backed up by some brilliant close-catching fielders, the best of whom was Eknath Solkar, who used to field so close on the leg side (before helmets) that it was lucky for the batsmen he wasn't a pickpocket.

[total-cricket.com, 21 March 2001]

Harbhajan Singh has reigned supreme over the Australians and dominated their batting like no one else has since Richard Hadlee took thirty-three wickets in three Tests (1986–87) and Jim Laker took forty-six in five (1956). Singh now has twenty-nine wickets in the series when the next best for India is three, and his fourth successive five-wicket haul has Australia on the ropes.

Batting in the second innings of a match where a result is on offer is a far different proposition from the same exercise in the first innings, when the sole object is to post a score. Australia would have been acutely aware of this difference when they commenced their second innings 110 runs in arrears, but you wouldn't have known it from the approach of Matthew Hayden and Michael Slater. Despite a paucity of runs in the series the feisty little right-hander hit a six in Harbhajan's first over and shortly afterwards Hayden followed suit with a huge hit off left-armer Nilesh Kulkarni. By reducing the deficit so quickly Australia maintained hopes of winning the game, but the early loss of the openers and Adam Gilchrist (who was promoted to number three) meant that Steve Waugh's team had to think seriously about preservation of wickets. Once again Harbhajan's ability to take a couple of quick wickets meant that India was able to wrest the initiative and dictate the terms.

With the three stroke-makers back in the pavilion the Australian approach changed, and both Mark Waugh and Justin Langer were conscious of survival, but the elegant right-hander didn't miss any opportunity to punish the loose ball. However, the scoring rate slowed to such an extent that Steve Waugh wasn't going to have the option of declaring, which would have been a great psychological boost in pushing for what would be a remarkable victory. Langer's vigil ended with a brilliant catch by V. V. S. Laxman and then the Waugh twins set up camp in the middle with the sole intention of occupation until stumps. So well was Mark playing (his fleet footwork had returned and his crisp timing was again evident) that it appeared a possibility they could achieve that target, but Rahul Dravid produced a marvellous reflex catch to end his resistance. Suddenly the sharp close-in work of the Indian fielders that once perfectly complemented the spin bowling of the talented triumvirate (Prasanna, Bedi and Chandrasekhar) had returned and this had the look of a successful team.

Into this gladiatorial atmosphere walked Ricky Ponting like a Christian being offered to the lions. He had a couple of near misses but his good fortune didn't last long and eventually he was out to Harbhajan for the fifth time (out of five) in a brief torture test that has lasted twenty-eight balls in total and accumulated only eleven runs. Never have I seen a top-order batsman so dominated by one bowler. Harbhajan completed yet another day as a one-man wrecking crew by trapping Shane Warne lbw padding up on the final ball of the day and, as has happened so often throughout his career, Steve Waugh was left to fight a lone battle for Australia's survival.

There is little chance of saving this match for Australia. They can only think of winning and, holding a meagre advantage, this will take courage and a lot of good bowling. They will rely heavily on the pace bowlers, and Glenn McGrath for one has a petrol tank showing close to empty, but any sign of the old ball swinging will quickly revive his spirits for one last charge to the line. Harbhajan has given India the chance to pull off a great comeback series victory but the batsmen will have to hold their nerve in what is sure to be a thorough examination on the final day.

In 1986–87, in the Madras tie, the last man dismissed was India's left-arm orthodox spinner Maninder Singh, who was also a (Sardarji) Sikh.

———

[total-cricket.com, 22 March 2001]

India produced the greatest comeback since Lazarus to win a thrilling series by the narrow margin of just two wickets, and the man to thank is Harbhajan Singh. Not only did the young man take thirty-two wickets for the series and fifteen in the deciding match but he was also expected to hit the winning runs. Harbhajan came through with a square drive for two from an exhausted Glenn McGrath, and it was time for India to salute the spinning Sardarji.

Harbhajan's bowling performance was even more meritorious because he had so little wicket-taking support at the other end, and at times his skipper's questionable tactics and field placings were a hindrance rather than a help. Nevertheless, Harbhajan was undeterred, and when he quickly removed Steve Waugh in the morning it meant Australia was going to struggle to forge a sizeable lead. Having prised out the opposing skipper the rabbits fell into the trap pretty easily and India had yet another opportunity to beat Australia after conceding virtually four hundred on the first innings.

There was never any question that this is Australia's greatest side: it isn't. However, it does rank pretty high when it comes to grit and determination. Defending only 155, every time India was about to shovel soil on their grave someone would kick open the lid of the coffin and they'd bounce back to life. The first time it was Sadagoppan Ramesh, who made a gift of his wicket by suddenly sprinting off for a run when he'd so often missed singles during the series. He could be a dangerous player (and was batting as well as he has in the series), but he must improve his running between wickets. Then Sourav Ganguly played a poor shot having received a sharp warning the ball before, and again the lid was opened a crack.

However, all was well as long as the cool, calm and classy V. V. S. Laxman was at the crease. He stroked the pace bowlers through the field and went for Shane Warne like an Alsatian after an intruder, spanking boundaries in all directions and quickly reducing the deficit. His contribution to India's turnaround in this series is nearly as great as that of Harbhajan. Then, just when it looked like Laxman would be the deserving hero for India, Mark Waugh displayed his nerveless skill in the field, diving metres to intercept a pull shot that was headed for the boundary and would have brought the target even closer. Laxman stood stunned for a few moments then departed the field he'd graced so successfully, but he left behind him a player with the resolve to see the job through.

Sameer Dighe summoned all his courage and skill to battle the fast bowlers as Waugh asked his lion-hearted quickies for just one more effort. Jason Gillespie and Glenn McGrath answered the call to arms bravely, but Dighe kept them at bay until only two runs were required, and a single would have gained Chennai the distinction of a second Test-match tie. This game reached the heights of the great encounter of fourteen years ago and the ground erupted as Harbhajan squirted the ball past point and took off for the most valuable runs in his short career. Right to the end the off spinner kept his head, even warning Dighe, who was ready to celebrate, to return to his crease until the umpires had confirmed the victory, just in case a run-out was effected.

This has been a classic Test-match to cap off a remarkable series. The Australians will not be thrilled with the result but they can hold their heads high, having fought to the end with their last drop of perspiration. India can be pleased that they've discovered a couple of young match-winners and one or two others who are ready to fight the toughest of opponents: this was a most meaningful home win. The fans of Chennai are indeed fortunate to have been witness to another encounter every bit as good as the tie, and they can be thankful that this time the Sardarji went one better than last time.

It has always irked me that a player's selection is subject to form but officials are not accountable. Perhaps there is a good reason: if the officials were subjected to the same selection criteria as the players there wouldn't be enough left to run the game.

[total-cricket.com, 30 April 2001]

A common complaint in life is: 'Who will judge the judges?' However, as judgement day nears in cricket's match-fixing affair, the closely scrutinised players are entitled to lament, 'When will the bosses be investigated?'

The players have been under serious investigation since the Delhi police first shocked the cricket world with their charges against Hansie Cronje, Herschelle Gibbs, Henry Williams and Piet Strydom. The eagerly awaited first report from the anti-corruption unit is due shortly and the investigators' tentacles have stretched far and wide to include the players (especially the overseas contingent mentioned in the CBI report), umpires and, it is rumoured, even commentators, but apparently the elasticity doesn't extend far enough to cover the administrators.

You might ask, 'Is there any need?'

Well, how about this list for starters. In the Mark Waugh 'payment for information' scandal the ACB covered up not once but three times. The Australian board's greatest crime was

331

to withhold information when Waugh was preparing to give evidence to the Pakistan inquiry into allegations about some of their players.

The English Cricket Board basically ignored the original suggestion from former international Chris Lewis that some English players might have been involved. Once his complaints were widely reported in the newspapers, Lewis was given a cursory hearing.

The irrational behaviour of South Africa's (then) cricket chief Ali Bacher immediately after Cronje was implicated should have brought some censure. In addition to ignoring rumours that some members of the South African team had contemplated 'a fix', Bacher lashed out like a wounded lion. He accused Pakistan of throwing a couple of matches in the 1999 World Cup, suggesting that match-fixing was solely a 'subcontinent problem', and then in a classic 'death-throe lunge', reported a conversation a South African businessman had with an aeroplane passenger posing as 'Shoaib Akhtar'. Bacher is yet to provide any evidence to back his claims.

At the height of the match-fixing furore Sri Lanka appointed a board president whose family business is bookmaking.

The Indian board was at least guilty of a poor impersonation of the three wise monkeys as it only saw and heard no evil. Nevertheless, around 1994–95 one official did speak to a senior Indian cricket writer, and asked him to desist when he published his concerns about two senior players and their association with some shady characters during the Sharjah tournament. Surprise, surprise, the CBI report later indicated the players were guilty, with Mohammad Azharuddin being banned for life and Ajay Jadega for five years.

The Pakistan board was tardy to say the least in checking out some of the accusations made by Rashid Latif, who was later vindicated in the Justice Quayum report and has now been included in the England touring party.

This is not the sort of list that instils confidence in the people running the game. If the bulk of those administrators had since gracefully fallen on their sword or been sacked and replaced by more dynamic officials that would help, but this is not the case. To make matters worse, many of the individuals involved in the cover-ups and complacency are still holding positions in cricket administration, and some of them are high up in the decision-making process.

Despite the fact that match-fixing is the one controversy that could bring the game to its knees, some of these officials have since admitted that they either 1) underestimated the depth of the skulduggery, 2) treated the rumours as a bit of a 'joke', or 3) were extremely naïve. When Mark Waugh admitted to being naïve he was fined. When are these officials, many of whom hold players' careers in their hands, going to meet their judgement day?

The following two irritations in the laws of the game have bugged me for a while.

With the first one, I suggested my solution to two referees and both told me you couldn't carry out the toss with only one captain in attendance because 'it's not in the laws.' Maybe not, but it would soon solve the problem.

In the second case, no one yet has tried to take advantage of the lax reverse sweep law, but it will happen if the administrators don't act. In the meantime there remains a hugely unfair advantage to the batsmen.

———

[total-cricket.com, 7 May 2001]

The subject of Sourav Ganguly's tardiness at the toss in the recent series against Australia (he's not discriminatory, he also kept Heath Streak waiting) received a lot of press at the time and was raised again by former Indian captain Sunil Gavaskar.

Sunny suggested that Steve Waugh was at fault because he should have been waiting for Ganguly to collect him to go to the toss. This certainly used to be the custom – the home captain would invite the visiting skipper to join him for the toss – however, that may have changed with the advent of referees.

There seem to be two simple solutions to ensure this doesn't become an ongoing problem. Either the referee goes to the dressing rooms to collect the captains for the toss, or he tells the skippers that 'the flicking of the florin' will occur half an hour before the start of play. If there is only one leader present at the appointed time the referee then asks that captain what he intends to do first, bat or bowl?

The second solution appeals, but I suspect the threat would be enough to ensure there was never again any tardiness at the toss. I doubt that even Ganguly (who travels to the chimes of his own clock) would be late under these circumstances, ensuring that his timing would always be precise, with or without the willow in hand.

Whilst on the subject of legislation there's another case looming where the players could be well ahead of the administrators. This happened with Bodyline and the underarm delivery. Whether or not you agree with Douglas Jardine in ordering his bowlers to pitch short to a packed on-side field, or Greg Chappell, who asked his younger brother to imitate Sir Francis Drake, no one can accuse them of operating outside the laws. If the administrators didn't want Bodyline field placings or underarm deliveries they should have thought of it before the event and legislated accordingly, rather than castigating the instigators after the event.

The same will happen with the reverse sweep if they don't act swiftly to clarify the situation. It is unfair to ask the bowlers to nominate beforehand the way they are going to operate (over or around the wicket, left or right arm) and then allow batsmen to change their mode of striking after the ball is in play.

I have no problem with a batsman who cleverly uses his hands to upset the field placings by reverse sweeping. This is no different from similar use of the wrists to sweep fine on the leg side. However, I can't accept that a batsman is allowed to change the order of his hands or feet after the bowler commences his run-up, as this in effect makes him the opposite type of player to the one who took strike. By this method a right-hander becomes left (or vice versa) and is rendering obsolete the field placings. This is taking an unfair advantage, whilst a batsman sticking with the first method (cleverly using his hands) is taking a chance and pitting his skill evenly against that of the bowler.

If that isn't reason enough to change the law, then administrators should ponder what would happen in a Test if a batsman decided to change his striking mode with his team needing one run to win, only a ball remaining and just a wicket in hand. If three slips and a gully were in position, in theory the batsman would be turning those fielders into four men behind square leg and would have a legitimate claim for a no-ball under the current legislation.

It couldn't happen? Well, I'll bet that's what the administrators were thinking before 1932–33 and again prior to 1980–81 when Jardine and then Greg Chappell jolted them out of their smugness.

I don't think most of the administrators or players understand what is involved with a lot of the so-called technology used on cricket telecasts. Until this is fully understood I don't see how a judgement can be made on whether more or less should be introduced. As one experienced television producer said: 'Qualification for the third umpire's job should be based more on knowledge of videotape than the laws of cricket.' He has a valid point.

[total-cricket.com, 21 May 2001]

When is it a human hand at work and not technology? The ICC should seriously consider that question when it meets this week to discuss the future of technology as it applies to umpiring decisions.

I'd be firmly in the negative camp in any debate: no to more technology being introduced to 'aid' officials, and yes to drastically reducing the number of decisions that are currently redirected to the third umpire. Only run-out, stumping and hit-wicket decisions should be referred to the third umpire, as that evidence is (mostly) conclusive, as long as the cameras are properly aligned on both sides of the wicket and at each end of the pitch. Any other decision involves a fair amount of guesswork from inconclusive evidence and therefore the umpire in the middle is best equipped to handle the appeal.

Television gimmicks like the 'snickometer' and 'ball tracker', which are used to evaluate snicks and lbw decisions, are not pure technology. Human hand is involved in obtaining the 'evidence' and therefore it's susceptible to operator error. Players are quick to assert that technology should be used in order to obtain more correct decisions, but I'm sure they'd be less hasty in their judgement if they knew exactly what was involved. No umpire should be on trial because of 'evidence' provided by these gimmicks, and any commentator who 'convicts' an arbiter on this basis seriously prejudices his credibility.

It's ludicrous to refer any catching decision to an umpire armed purely with videotape evidence. I've seen many of these decisions referred lately and almost all have resulted in prolonged controversy, because the evidence is inconclusive. If the administrators had taken the trouble to think the matter through fully before adopting some of these ideas then they wouldn't be saddled with a game that has slowed dramatically and is racked by declining umpiring standards and an increase in on-field bad blood between players.

An experienced television commentator did an unofficial experiment a few months ago whereby he re-enacted a disputed catch decision from the previous day's play. Despite the fact that the commentator deliberately placed his hand with the ball in it so that he was emulating a fair catch, some videotape evidence appeared to show the ball touching the ground. I'm not sure what quirk of nature produces this effect but it should render all such evidence inadmissible.

As for boundaries being referred to television replays, this is ludicrous. The laws should be simplified so that the umpire in the middle can easily decide the fate of a shot to make sure that play is continuous. The law only needs to say that a ball hitting the boundary is a four and clearing it is a six: if the ball doesn't do either then it's what the batsmen run. It would help umpires if all grounds had a fence, even if it's low, but there's no need to complicate what should be a simple matter of what happens to the ball. The game is slowing up enough without the administrators contributing to the sluggishness.

The hasty acceptance of technology came about because administrators were keen to protect against 'umpire bashing' by commentators supposedly armed with superior 'evidence' to the arbiters. This has resulted in the baby being thrown out with the bathwater, and not only have umpiring controversies not been reduced, but the decision has also contributed to the adverse side-effects listed above.

One of the best umpires I played under was Australia's Colin Egar. When asked if he'd ever given an incorrect decision, Colin replied, 'On the evidence available to me I got every one right.' If he'd given any other answer he would have been an incompetent umpire or a cheat.

Umpires shouldn't worry about commentators' opinions (I'm sure the good ones don't), as they should be judged solely on decisions they make on the evidence available to them. In a lot of cases their evidence is superior to that being offered to the off-field adjudicator.

Although they are virtually unrelated subjects apart from the fact that Mark Waugh was taking part in the 2001 Ashes series, it was worth including the relevant and insightful comments of Sir Donald Bradman.

In 2001 England played a two-Test series against Pakistan in the lead-up to the Ashes contest. It was an omen: that the day Australia started their English campaign the home side had a bad day.

Bradman's letter was written in 1991 to Jack McHarg, who had just written a book on Bill O'Reilly. A copy was sent to me by ABC cricket commentator Jim Maxwell. I wrote about it because I was bemused by the way many batsmen are so keen to charge onto the front foot that they not only create problems but also leave themselves with virtually no shot options off the back foot.

—

[total-cricket.com, 4 June 2001]

As another Ashes battle looms it was significant that the renascent England went wobbly at the knees as soon as the Australians landed on UK soil. No sooner had Steve Waugh's warriors unpacked their gear at the picturesque Worcester ground than the much-vaunted England pace attack was giving away runs the way Santa Claus hands out gifts at Christmas.

At Old Trafford, Darren Gough, Andrew Caddick and company

had Pakistan on the ropes at lunch on the first day, and yet, led by a blistering assault from Inzamam-ul-Haq, the visitors had amassed 380 by stumps. These are the same bowlers who are expected to take Australia's batting line-up (a more settled group than Pakistan) to the cleaners. The problem for England is that these bowlers (with the exception of Gough) have previously been trampled by the Australian batsmen, and the sight of them receiving a pounding will only boost the confidence of Waugh's team. If there was any doubt that Michael Slater would be given a licence to mount an onslaught against Caddick in particular, it has been dispelled by the Pakistan assault. If this ploy works and Australia wins the opening encounter it won't surprise me if England buckle and go under like a skilled limbo-dancer.

The fact that England bounced back from that first-day hammering at Old Trafford is a sign that they are now a more resilient bunch than those who have capitulated to Australia on previous occasions, but they will find Waugh's warriors a much more ruthless combination than Pakistan. If Australia puts England down on the mat they won't let them up and they possess the bowling attack to take full advantage of any scintillating batting displays. If Australia's batsmen dominate the England attack the Ashes series will be another lopsided contest.

One of the batsmen who'll be expected to exert a strong influence over the England attack is Mark Waugh. As an admirer of Mark's skill and an advocate of the advantages of back-foot play in an era where we're surrounded by many batsmen who prefer front-foot play, I was interested in a comment by Sir Donald Bradman that I unearthed the other day.

Bradman's comments were made in a letter dated 29 January 1991:

I was thrilled by Mark Waugh's century in Adelaide largely

because so much of his play was off the back foot in marked contrast to his colleagues. Sadly I think most of the present crop of batsmen are coached to indulge in the front-foot prod method of play, which is most unattractive and negative. I find it great that Mark is not so inhibited. His batting was like a breath of fresh air.

I assume this was also one aspect of Sachin Tendulkar's play that brought Bradman so much pleasure when he watched the Indian champion bat. I have suspected for some time now that the current players are being subjected to a narrow-minded brand of coaching that doesn't do them any favours and is also a deterrent to attractive batting. It's no coincidence that the more successful batsmen in world cricket are all at the very least competent off the back foot and in general are among the more attractive players to watch.

If back-foot play was good enough for Bradman it should be a sizeable hint that younger players would do well to improve that aspect of their batting. As far as the coaches are concerned it should be a case of: 'A wink is as good as a nod to a blind horse.'

On this occasion there were huge screams from England because a couple of deliveries that were shown by the side-on television replay to be front-foot no-balls weren't called by the umpire and resulted in a batsman's dismissal. If Bradman and Benaud can't make the administrators and umpires see sense, then I doubt there will be a return to a back-foot no-ball law, but it would cure a few of the ailments plus bring a number of positives to the game.

––––––

[total-cricket.com, 11 June 2001]

The fuss over the no-balls that weren't called in England's loss to Pakistan in the second Test highlights the stupidity of the current legislation.

Most no-balls are only illegal by the trifling matter of millimetres and they make absolutely no difference to the delivery when it reaches the batsman. That is the first and most important point. In each case the aggrieved batsman played the shot as if the delivery was a legal one, and he was beaten by a ball that wasn't altered by the bowler's front foot being a few millimetres over the front line, so why not improve the law to rectify the situation? A back-foot no-ball law would achieve that purpose and bring so many other positives to the game: it's amazing that the administrators and the umpires baulk at making what would be a beneficial change.

The benefits to the game would come in the form of improved umpiring. The umpires would have longer to focus on the important end (where the striker is), and hopefully this would result in more correct calls, particularly with lbw and caught decisions. Then there would also be fewer no-balls, which would have a positive effect on over rates, and they need as much assistance as a cripple trying to cross a busy road. And finally, the few no-balls that did occur (under a back-foot law) would be exciting and a punishment to the bowler, because the batsman would have time to crack them for four or even six. That should be enough pluses to excite even the sleepiest of Lord's members, who were probably tut-tutting the loudest when they received the bad news about England's collapse on the final day at Old Trafford.

However, if that isn't enough reason to spark the administrators into action there are a few other points that need to be made about the sudden rash of deliveries that are being replayed on television to show that the umpire has made a mistake.

Firstly, why are side-on replays being shown in some of these dismissals? For instance, we're being told Adam Gilchrist was bowled in the first one-day international by a delivery from Shoaib Akhtar that should have been called a no-ball. What can a side-on replay show you that is of any worth in the case of a bowled dismissal? As I said before, a no-ball by a few millimetres makes absolutely no difference to the batsman's reaction, and if the side-on replay hadn't been shown then no one (apart from an eagle-eyed non-striker and an alert tape operator) would have known that the bowler's foot was slightly over the line. It should also be pointed out that an umpire standing back a few metres from the bowler's-end stumps is subject to parallax error, and this makes it harder to judge exactly where the front foot is landing. So, apart from giving television commentators something to stir up trouble about, and batsmen an excuse for getting out, the side-on replay, when it is not required, only shows viewers that umpires are probably lifting their eyes a little early in order to have more time to make a judgement at the batting end.

Nevertheless, this spot of trouble-making may have served a worthwhile purpose. It highlights how useless the current law is and should have the administrators looking for a version that would give the umpires more time to focus on the batting end. They need only look as far as the advice that ex-players of the ilk of Sir Donald Bradman and Richie Benaud have been giving them for around twenty years and adopt a back-foot no-ball law. If they did then the side-on replay could be used to judge where each international bowler would have to land in order to be delivering from a legitimate distance. Now that would be a useful replay.

The Australian selectors continued a trend they started in late 1997. On that occasion they sacked Mark Taylor as the one-day captain, and at the conclusion of the 2001–02 VB series they sentenced his successor, Steve Waugh, to the same punishment. The selectors were saying to the players, especially in the one-day game; we aren't prepared to let you grow old gracefully.

———

[*The Sunday Telegraph* UK, 16 February 2002]

The one-day captain has become an endangered species in Australia, with the last two being unceremoniously dumped whilst enjoying a winning record. And not only did Steve Waugh have a sixty-four per cent winning record, he was also skipper of the reigning World Cup champion team.

Despite the enormity of the decision to sack Waugh, the greatest surprise is that the selectors actually made it; that they had the courage to chop one of the four pillars of strength supporting the Australian cricket team rather than let them crumble in unison and bring the whole structure crashing down. The upshot of their decision is that twin brother Mark (who must have thought the sacking was a case of mistaken identity) and Shane Warne (following a lacklustre VB series) will now be nervously looking over their shoulders. Especially as the appointment of Ricky Ponting suggests the selectors will look to some younger

346

players to go with a leader who is at the right age to be a long-term captain. However, it'll be interesting to see what effect these two decisions have on the Test side, with neither the captain nor his deputy at the helm in the one-day team.

There can be no doubt that Waugh's sacking will have an effect on the Australian team, but the initial one may be positive. Steve has built an excellent career on utilising setbacks for self-motivation and the selectors' brutal decision may well have prolonged his Test career. The South African Test side should beware, as they of all people will know a wounded lion is at his most dangerous.

In fact the upcoming series will be a litmus test of the selectors' judgement of Waugh as a player. The selectors had to decide whether Steve's dip in batting fortunes over the summer was due to a lapse in form or the terminal decay of a once impregnable batsman. They obviously decided it was the latter, and if his sacking doesn't bring about a revival in Waugh's Test-match batting then they will know they made the correct decision. Not that the selectors are likely to change their minds about him as a one-day player, as this would require them to admit their original decision was wrong, which happens about as often as a confirmed sighting of the Tasmanian tiger.

There's no doubt Steve's batting slipped a lot this summer after he was initially exposed by medium-pace tyro Craig McMillan during the Gabba Test. From thereon his refusal to play horizontal bat shots on the leg side, a move that had stood him in good stead throughout his career, suddenly became a burden when a bowler maintained a short-pitched attack aimed at the body. In the end he was forced to dabble with the hook shot, which is ironic, as he'd recently answered a question on the timing of his retirement with: 'You'll know because I want to play a hook shot in Test cricket before I retire.' Trouble was, the bowlers had forced Steve to play the hook rather than him executing it when he felt the time was right. When that happens the shot appears to be a panic move.

In an era where Australia's cricketers are better paid than their predecessors, the top-class players are likely to stay in the game longer, leaving them vulnerable to the selectors' whims. The really good players of any era have a decision to make on retirement. Former great all-rounder Keith Miller summed it up best when he said, 'I wanted people asking, "Why did you retire?" rather than, "Why don't you?" ' However, this is a more difficult decision for the modern player because it means turning your back on a lucrative wage with very little prospect of repeating those earnings elsewhere, especially at the same level of enjoyment.

Converging with this line of thinking is the selectors' perspective: if there isn't a natural attrition rate with players retiring to concentrate on business then they have to do some culling of their own. Selectors need to be brutal more often under the current system.

Now, when the question is asked, 'Did he jump or was he pushed?' the answer is more often the latter. Mark Taylor, Ian Healy and David Boon were all shoved out of the one-day side, and the latter two along with Allan Border were given a gentle nudge when it came to their departure from the Test side. Only Taylor left the Test arena of his own volition, so it's not surprising that with Border and Boon on the panel, Waugh was pushed (although if reports are true that he was told a couple of days before the announcement was made public then he was effectively given the opportunity to jump).

The sacking of Steve Waugh was a momentous decision and Border said he felt 'physically ill' when it was made. I'll bet that's nothing compared with what Waugh felt when he heard the news, and Border's original discomfort will be only mild if Ponting turns out to be a flop as his replacement.

The cancellation of Australia's tour to Zimbabwe in 2002 may have been well received by the human rights' activists but it wasn't the news a couple of aging Test players wanted to hear.

[*Hindustan Times*, 5 April 2002]

Apart from being a severe blow to Zimbabwean cricket in particular and the game in general, Australia's decision to abort the 2002 tour of the beleaguered African nation was not the news the Waugh twins wanted to hear.

Both Steve and Mark would have been like eager up-and-coming first-class players, having just completed an excellent Pura Cup season, awaiting the announcement of Australia's Test squad. Their inclusion in the Zimbabwe squad would have provided heaven-sent opportunities to score a mountain of runs against a moderate attack and in the process prolong their Test-playing careers. Instead they now have another anxious wait to hear the selectors' choice for the Test leg of the upcoming Pakistan tour.

The selectors are likely to retain Steve for the Test series against Pakistan, but sadly they could decide it's the right time to discard Mark. There's no way the selectors will want to replace two such important players as the Waugh twins simultaneously, and Steve, as a successful captain, has the advantage. If that happens it'll be a sad day as Mark is currently playing with a little more assurance than Steve and is by far the better player to watch as well as being the best catcher in the team. If the selectors picked the best eleven solely on playing ability then Mark would be in front of Steve, but as we saw during Mark Taylor's 1997 run drought, the meritorious Australian system of choosing the best team and then appointing a captain from within is occasionally blurred by sentiment.

If the selectors do choose it's the right time to end Mark's international career that will lead them to another tough decision. First they have to decide on the immediate replacement for Mark, and that's easy – Darren Lehmann, the next best batsman outside the Test team by a wide margin, and despite all the rhetoric about Australia's great depth he's the only one with a legitimate claim for inclusion. Having made that decision the next move is critical: the choice of the extra batsman who will tour purely to gain international experience.

This is where the selectors need to look into the crystal ball. There's no point in picking one from the group of Michael Bevan, Matthew Elliott or Greg Blewett, as they already know what they can do at international level. Then there's a group of Jimmy Maher, Martin Love, Brad Hodge, Simon Katich and Michael Hussey, who, aged between twenty-six and twenty-eight, aren't going to be long-term replacements, but like the senior players in the batch above could play useful cameo roles. The selectors would be better advised to look at a lower age group (around twenty to twenty-two) to unearth the next long-term batsman who has the potential to be a heavy run-scorer. This is where the job becomes difficult, as there's only one standout in that group, former under-nineteen Australian captain Michael Clarke of New South Wales.

However, herein lies a problem that's largely ignored when assessing Australia's depth. Clarke is the best of the young batsmen, but like most contenders he's not threatening to bury the selectors beneath an avalanche of runs whilst facing attacks that are minus the international bowlers. Any young player with ambitions to be a long-term fixture in the Australian side and emulate the Waugh twins should be mounting a good argument for inclusion with relentless high scoring.

The fact that no player (apart from Lehmann) has provided the selectors with such a dilemma should mean that Mark Waugh has a good chance to retain his place. However, whilst he may well have been included for Zimbabwe I'm doubtful about him surviving to tour Pakistan. With all the trouble Pakistan has experienced on its borders recently the absence of a Waugh should be good news, even if it only lessens the threat on the cricket field.

As a kid I was never a cricket card collector. However, early in the new century I was presented with a set of cricket cards that were being endorsed by the ACB. I noticed they were double-sided and Mark Waugh was on the other side of my picture. I saw Mark at a cricket match not long afterwards and I said, 'I'm proud to be on the same cricket card with you, mate.' He looked a little taken aback and then just smiled and said, 'Me too.' I hope he doesn't get embarrassed when I say that in 2003 a cricketing genius retired from the international arena.

———

[*Inside Edge*, 5 February 2003]

Mark Waugh was one of the most 'watchable' cricketers I've seen. His elegant stroke play, which made run-getting seem as simple as kindergarten maths, combined with his sure-handed fielding, where intercepting a speeding ball looked no more difficult than plucking a ripe apple off a tree, made him a player to watch constantly.

The fact that he would bat brilliantly for a while and then appear to become bored with the ease of it all and look for ways to add to the difficulty of making runs (and in doing so short-circuit a sure century) just added to Mark's mystique. It's been claimed the Waugh twins are different – well, this is one obvious example. Whilst Mark was as likely to squander a certain century as reach three figures, Steve would relentlessly grind out the runs long after he'd reached a hundred and would more often than not outstay his partners. I preferred Mark's brilliant but unpredictable style.

Mark's first Test innings stamped him as a special player. He made a lot of first-class runs before earning his first Australian cap and also had the unnerving experience of replacing his twin brother in the team. Following his glorious century in his first Test innings, at the Adelaide Oval, both his place in the team and his spot at second slip became permanent. His wristy on-side play in his debut 138 established Mark as the best leg-side player among Australians since Greg Chappell. Mark would play with a straight bat and then, when he felt leather on willow, he'd gently ease the ball into a gap on the on-side with a well-timed flick of the wrists. He was such a superb on-side player that his off-side play was often overlooked, but he was an excellent cutter and no one drove through the covers better than Mark Waugh on a good day.

Perhaps it was his superb on-side play that reminded Greg Chappell of himself, but he obviously felt some empathy for Mark, backing him to score twenty Test centuries. Greg placed the bet in England in 1993 following Waugh's fourth Test century, a fine 137 at Edgbaston. Greg may not have parted so easily with his 'hard-earned' if he'd seen the second Test at Lord's where Mark was out playing a reverse sweep to Phil Tufnell on ninety-nine.

It was that outrageous dismissal that typified Mark's approach to the game. When he returned to the dressing room, instead of admonishing himself he simply asked with a bemused look on his face, 'How did that hit the stumps?' That was the attraction with Mark Waugh: as a spectator you paid your money and you took your chance. Mark certainly took chances both with the bat and in the field.

Catches that would be difficult for most players (like the one in the 1999 World Cup final) Mark made look easy because he was so well balanced. His footwork was exemplary, so that even when he had to fling himself one way or the other he was still perfectly balanced. He would watch the ball on its flight and then land so softly and retain a firm grip on the pill. Mark was better than anyone else in his time at first slip to Shane Warne.

His catch off a top-edged cut from the bat of Inzamam-ul-Haq at Bellerive in 1999–2000 was the classic combination of great technique and tremendous reflexes. Mark backed off as Inzamam shaped to cut, which meant his hands were already rising with fingers pointed skywards. When the edge flew high and to his right Mark pounced like a hungry lion. The kill was swift and merciless.

Despite his undoubted skill at catching I gained just as much pleasure from watching Mark stop ground balls and plot run-outs. I couldn't count the number of times a player smashed a drive at Mark fielding at short cover in amid the scarring of a used pitch, and every time it would disappear softly into the middle of his hands. It's impossible to describe how difficult this is to repeat even a few times, never mind maintaining a one hundred per cent record.

When Mark fielded at silly mid-off a batsman would hit the ball to him on the bounce and he would unerringly parry it back at the stumps without first catching it. Mark never ran anyone out with this ruse but he kept all batsmen on their toes. Mark had an astute cricket brain, always plotting the downfall of his opponents. Whilst he may have looked like he was in the middle of a Sunday pick-up game with friends, Mark's brain was always on full alert in the field.

His team-mates were also quick when it came to giving Mark a new nickname, most of which reflect on his cricket career.

When Steve was making his name as an international player and Mark was fighting to cement a place in the NSW side he was 'Afghanistan': the forgotten Waugh. When he had a horror run in Sri Lanka (1992–93) and scored four ducks on the trot he was 'Audi': four rings, one short of the Olympic symbol. Ian Healy often used to call him 'Pretty' when he was bowling, a reference to a fastidious concern with his appearance. And when there were no other gems forthcoming he was simply 'Junior', born a few minutes after Steve.

Whatever name he answered to, Mark Waugh made compulsive viewing. He was an exemplary cricketer. He had great skill and unselfishly utilised it to entertain, and he never put a foot out of place on the field. He only appealed when he thought it was out and never indulged in an outburst, let alone a tantrum. The only black mark in a great career was the 'bookie affair', when he was fined by the ACB for passing on information about weather and pitch conditions in return for money.

It's no wonder Greg Chappell bet (and won) on Mark Waugh – they had much in common. Both were wonderfully elegant batsmen, excelling through the on-side, as well as being exceptional fielders. Both only made the one major blunder in their career: Greg with the underarm and Mark with the bookie. As Greg said at the time of the underarm incident: 'If that's the only mistake I make it'll be a good career.'

Some thoughts on Steve Waugh as he became statistically the most successful captain of all time.

[*Hindustan Times*, 25 July 2003]

With a comprehensive victory over lowly Bangladesh Steve Waugh has become the most successful captain in Test history, winning for the thirty-seventh time in fifty matches. Does that make him, as some are suggesting, the best captain of all time?

I don't believe Waugh ranks even as the best of the last two Australian captains. To me Mark Taylor was a superior skipper and I would place Waugh on the same rung with Allan Border: both good captains but more inclined to take a defensive option when things got tight.

Good captaincy is like pornography: it's hard to define but you know it when you see it. So why do I place Taylor, who had a lower winning percentage (fifty-two to seventy-four) ahead of Waugh?

Taylor had more flair and didn't resort to seven men on the off-side with Glenn McGrath bowling half a metre outside the stumps. Waugh has utilised this form of patience game a few times, most notably during the two losses to India in 2000–01, the last series he lost. When the going got tough Taylor was more likely to go on the offensive, employing the Warne–McGrath combination to test the opposition's nerve.

The best time to judge a captain is in tight games when the team is bowling. In these situations Waugh has a history of allowing the opposition to dictate, albeit thanks to some exceptional batting. It happened twice in his first series as captain, when Brian Lara played brilliantly to pull off a brace of remarkable victories for the West Indies. V. V. S. Laxman then produced a memorable innings at Eden Gardens to turn that series on its head, and finally in Antigua (2003–04) Waugh totally lost the plot and the game as the West Indies scored a mammoth 418 to win by three wickets. You might argue that's not a lot of mistakes in fifty Tests but I'd counter by saying the bulk of the times Waugh has been put in that position by the opposition he has faltered. Consequently, if he met stronger opposition more often his record might not be so unblemished.

Waugh's tendency to succumb to skilfully aggressive batting highlights a flaw in his captaincy. He allows his players to get angry when things get tight, which often leads to ugly clashes if an opponent has the temerity to stand up to what Waugh calls 'the process of mental disintegration'. This is a dangerous path to go down if you can't 'take as good as you give'. James Sutherland, the CEO of Australian Cricket, alluded to this when he told Waugh after an ugly incident in the Caribbean: 'It's all very well to be playing the game in the right spirit when things are going your way, but if things are not going your way, that's when the real test is on. If you can't carry yourself in the true spirit of the game at those times, perhaps you need to have a good look at yourself.'

Waugh has a better pace attack at his disposal than either of his recent predecessors. In thirty-eight per cent of his Tests Waugh was able to sool the formidable trio of McGrath, Jason Gillespie and Brett Lee on to the opposition. This was a distinct luxury that Border and Taylor could only dream about, although the latter had a very good attack built around the excellent pairing of McGrath and Warne at their peak. Taylor utilised this superb combination brilliantly, and I would class him as a good all-round captain who treated spinners and fast bowlers as equals in stressful times. With his 'crush the opposition' approach, Waugh is more comfortable resorting to his quicks in tight situations.

The difficulty in judging Waugh and his team is the number of weak opponents who haven't fully tested the Australians. It is only when a side comes up against strong opposition that you can best judge their capabilities. Waugh can do no more than beat the opposition presented, and he has done that more often than any other captain. However, on a number of occasions when Waugh has been tested by the opposition he has shown signs of frailty that I didn't see in his predecessor.

In 2003 Channel Nine introduced a reality television show called *The Block*. It was a big hit, as was the Steve Waugh farewell tour that began a little later that same year. On greater reflection since writing this piece I came to the conclusion that Allan Border was a better captain than Steve Waugh.

[*The Bulletin*, 27 November 2003]

Retirement is a very personal decision; different people choose their right moment for a variety of reasons. However, sportsmen basically have two choices that are best illustrated by former Australian all-rounder Keith Miller: 'I wanted people to ask why did you, rather than why don't you?'

Remaining true to his image as an independent thinker, Steve Waugh has managed to unearth a different slant on the two options. He has announced he'll retire at the end of the upcoming Test series in Australia, which affords him a farewell tour of the country culminating in an emotional send-off at his home ground. Waugh, a man who has thrived on challenges to drive his successful career, has set himself one final demanding assignment before he hangs up his boots.

The 'motivation by termination' approach can work very well, as Greg Chappell showed when he announced his retirement knowing it only left him one last chance to score the sixty-nine runs (he made 182) required to pass Sir Donald Bradman as

Australia's highest Test-match run-scorer. Maybe Waugh has adopted a similar approach with Allan Border's world record beckoning, only an enticing 515 runs from Waugh's flashing blade. The difference is that Chappell's ploy was a calculated gamble to jog his mind for one last supreme effort, whilst Waugh is asking a lot to 'maintain the rage' for four Tests.

The danger in a player prolonging his career with a premature retirement announcement is his mind can then begin to drift into 'pipe and slippers' mode. Whilst it's difficult to imagine the taciturn Waugh in any state other than 'red alert' on the field, remaining focused when you are no longer playing each innings for your place in the team, and with everyone slapping you on the back wishing you well through a constant round of farewell occasions, is a challenging assignment. If anyone can achieve this difficult feat the doggedly single-minded Waugh is the man.

As a player Waugh was strong-minded enough to re-invent himself in the early Nineties. He began his first-class career as a swashbuckling stroke-maker willing to challenge the bowlers, but after a period in the Test wilderness he reappeared as a batsman who minimised errors in order to become a run machine. His makeover produced a bigger upside than *The Block* and his average rocketed from the high thirties to the fifties, where it has resided for more than six years. As a batsman he became Australia's right-handed Border, the man to have at the crease in a crisis, which is not surprising because he greatly admired his first international skipper.

As a captain I rank Waugh on a par with Border, one rung below his predecessor, Mark Taylor, who had more flair than either of the men who book-ended his leadership period. As with his batting, Waugh adopted many of the captaincy philosophies of Border, including a strong desire to grind the opposition into the turf. For a period when he had Glenn McGrath, Shane Warne,

Jason Gillespie and Brett Lee firing on all cylinders Waugh had a superior attack to that of his mentor, and he also encouraged his team-mates to take a more aggressive batting approach than the slightly pessimistic Border.

Former Pakistan captain Imran Khan said that where he came from, 'A warrior is judged by the calibre of his opponents.' In this regard Waugh was unlucky to strike a period where much of the opposition was weaker than in either Border's or Taylor's time. On the few occasions when he was challenged, Waugh's captaincy relied more on containment as a method of breaking down the opposition rather than any flashes of brilliance. Asking an attacking bowler like Warne to operate with everyone on the boundary when Brian Lara was dominant in Barbados was perhaps a captain being over-cautious early in his term, but there were also times in India when he allowed the game to drift. His ploy of having the faster bowlers direct deliveries outside off-stump with only two men on the leg side often achieved success in times of domination, but it failed to disrupt the crucial series-turning partnership of V. V. S. Laxman and Rahul Dravid in Kolkata.

Despite having a spin bowling artist like Warne for much of his reign, deep down Waugh appeared more comfortable as a captain when the quick bowlers were operating efficiently. His greatest achievement as a captain would have to be the way he inspired many of his players who had previously struggled in Test cricket to suddenly perform at a lofty level. Openers Matthew Hayden and Justin Langer are prime examples, and Waugh perhaps recalled something of his younger self in their early struggles.

Waugh's mantle will now surely pass to the deserving Ricky Ponting, who has done everything asked of him as the one-day captain. If Waugh's upcoming assignment is demanding then Ponting's will be daunting. Not only does he take over from one of Australia's most successful skippers; he will also be handling an attack that has been diminished by injury and aging bowlers. At least he's had some experience coping with this situation in the one-day game, but in the Test arena it will be a far greater challenge to his inventiveness. In this regard his greatest asset will be his background as a punter: if he retains his gambling instincts on the field he will succeed as a Test skipper.

The ideal time to promote Ponting to the captaincy was probably after Waugh's triumphant Test at the SCG last summer. However, Waugh decided to stay on and he was good enough as a batsman to retain his place on form and delay Ponting's ascension to the top job. However, I doubt the selectors were prepared to be patient any longer and Waugh may well have got the message that following this summer's series against India he would remain in the team as a player only. If this was the case Waugh has wisely decided to retire, as playing on without the challenge of captaincy would have been an anticlimax for a player of such pride.

In 1987 I wrote in *The Bulletin*: 'In recent years Australia has been crying out for cricketers with character, some hard-nosed competitors. I think we have one in Stephen Waugh.' He proved to be a fierce competitor and an extremely hard-nosed cricketer right to the end he has chosen.

The original request from the *Sunday Telegraph* was for a column on Steve Waugh's triumphant finale at his beloved SCG. That all changed when Sachin Tendulkar reigned on Waugh's parade.

[*The Sunday Telegraph* UK, 3 January 2004]

It was Jonny Wilkinson playing the World Cup final in a pair of slippers. It was Tiger Woods in contention in the last round of the British Open using his mother's clubs. It was Pete Sampras trying to win his record seventh Wimbledon title wielding a wooden racquet.

In reality it was Sachin Tendulkar using his equipment of choice but battling a severe case of self-doubt as he defied the Australian attack at the SCG. Nevertheless, the final result was that the batting maestro turned mere mortal reigned on Steve Waugh's farewell parade. Tendulkar was hit on the arm when he ducked into one Brett Lee thunderbolt and a couple of other short ones had him jumping awkwardly in the air: if he was doing a mickey-taking impersonation of a tail-ender in the nets he would have received a ten for style. Then all of a sudden he'd produce an exquisitely timed on-side shot to the boundary just in case any policeman on duty was tempted to march onto the field and arrest him for being an impostor. This was Tendulkar, one of the best batsmen of his time, struggling, but he could thank the man the SCG crowd had come to farewell for the fact that he was able to survive his early tremors to equal Waugh's number of Test centuries.

Waugh's final Test provided a dramatic example of why a tactic that has developed under his leadership needs to be revised under the new captain, Ricky Ponting. Years of watching Glenn McGrath successfully bowl a line just outside off-stump has obviously convinced Waugh of the merit of this ploy. However, on Waugh's big occasion it backfired badly and Lee and Jason Gillepsie's persistence with this line in their opening spell meant the new ball was wasted. This must have been a relief to the Indian openers, and it meant a reprieve for the struggling Tendulkar, who could so easily have been in early if Waugh hadn't insisted on such a negative line.

McGrath is the only bowler who is likely to have much success using this method. This is perhaps an example of where Steve's stubborn streak has had a negative rather than positive effect on the team. It's also a measure of the difference in thinking between the twins, that when the discussion became a bit too cerebral in team meetings Mark would bring matters back to earth with a concise: 'Hit the top of off with the occasional bumper – that generally works.'

The positive legacy Steve will leave the Australian side is a ruthless streak and the determination to produce a spirited fight-back like the recent one against India at the MCG. He has also been the inspiration for an incredible turnaround in the careers of both Matthew Hayden and Justin Langer, whose aggressive batting has propelled Waugh's team to many of the wins collected in his record-breaking reign.

As a player Steve will be missed for his dogged defiance when the team is in trouble. This admirable trait was probably appreciated more by his predecessors Allan Border and Mark Taylor, as it wasn't often required during his own incredibly successful reign. He should also be recalled as the young player who brought a take-no-prisoners attitude to a team that was downtrodden. In the mid-Eighties he was prepared to bounce players of the reputation of Viv Richards and Ian Botham. He also gained the nickname 'Ice Man' by holding his nerve whilst bowling at the death in the winning World Cup team of 1987.

Despite all the success he's had as a captain, Waugh hands over an attack that was beaten into submission by a superb Indian batting side – further evidence of how critical was the presence of McGrath and Shane Warne during Australia's golden run.

Ponting takes over the leadership at a time when he is in prime batting form, which is an important confidence-builder for a new captain. Ponting has been a great success as a one-day captain and he confirmed that his temperament is ideally suited to the leadership role when he scored an exhilarating hundred in the World Cup final. Some players are burdened by the extra load captaincy brings, whilst others are inspired by the responsibility and revel in the role. Ponting appears to fall into the latter category. He's potentially a more aggressive skipper than his predecessor, who tended to try to wear the opposition down except when he had them at his mercy. If Ponting lives up to his nickname 'Punter' he'll be a good Test-match captain. If he retains his gambling instincts and runs the team himself, as Taylor did when he took over the leadership role and immediately sidelined coach Bob Simpson, then Ponting will not only be a good captain but also one worth watching. The biggest obstacle Ponting will face is the prospect of handling an attack that is diminished from the much-vaunted one Australia has become used to for most of Waugh's era. In addition he will also inherit a fielding side whose standard has slipped alarmingly in the last couple of years.

Ponting had a first-hand look at those failings in the Australian side as the Indians, led by Tendulkar and V. V. S. Laxman, flayed the bowling to all parts of the SCG. As the Indian maestro reigned on Steve Waugh's parade for a second consecutive day, the Australian captain was probably quite pleased he wouldn't have to face this agony ever again.

In the New Year Test of 2004, Steve Waugh's illustrious international career came to an end at his beloved SCG.

[*The Bulletin*, 9 January 2004]

In the end it was 'close, but no cigar' for India, whilst in the Australian dressing room the only cheroots handed out at the conclusion of the series would have been to celebrate Steve Waugh's successful career.

For a team often billed as 'the best ever' and supposedly with enough good replacements to 'field a second team', Australia faces some serious questions after a series in which they were outplayed by India. The only firm conclusions at the end of the enthralling series are 1) Australia's attack *is* dramatically diminished in potency without Glenn McGrath and Shane Warne, and 2) The claims of a second side capable of beating the world are nothing more than jingoistic propaganda.

Without McGrath and Warne to prop up the attack against a strong batting side, the only bowler who consistently troubled the top order was Jason Gillespie. Of the second-stringers Brad Williams appeared to be the one most likely to unsettle good Test-match batsmen, whilst the form of Brett Lee on return from injury must be of grave concern.

Lee may well benefit from a new captain because Waugh's tactics at both the MCG and the SCG severely hindered his speed

367

man. Waugh's insistence on placing a seven–two (on-side) field and having the bowlers operate on a line outside off-stump makes no sense at all. It has worked on occasions for McGrath but suits no other bowler I have seen. These tactics hurt Australia in general and Lee in particular on the first day at the SCG, when the ball was swinging. Despite favourable conditions early on there was only a short period where Lee made the batsmen play, and in that time he had a catch taken off a no-ball and another one dropped. In addition, Waugh's constant pre-match reference to Lee 'shaking up' the Indian batsmen (cricket speak for a bouncer barrage) has encouraged the blond speedster to regularly bang the ball in really short. Apart from rattling a few helmets at the MCG and causing Rahul Dravid to have a couple of stitches in his ear at the SCG, this tactic brought zilch to the wicket column.

Ricky Ponting would be well advised to place fields which encourage Lee to employ his dangerous outswinger, and to counsel him to adjust the length of his short-pitched deliveries to cause the batsmen maximum discomfort. And whilst he's at it, Ponting should use his elevation to the Test-match captaincy to take control of the team and relegate John Buchanan to a servant rather than master role. Only one man can run a cricket team and that is the captain. Mark Taylor pursued this path when he took over from Allan Border, pushing Bob Simpson more into the background, and the move contributed to his successful reign.

Australia's catching has slipped so badly since the retirement of Mark Waugh that it has made his absence almost as critical as that of McGrath and Warne. Judging from the flaws in the Australian catching cordon it's time for a specialist adviser to spend time with the culprits rather than continuing with a practice policy designed to improve run-saving techniques. There has been no better slip fieldsman for Australia than Simpson, and his advice and catching-related drills should be the subject of Ponting's first call for assistance. His second call should be to former Australian pace bowler Dennis Lillee to help get Lee sorted out and, in particular, overcome his chronic no-ball problem.

What India's spirited opposition has done is put the Australian team and the captain in perspective. The side has been in decline since Mark Waugh retired and any reference to it being one of the greats should have ceased following his farewell party. A series of matches against hapless batting sides has done for the bowling line-up what wallpaper does for houses built in a slip zone. The appearance of an excellent Indian batting line-up has dispelled any thought that Warne shouldn't be recalled as soon as his suspension is served. And the selectors should promptly check with the medical staff to see if McGrath's return can't be hastened.

When Warne does return he should bowl in tandem with Stuart MacGill whenever two spinners are required. They should be as inseparable as conjoined twins in Sri Lanka, where Warne's accuracy will allow MacGill's excesses to be forgiven if he's bowling enough wicket-taking balls. In return, MacGill's extravagance encourages batsmen to play shots, which in turn ensures Warne is a more dangerous opponent.

The other aspect of this Indian uprising was to confirm the deficiencies in Waugh's captaincy. They were evident during the 2–1 series loss in India in 2001, when Waugh was unable to get the better of the home side even with McGrath and Warne at his disposal. This was basically due to his habit of attacking a lot when on top but resorting to a waiting game once the batsmen were set. There was little chance of this ploy being successful with McGrath and Warne missing in action. The fact that in the space of six Tests V. V. S. Laxman was involved in three triple-century partnerships is a tell-tale statistic.

Waugh was an excellent captain with a full-strength attack that was totally dominant. However, he lacked the flair of Taylor when a game was finely balanced and this conservative approach wasn't suited to the depleted attack he led on his farewell tour. He leaves the legacy of a strong Australian side, but one that needs to regroup quickly under Ponting. The Australian selectors were spot on: it was the right time for a new captain.

Where Waugh will be greatly missed is in the middle order when the team is in crisis. The player who takes over his position in the batting order could do worse than adopt the Steve Waugh adage, that a crisis is only an opportunity in drag.

Ricky Ponting's first Test as Australian captain, in the later-to-be-devastated Sri Lankan coastal city of Galle, was one to remember. Australia trailed by a mammoth 161 runs after the first innings.

[*The Sunday Telegraph* UK, 12 March 2004]

I n the record books it will simply say victory to Australia by 197 runs. When people read the scorecard in years to come they'll mutter: 'Easy victory for Australia.'

Try telling that to Test-captaincy debutant Ricky Ponting. That stark one line in the record book will never explain the ulcer-producing jangling of his nerves, the emotional drain of battling back from a substantial first-innings deficit and then the joy of watching Shane Warne return from suspension and help bowl Australia to victory whilst in the process capturing his five-hundredth Test wicket. By holding his nerve as captain and supporting his team-mates, two of whom were making highly successful personal comebacks, Ponting oversaw the greatest reversal in a Test match since India turned the tables on Australia at Kolkata in 2001.

Cricketers have a saying when a team-mate scores an edgy boundary: 'There's not room on the scorecard to write down anything other than four.' Well there isn't room in a newspaper column to describe the range of emotions Ponting must have endured in his initial Test as captain of Australia. Suffice to say he'll have a hard time making the rest of his captaincy reign anything other than an anticlimax.

After this one enthralling Test match it's apparent there's a major difference in captaincy style between Ponting and his predecessor, Steve Waugh. Under Ponting the Australians have remained predatory but they've also shown a willingness to fight for a draw when they are in a seemingly hopeless position.

Under Waugh, the Australians, in their mad dash to clinch one overwhelming victory after another, very occasionally went plunging to defeat. They lost a mere nine of the fifty-seven Tests Waugh captained but they also only drew seven, and two of those were in his final series, when India reigned on the parade. It's a laudable trait to exude invincibility, but it is equally admirable to be humble enough to occasionally accept the opposition has you in a 'squirrel grip' and that surviving to fight another day is a brave option.

Only by showing the opposition he wasn't prepared to concede victory without the cricketing equivalent of hand-to-hand combat did Ponting manage to conjure up a great Test victory. Ponting wasn't too proud to seek an island when he looked like drowning, but when the waters subsided he was shrewd enough to swim with the tide rather than wait to be rescued. This will concern his Sri Lankan opponents and also the other teams lining up to have a crack at dethroning Australia.

The Sri Lankans will be particularly disturbed as they rely more on individual brilliance to bring them victory than Australia's team-effort approach. They may not admit it, but deep down Sri Lanka will feel that in the shadow of the ancient fort at Galle all the artillery was fired, and with two battles remaining they are now left with a bunch of cannons and no ammunition.

Even before the 'be prepared to draw' mentality surfaced there were glimpses of the differences in the leadership style of Ponting and Waugh. In a warm-up game against the Sri Lankan President's XI, Ponting, acting as twelfth man, brought out the drinks and was mocked by his team-mates: 'Who is this guy?' they joked. 'Where did they find him?'

Ponting willingly accepted being the butt of the players' humour (but probably also returned it in kind) in a display that clearly established him as still being 'one of the boys' whilst commanding the respect required to lead a team. Waugh never was a one-of-the-boys character, preferring instead to lead by example.

What will also help cement Ponting's reputation was his unselfish sacrifice when Matthew Hayden was seeking the single to reach a hundred in the second innings. Ponting was run out trying to complete the vital single, but players will always give that little extra for a captain who doesn't adopt a 'me Lord, you serf' attitude towards his own wicket.

Hayden eventually reached his century and his value to this Australian team shouldn't be underestimated: he probably ranks third in the pecking order behind the skipper and Warne, who has an uncanny knack of either taking wickets or tying the opposition down. In the Test at Galle, Australia would have lost if Warne hadn't restricted the Sri Lankan first-innings lead, but despite his Herculean effort they would still have crashed to defeat if Hayden hadn't ensured the deficit was erased with a minimum of victims surrendered.

Prior to Ponting making his debut in this Test as Australia's captain, a lot of people wondered: 'How will the team cope without Steve Waugh?'

My answer was simple: 'Have a look at Lindsay Hassett's captaincy record.'

Hassett won fifty-eight per cent of his twenty-four Tests as captain of Australia, which places him right up there among the best records. More importantly, he was only five per cent down on Sir Donald Bradman's excellent winning record of sixty-three per cent, and Hassett was the poor unfortunate skipper who followed The Don in the job. If Australia only missed Bradman slightly then they weren't about to wilt following Waugh's retirement.

Not only did they not wilt, they flourished in adversity. Thanks to a remarkable victory in Galle, Ponting has a great opportunity to do something Australia couldn't achieve under Waugh's leadership – win in Sri Lanka. That's the sign of a good captain: one who gets the best out of his team.

In 2004 Sri Lanka became the second team to tour Australia in the winter (following Bangladesh in 2003) but they arrived without star off spinner Muttiah Muralitharan. Murali chucked a wobbly and in doing so helped highlight the nonsensical law on illegal bowling actions.

[*The Sunday Telegraph* UK, 18 June 2004]

Muttiah Muralitharan's decision not to come to Australia was no great surprise considering he has been no-balled (by local umpires) for throwing on two separate occasions whilst touring the country and now the Prime Minister has labelled his action illegal.

Whether you think, as the Sri Lankans do, that his snub is justified, or, like Shane Warne, that he needs to be a little less touchy about criticism, Muralitharan's plight only serves to highlight the quagmire created by the complicated law on illegal bowling actions.

I have no doubt that according to the law Muralitharan's action is illegal, but in this case 'the law really is an ass'. As if it isn't confusing enough to have one type of bowler (fast) allowed to bend the arm more than another (slow), how can the square-leg umpire then be asked to adjudicate on degrees of 'crookedness' with the naked eye? The law needs to be overhauled and the whole process surrounding illegal deliveries simplified.

However, before the administrators work on simplifying the law, they must first decide what they are trying to achieve with the legislation. If they want a batting exhibition then a law that allows for no flex in the bowler's arm is in order, but please don't ask me to watch games where one team scores 1,200 and loses on the first innings. If the administrators come to the (correct) conclusion that this isn't in the best interests of the game then the answer is a simple law like: 'If, in the umpire's opinion, the bowler is not gaining an unfair advantage from his action, then the delivery is legal.'

A simple law allows the umpires on the field to make the judgement. This is critical because a bowler who pelts only the odd delivery is far more difficult for a batsman to handle than one who chucks them. All a batsman asks for is protection from those 'sneaky' deliveries, and that requires a call from an umpire on the field.

A simple law also allows for a bit of flexibility in the bowling action, which is necessary if bowlers are to remain competitive in their battle with batsmen. And finally, it keeps to a minimum the influence of the legal eagles and ensures that cricket matches, unlike America's Cup races, can't be decided in the courtroom.

These outcomes are predicated on the premise that: 1) A throw is discernible with the naked eye and has to be blatant to gain a real advantage, and 2) The umpires work out among themselves which actions have the potential to give a bowler an unfair advantage. There are enough tell-tale signs with a chucker (bent and splayed front leg and open-chested action) that the umpires could utilise video footage to check up on those bowlers who need watching closely. However, the use of video to decide whether a bowler's arm action is legal or not is fraught with danger. All bowlers who use a 'cocked-wrist' style look dubious when the action is in slow motion.

Most of the doubt in Muralitharan's action is created by an extremely flexible wrist. It's not right to penalise Muralitharan (or any other player) because he's physically able to do things others aren't capable of achieving. Mark Waugh wasn't penalised because his wrist-work was superior to the West Indies' Phil Simmons', so why apply the principle to bowlers? It's this bias in the laws towards batsmen that often leads bowlers to resort to ball-tampering and chucking to try to redress the balance.

Throughout his career Muralitharan has polarised people, and this situation has been exacerbated by him recently achieving world-record-holder status. He hasn't helped his cause by declining the invitation to tour Australia. His non-appearance against the top team in Test cricket will add strength to those who argue that Warne is a better bowler, both because his action is legal and because he has never shied away from a challenge against strong opposition.

Nevertheless, Muralitharan (and others) haven't been helped by the shameful way the administrators have tiptoed around this issue as though it were a Cambodian minefield. Players will always try to bend laws and will push them to the limits, but if they are penalised for breaking them then they know the boundaries and won't continue to transgress. Currently no bowler has a clue what constitutes an illegal delivery, and consequently they will keep trying to expand the parameters.

If the administrators are really serious about cleaning up bowling actions then the problem needs to be sorted out at the lower levels of the game so bowlers with dubious deliveries never even reach first-class level. In the meantime what the game desperately needs is a simple law on bowling actions and Muralitharan playing in Australia rather than being yet another person John Howard doesn't want in the country.

A look at Ricky Ponting from academy to captaincy graduation.

[*Inside Cricket*, 19 July 2004]

Ricky 'Punter' Ponting was easily the best batsman to attend the Commonwealth Bank cricket academy in my ten-year association with the Adelaide-based establishment.

He arrived in 1992 as a rare seventeen-year-old talent, and by the time he returned in the 1993 intake he was a fully fledged first-class batsman. In his second term it became obvious that here was a young man who not only played the game proficiently but also gave it plenty of thought. It's not surprising he has successfully turned his hand to captaincy and has the potential to be one of Australia's really good skippers.

His captaincy in the one-day game after taking over from Steve Waugh was steady rather than spectacular until the VB finals series against England. He suddenly transformed into Superman in a gold uniform as his leadership skills soared in coping with some demanding challenges, which culminated in a spectacular World Cup campaign.

In the space of two months his team won two major titles: the VB series and the World Cup. In this period Ponting was authoritative: he promoted Brett Lee (30 wickets at an average of 15.1) to the spearhead role and then pleaded the case for the talented but inconsistent all-rounder Andrew Symonds (a decisive century in the opening match) to be included in the World Cup squad. Off the field his leadership skills were further tested by the loss of Shane Warne to a doping charge on the eve of the World Cup and the controversy over whether or not to play in Zimbabwe. To underscore his maturity as a leader he amassed a dazzling century in the final of the World Cup and was rewarded for his brilliance with a Man of the Match award as well as the trophy.

His handling of the Warne drug revelation was textbook: 'He's gone and it's a big loss, but we're still here so let's concentrate on how to win without Shane.'

In the case of the Zimbabwe dilemma he relied on a similarly successful mixture of pragmatism and commonsense: 'We're going, so let's start thinking about how to win in Bulawayo.'

Compare Ponting's no-nonsense, clear-thinking approach to the Zimbabwe problem with the dithering of his England counterpart, Nasser Hussain. A week before Australia was due to travel to strife-torn Zimbabwe, Ponting publicly declared his team would be playing their scheduled World Cup match. His decisiveness cleared the air and allowed his players to focus on the fact that despite any personal feelings about President Robert Mugabe, they should now prepare for an important contest against Zimbabwe.

Hussain, on the other hand (who admittedly wasn't helped by his own board's muddled thinking), kept waiting for someone else to make a decision. In the end England (and New Zealand) refused to travel to Zimbabwe and the points forfeited cost both teams any hope of advancing to the Super Six stage of the tournament.

A sign of maturity beyond his years prompted academy head coach Rod Marsh to call for the eighteen-year-old Ponting's inclusion in the 1993 Australian squad to tour England. As it was, the selectors rejected Marsh's plea but almost included Glenn McGrath, another academy graduate from the same intake, in the squad. The battles in the academy nets between

Ponting and McGrath were uncompromising and a sheer joy to watch. I remember one particular day when McGrath got the better of Ponting, who displayed his exasperation by throwing his bat twenty metres out of the Adelaide Oval number-two nets.

Recalling those feisty duels it was interesting to watch as, more than a decade later, Ponting ran to the side of McGrath following the disallowance of the fast bowler's confident lbw appeal in the Cairns Test. On this occasion Ponting made McGrath smile and this immediately diffused a potentially explosive situation where a fast bowler had smoke coming from his ears. McGrath was later fined twenty-five per cent of his match fee for his initial outburst, but Ponting's quick thinking ensured the incident didn't escalate. Ponting and McGrath may be uncompromisingly competitive in the nets but there is an underlying mutual respect for each other's ability.

Compare Ponting's handling of this tricky situation with his predecessor's lack of intervention when Michael Slater blew his top in India. Not only was Slater allowed to remonstrate with umpire Venkataraghavan, but he also marched unhindered to the other end of the pitch to inform Indian batsman Rahul Dravid of his displeasure.

During the second Test against Sri Lanka it became obvious that there's another major difference between Ponting's and Steve Waugh's captaincy. Often, in periods where wickets weren't forthcoming, Waugh would resort to a seven–two (off-side) field and have the bowlers operate on a line outside off-stump. There were times when Ponting tried the patience of the Sri Lankan batsmen, but never with unbalanced field placings, and his bowlers will appreciate being allowed to bowl at the stumps.

Whilst Ponting's transformation as a captain can be traced back to his move to anoint Lee as the strike bowler, there were distinct signs he was a changed person from the time he met wife-to-be Rianna.

His career was in danger of disappearing down the plug-hole like illicit alcohol in a prohibition raid following a couple of late-night altercations in Kolkata and then Sydney. His tangle with a bouncer at a Sydney nightclub resulted in suspension, which prompted Ponting to publicly declare he had a drinking problem and was going to address the issue. This was a courageous and correct move. Nevertheless, it didn't appear as though Ricky had fixed his problem after seeing him in a bar following the Allan Border Medal presentation. However, that was before he met Rianna, and with her love and understanding Ponting is now a much more calmer person and it shows in his batting and the way he handles the captaincy.

His relaxed frame of mind has translated into a different batsman. Gone is the angry young man so hell-bent on dominating opposing bowlers that he played reckless shots early in his innings. In his place is a man confident of his ability to dissect attacks by playing each ball on its merits and relying on his wide range of shots to dominate.

On the field Ponting has learnt to control his aggression, and in handling some difficult media encounters he has displayed a calm and occasionally humorous side to his nature. His international captaincy career began with an already successful Australian one-day side not missing a beat. He then performed the same feat with the Test side, as Australia claimed a rare whitewash in Sri Lanka after trailing on the first innings in all three Tests.

Later this year, Ponting faces his greatest challenge as a leader when his Test side takes on a strong Indian line-up. Australia hasn't won a Test series in India since 1969–70. It will require all his leadership skills and newfound patience for Ponting to achieve this distinction, but I for one wouldn't bet against a 'Punter' who looked all the way a winner back in 1992.

For a lot of people there would have been mixed emotions in October 2004 when Shane Warne passed Muttiah Muralitharan to become the world Test-wicket-taking record holder.

[*Hindustan Times*, 15 October 2004]

It's ironic that Shane Warne should claim the title of world-record holder in India, a country where he is revered by the fans but often battered by their batsmen.

When you tell an Indian that if he walked into a restaurant in Australia and called out, 'Shane Warne is a good bloke,' only about fifty per cent of the patrons would nod in agreement, he is stunned. In a country where Sachin Tendulkar is a virtual deity, the sheik of tweak is looked upon as nothing short of royalty. However, in Australia his occasional indiscretions ensure the population is divided into opposing camps regarding Warne's popularity.

I occasionally play tennis with Peter O'Malley, a young sports enthusiast. O'Malley is a tennis coach, but as an eighteen-year-old he attended a veterans' tournament in Sydney for work experience. At one stage he was sent to get drinks and ran into Warne, who was at the fridge grabbing a beer. 'Do you drink, son?' inquired the blond bamboozler.

'Yes, Mr Warne,' came the reply.

With that Warne pulled an extra beer from the fridge, handed it to O'Malley and they sat down and chatted. Years later,

O'Malley still beams when he recounts the story of a lengthy chat with Warne encompassing everything from leg breaks to spin serves. Try telling Peter O'Malley that Warne isn't a good bloke.

Then a couple of years ago I was at the dog park on a day when Warne had once again hit the headlines for the wrong reasons. As I innocently wandered along behind the family dog a woman demanded of me, 'When will Shane Warne make his country proud?'

'He already has, madam,' I responded, 'many times over,' and before she could reply I took off, jogging after the dog. I doubt very much that my short, sharp dissertation changed her mind to my way of thinking.

With Warne, people either like him immensely or are intense in their dislike. That is why fifty per cent of the Australian population would have cheered when he had Irfan Pathan caught and the other half would have muttered 'Damn', and in most cases it wouldn't have been under their breath.

In an odd quirk of humanity, the man Warne passed to claim the record, the much-maligned Muttiah Muralitharan, is probably in the same boat. In Sri Lanka he enjoys the same appeal Tendulkar has in India and no one there will have a word said against him. However, a considerable portion of the rest of the cricket world believes Muralitharan doesn't deserve the record because his action is illegal. Ironically, most of those people are probably cheering like hell for Warne to retain the wicket-taking record.

The one section of the community where Warne's popularity is unanimous is among kids. If that mythic Indian gentleman made the same pronouncement about Warne in a McDonald's restaurant he would be loudly applauded. Kids are good judges until they are influenced by their parents' prejudices.

There is one inescapable conclusion that not even Warne's

severest critics can dispute: he is a magnificent bowler who has brought many positives to the game of cricket. Not only has Warne been successful at a difficult art; he has also influenced many of the next generation to take up leg spin bowling. It's crucial that leg spin and swing bowling remain viable forms of attack in top-class cricket because they both foster aggressive play: the ball has to be pitched up to bring success and that often results in either a boundary or a wicket, either conclusion assured to please somebody. There's also probably a fair chance the next generation will produce at least a few aggressive leg spinners who want to emulate Warne's approach to ambushing batsmen.

In this regard Warne is probably second only to former great Australian leg spinner Bill 'Tiger' O'Reilly, who adopted a fast bowler's mentality to dismissing the players he loathed most: batsmen.

Sadly, Tiger passed away before Warne reached his peak, but he would have approved of the blond bamboozler's approach. And to anyone who complained about Warne's methods Tiger would've given them short shrift. I can just hear him saying: 'Warne is a great bowler – like it or lump it.'

Glenn McGrath, the metronomic miser, reached one hundred Tests. For the record, Lindwall took 226 wickets (at the time an Australian record) and Lillee, 355 (at the time the world record).

———

[*Mid-Day*, 23 October 2004]

The question is often asked, 'Who is the best Australian fast bowler – Dennis Lillee, Ray Lindwall or Glenn McGrath?'

I guess I've tipped my hand with the order of preference above, as I consider both Lillee and Lindwall excelled in the same skills as McGrath but they did it at greater speed. However, it's not really important in what order you place those excellent Australian fast bowlers, the fact is that McGrath is always considered good enough to be included in such august company.

McGrath is about to play his one hundredth Test and the word that would best describe his sterling career is consistency. It really took off when Craig McDermott flew home from the Caribbean in 1994–95 and McGrath slipped into the spearhead position as though it was a comfortable pair of slippers. He not only relished the role of leading the attack but also announced himself by becoming one of those rare breed who are prepared to bounce the opposition pace bowlers, who, in this case, were the formidable pair of Courtney Walsh and Curtly Ambrose.

This took a fair amount of courage on McGrath's part as he is about as comfortable with a bat in his hands as a blacksmith holding a newborn baby. However, seventeen wickets in four Tests was ample testament to McGrath's ability. The fact that Australia also defeated the West Indies in the Caribbean for the first time since 1972–73 suggested McGrath's aggressive approach paid dividends.

He has now progressed to almost 450 scalps at the excellent strike rate of a wicket every fifty-two balls. He has those rare qualities that only the truly top-class fast bowlers have: he claims top-order scalps with the new ball, he's good enough to pick up wickets in the fourth innings, and he's durable because he has remained crafty even when his pace dropped.

McGrath differs greatly from both Lillee and Lindwall in that he was never a tearaway fast bowler. It was a greater adjustment for them when their pace started to wane, as McGrath never relied on speed as a weapon, only accuracy and guile.

Despite the difference in pace, McGrath has quite a bit in common with Lillee apart from their identical strike rate. They both have a highly developed competitive streak and iron-willed determination, although their method of claiming victims is radically different. McGrath's favoured ambush is a subtle one, where he tests the patience of a batsman until he succumbs to temptation, much like a spider enticing a fly into his web. Lillee, on the other hand, was eager to confront his opponent right from the outset, in the manner of a redback spider biting a victim on the backside whilst they're sitting on the toilet.

McGrath considers a boundary taken from his bowling as a personal affront, whilst Lillee shrugged it off as a lucky shot that would soon lead to the batsman's downfall. Both dislike batsmen intensely when they have a ball in their hands, but they're excellent company once the day's play is over.

He has always had a measured approach to the crease with no wasted effort – each delivery is aimed at a precise spot on the pitch, calculated to make scoring difficult for the batsman. The batsmen who have had the most success against him have been the likes of Sachin Tendulkar and Aravinda de Silva, who both recognised his tendency to become extremely angry when attacked. I've seen both batsmen deliberately bait McGrath by clouting boundaries off him early in their innings. This led to McGrath abandoning his plan to bore the batsman out and begin trying to bowl him out. What usually follows an onslaught from a batsman is a muttering and mumbling fast bowler who snatches his cap from the umpire and pulls it on so firmly you fully expect McGrath's head to pop through the top.

This provides great humour in the commentary box but not prolonged relief for the batsmen. McGrath is smart enough not to allow this state of intense anger to last long, as he's not a sulker but rather a bowler who quickly regathers his thoughts in order to return to being a valuable member of the team.

McGrath and Shane Warne have been a constant thorn in the side of opponents since the faster bowler rose to prominence in 1994–95. They have regularly combined to bowl Australia to victory in the fourth innings and their records are remarkably similar in these circumstances.

There's no doubt they would have been the greatest threat to India winning the second Test if the rain hadn't intervened. They may not pose this threat to opponents much longer, and that will be the day of reckoning for this Australian side. That day was never going to be after the Waugh twins retired, but always when Warne finished and McGrath hung up his boots to join Lillee and Lindwall as one of the three greatest Australian fast bowlers no longer playing the game.

At the completion of the 2005 Ashes series I said Australia had been lulled into a false sense of security by beating mostly moderate opposition in the lead-up. That state of mind also contributed to some poor predictions.

[*Inside Cricket*, 10 January 2005]

Despite England's considerable improvement in the last twelve months, and the fact that they are playing at home, Australia will win the upcoming Ashes series comfortably.

The two major reasons for this confident prediction are Glenn McGrath and Shane Warne – but there is another Australian player who gives a significant boost to that already considerable difference between the two teams. The psychological effect of Adam Gilchrist's plunderage from the middle order is a large positive for Australia and a huge hurdle for England to overcome. Gilchrist's ability to consistently turn a dire situation for Australia into a calamitous one for the opposition is a major reason why the top-order batsmen can afford to play with such unbridled aggression.

However, it is bowlers who win matches, and therefore the ability of both McGrath and Warne to either dominate or suffocate opposing batsmen is pivotal to Australia winning. Warne's biggest attribute will be his talent for keeping in check England's dashing all-rounder Andrew Flintoff. Where Flintoff has the ability to play Gilchrist-like innings against other teams, he won't be able to batter Warne into submission and this will reduce his effectiveness with the willow. On the other hand, Gilchrist will relish facing England spinner Ashley Giles, and the left-arm orthodox spin bowler will also have his work cut out removing Australia's stubborn lower-order batsmen. Warne, on the other hand, won't allow the England bottom half of the order any peace of mind, and this will ensure their contributions are minimal.

Throughout his career McGrath has been exceptional at removing top-order threats with the new ball, and already he'll be formulating plans for England's latest star, Andrew Strauss. In addition to McGrath targeting Strauss, Jason Gillespie has already had great success (seven dismissals in twenty innings) against the leaden-footed Marcus Trescothick, so both openers are in for a torrid time. In addition to those duels favouring Australia, Michael Kasprowicz was dynamite against left-handers in 2004 (forty-two per cent of his victims) and England's top three are all mollydukers.

The one England batsman who would have been favoured to win a stoush against the Australian attack is skipper Michael Vaughan. He had an outstanding record against a strong Australian attack in the last Ashes series and it was as much the method of his dominance as the mountain of runs he scored that created such a good impression. He adopted an aggressive approach in conditions well known to the bowlers, and had great success by employing horizontal bat shots to subdue the quick men and liberal use of the feet to neutralise the spinners. Strangely, since assuming the captaincy role he has demoted himself to number four and hasn't had anything like the success he experienced at the top of the order against Australia. England would be better served with Vaughan opening against Australia in place of Trescothick, but this move won't be made until it's forced on the selectors and by then the Ashes will be decided.

It's crucial for England to make good starts; otherwise, their middle order, whence comes so much of their aggression, will struggle to cope with Australia's talented and varied attack. Even if the openers do survive the new ball, England will not be able to dominate the Australian attack as this is when McGrath and Warne really come into their own. They slip into 'suffocate and succeed' mode, the runs dry up and eventually a wicket falls.

The flip side is England don't have a combination of bowlers to produce the same effect on the Australian batsmen. For instance, take the recent form of Jacques Kallis against England. If they struggled to get rid of Kallis cheaply it doesn't bode well, as Australia has a number of batsmen with the capabilities of the burly South African. Consequently, if Justin Langer and Matthew Hayden continue to rewrite the record book for opening batsmen then England is in big trouble. This is where Stephen Harmison looms large for England. If he can rid England of the Langer–Hayden nuisance early in the innings then England has a chance to restrict Australia's totals to manageable proportions. If not then the England bowlers will be facing a sentence of hard labour. Flintoff will cause problems if Harmison does some early damage, and so might Matthew Hoggard in the same circumstances, but they'll be expensive wicket-takers if the Australian batsmen get set. Giles is purely a defensive bowler and there are too much nous and too many left-handers in the Australian batting line-up for him to create major headaches.

Normally Australia's fielding gives them a huge advantage over their opponents, but the catching has slipped dramatically in recent times and so the difference is marginal. However, Australia's bowling being superior, they will create more chances and therefore spilt catches will hurt them less. England's wicket-keeper,

Geraint Jones, is a mini-Gilchrist with the bat, but he's suspect with the gloves and at some stage this will come back to bite the team.

The good news is this will be the most competitive series since Australia regained the Ashes in 1989. The bad news for England is the result will still be the same: a loss.

Twenty20 hit the cricket world with all the force of an Andrew Symonds scorching six.

———

[*The Bulletin*, 3 February 2005]

Just because cricket administrators are embracing Twenty20 cricket doesn't mean they have perfect vision.

The immediate popularity of Twenty20 cricket, especially among young supporters, means that Cricket Australia would be negligent if it didn't include some matches in its schedule. Nevertheless, the more the length of a match is trimmed the greater the chance a 'limited' player's shortcomings will be laid bare. Played by cricketers with obvious limitations, the Twenty20 game is about as enticing as another English invention: the cucumber and watercress sandwich.

The advent of 'quick cricket' in next season's interstate competition begs the question: 'How many games should be played at international level?'

The main considerations are the economics of the game and the wear and tear on players and the paying public. The financial reality of the Twenty20 game is it costs about the same as mounting a one-day International (ODI), but the return from a crowd of equivalent proportions is less. The same economics apply for television coverage. Judging from the decision-making of the International Cricket Council in recent times the bottom line takes priority.

Prior to World Series Cricket player welfare ranked alongside stadium catering in administrative priorities, but officials can't be blamed for the current situation where the lemon is being squeezed till the seeds pop.

Whilst players complain about administrators exceeding the agreed-upon parameters for matches in a calendar year, they are quick to sign a lucrative contract to play county cricket in the UK if there's a gap in their schedule. Nevertheless, both sides need to be aware that if players reach the point of 'just going through the motions' the public will tire of dull fare and then the game is in trouble. Already the patience of some fans is being tested by Australia's dominance at home, which is leading to a plethora of one-sided matches and star players being rested via the rotation system.

Since they defeated the West Indies in the Caribbean in 1995–96 to attain number-one status, Australia has only lost twenty-seven per cent of its ODI games and ten per cent of its Test matches at home. Whilst this is a credit to Australian cricket it is an indictment on the other nations. In the long run any form of cricket will only survive because of the skill of the players and the competitiveness of the matches.

The rejuvenation of the one-day game depends more on encouraging captains to be imaginative than on introducing 'gimmicky' laws. One answer could be to incorporate the popular 'shortness' of Twenty20 cricket into the ODI game. If both teams had a 'first innings' of twenty-five overs and a 'second innings' of the same duration this could correct any inequality arising from the toss or batting under lights. This type of 'two-innings ODI' would also be an attractive option for young fans who can't stay for a full game, and add opportunities for captains to be innovative.

'The game is not the same,' is a catchcry that has become as jaded as a dull ODI. As long as players and administrators have a vision for improvement rather than constantly looking for a quick fix, cricket will remain an entertaining game.

In early 2005 Adam Gilchrist was in the zone and plenty of balls were going out of the park. Unfortunately for Australia his extraordinary run of form didn't last for the Ashes series.

[*The Bulletin*, 24 March 2005]

By the time Adam Gilchrist strode to the wicket in only his third Test innings, such was the keeper's reputation for clean striking and aggressive batting that a nervous opposing skipper Wasim Akram quickly resorted to ultra-conservative field placings.

Gilchrist proceeded to vindicate Akram's fears and raced to his initial Test century, and, with the help of a gritty Justin Langer, led Australia to an improbable victory. If the then wary Wasim had to confront a rampaging Gilchrist nowadays how would he approach the job?

In his last seven innings Gilchrist has amassed an amazing 689 runs, including four centuries. Most of his three-figure innings have commenced with Australia in a less than dominant position, but his audacious stroke play has quickly led to them taking charge of the match. In all but the last one, where rain ruined any chance of a result, Gilchrist's gladiatorial style of batting has resulted in Australia going on to pulverise the opposition.

In his Test career the gluttonous Gilchrist has slammed fifteen centuries and scored at around eighty-three runs per hundred balls. Ricky Ponting, a player currently rated among the best five batsmen in the game, has only scored two more centuries and his run rate is twenty less than Gilchrist's. All this mayhem created by a player whose primary job is to keep wickets.

However, those figures only tell half the story of Gilchrist's impact on international cricket. His batting is equally devastating in the shorter game (the main cause of Wasim's nervousness in 1999), where his role is broadened to include opening the innings in dynamic style, and he has also captained Australia in six Tests and eight one-day internationals. As Gilchrist nears thirty-four, the question is: how long can he keep on terrorising bowlers?

The simple solution to prolonging Gilchrist's glittering career would be for him to give up keeping soon and play both forms of the game purely as a batsman. That wouldn't be a wise choice. Firstly, a good keeper has to love the job and Gilchrist didn't originally take on the role purely to find a place in the team. Giving up keeping would diminish Gilchrist's enjoyment of the game and therefore make retaining his place as a batsman more difficult. Secondly, Gilchrist played purely as a batsman for New South Wales, albeit at the start of his career, and only managed to average twenty in fifteen innings. Playing a single role after a long and fulfilling career in a dual capacity is not easy, as England all-rounder Ian Botham found out when his batting, devoid of any meaningful bowling support, couldn't sustain his place in an ordinary 1989 line-up.

If Gilchrist does want to prolong his career he may have to consider retiring from one form of the game and continuing his dual role in the other. So far his knees have held up reasonably well (and he works hard at preserving them). Nevertheless, deterioration of a keeper's knees, when it starts, takes on the proportions of a snowball in an avalanche once the downhill slide commences.

I suspect Gilchrist, a wholehearted and dynamic cricketer, may not get the fulfilment he requires from any bit-part roles and he may well quit all forms of international cricket at the same time.

In 918 innings before Gilchrist came along, Australian wicket-keepers (some handy batsmen among them) had accumulated a total of eight Test centuries. In ninety-six innings so far, Gilchrist has personally almost doubled that total and in the process accelerated the incidence of ulcers among opposing captains.

If Glenn McGrath were a marksman he'd claim plenty of bulls-eyes.

[*The Bulletin*, 19 May 2005]

Targeting, as practised by the Australian team or, more precisely, Glenn McGrath, has become the cricketing equivalent of the Aboriginal custom of 'pointing the bone': an opponent generally pays a hefty price.

Under the captaincy of Steve Waugh, targeting an opposition player became public knowledge as part of his 'mental disintegration' warfare. McGrath quickly picked up on the tactic and is renowned for targeting former England captain Michael Atherton and dismissing him nineteen times. McGrath also nominated West Indies champion batsman Brian Lara as the preferred victim for his three hundredth Test wicket and lived up to his prediction in December 2000.

It has reached the stage where, two months out from the first Test at Lord's, McGrath has targeted two Ashes opponents. With Atherton now ensconced in the media centre out of harm's way, McGrath has chosen opposing skipper, Michael Vaughan, and emerging opener Andrew Strauss as his prospective bunnies. With his five hundredth Test victim beckoning just one wicket away, it's a fair bet, with McGrath's legendary ability to strike early, that one of this pair will provide him with the cherished celebration.

It's not unusual for the hyperboles to start well before an Ashes series. The jockeying for mental superiority generally parallels the thinking in the old political gag 'Vote early and vote often', as the media patriotically join in the opposition-baiting. In 1972 the English press picked up the chant of 'worst Australian team to leave their shores', and despite our side drawing a very entertaining series two-all they tended to trot out the same headline prior to most succeeding Ashes tours up to 1989.

Wisely, with Australia convincingly winning every Ashes series since Allan Border's team regained the urn, that line has now been consigned to the archives. Nevertheless, Waugh (whose first UK tour was in 1989) may have been motivated by that taunt in his fierce desire to crush opponents. Whatever his motive he was the first skipper to publicly make known his feelings about the opposition. He certainly wasn't the first to have opinions and plans for opponents, but prior to Waugh players tended to keep those to themselves.

There's a good reason. Cricket is a game governed by laws but with one overriding rule – swift punishment for any player who dares to challenge its authority.

'Don't upset good players because they perform better when riled,' was a lesson rammed home to me during a Sheffield Shield encounter between Victoria and a South Australian side featuring Garry Sobers. After stumps a Victorian player was goaded into expressing his thoughts when he finally blurted out: 'Your illustrious recruit doesn't make too many against us at the MCG.' A jubilant SA player then dashed into the visitors' dressing room to inform an attentive Sobers, who duly made a scintillating century the next day.

The fact that Waugh managed to leave the game unscathed and McGrath is still unscarred could be an indictment on an era that has largely been dominated by Australian sides possessing the only lethal bowling attack. If Vaughan and Strauss do turn the tables on McGrath in this Ashes series, targeting may have something else in common with pointing the bone. These days the custom is rarely mentioned in public.

In July 2005, at the historic Lord's cricket ground, Glenn McGrath created his own bit of fame when he reached five hundred Test wickets.

[*Hindustan Times*, 22 July 2005]

Glenn McGrath became only the second fast bowler to claim five hundred Test victims when, as surely as Bangladesh has a flood and Norway experiences a midnight sun, he dismissed Marcus Trescothick.

It was a typical McGrath performance: he has the patience of Job, the discipline of Gandhi, and the confidence of Muhammad Ali. For a guy who has an abundance of the first two qualities, it's amazing that he displayed a similar characteristic to the former boxing champion in nominating who he would dismiss for the landmark wicket. Ali would have been proud of McGrath when he accurately nominated Brian Lara as his three hundredth victim and then topped it off by completing a hat-trick with the following delivery.

The fact that McGrath has, for the bulk of his career, been allowed to get away with publicly announcing who he is going to target is an indictment on an era of batsmen who, in the main, have reacted to his bowling rather than looked to be proactive. This doesn't detract from what McGrath has achieved in his career but just makes it harder to judge where he fits in the lexicon of the game's great fast bowlers. I have him placed along with Dennis Lillee and Ray Lindwall as the best three Australian fast bowlers. However, I believe the other two champions could do everything McGrath does and they did it at a considerably faster pace and so have to rank slightly ahead of the current champion.

The fact that McGrath hasn't had to confront any champion opening combinations in his career is another reason why it is difficult to judge his greatness. Lindwall came up against Len Hutton and Cyril Washbrook, whilst Lillee had many new-ball duels with Gordon Greenidge and Desmond Haynes. Both pace bowlers won and survived enough of those encounters to display their class for all to witness. Unfortunately McGrath was injured when Virender Sehwag launched himself as a genuine Test-match opener of destructive qualities, as this would have been the ideal opportunity to see the Australian tested by a skilfully aggressive opponent.

Trescothick has neither the technique nor the temperament to provide any more than token resistance against McGrath. With his flimsy defence Trescothick only has one way to succeed against McGrath: launch an assault on the bowler so he has something to think about other than clinically dismembering his opponent's batting with his metronomic accuracy. When he's attacked, McGrath tends to become angry and starts bowling yorkers and bouncers in an attempt to claim dismissals via aggression, rather than his preferred method of winning a war of attrition.

McGrath's milestone and the lure of a competitive Ashes series was the ideal distraction from a game that insists on self-inflicting damage to its credibility. In recent times cricket has been devalued by a rash of ill-advised decisions to make official matches that are not between two countries and some that also involve teams of dubious quality. Added to that is the puzzling decision whereby a bowler (Jermaine Lawson of the West Indies in this case) is cited for a questionable action by the umpires but is still able to play in a Test match against Sri Lanka without the threat of being called from square leg.

The law on illegal deliveries (chucking) shows a complete lack of understanding of the game. All a batsman asks is that he's protected from the odd illegal delivery: he is afforded this courtesy if a bowler oversteps the front line so why shouldn't he expect the same treatment if the ball is chucked? It's not much help to a batsman if he receives a letter from the ICC explaining that the judiciary process has decided the delivery which dismissed him six months previously was an illegal one.

Therefore it was a welcome relief when for around four hours the English dream of an Ashes victory was alive and many good things about the game were on display.

However, McGrath soon put an end to English dreams and made them realise any Ashes victory will be hard-earned. In the process he also claimed a memorable personal milestone by utilising those timeworn virtues of a classic action, consistently producing menacing deliveries of impeccable line and length.

As it turned out, the fans had no reason to fret over Kevin Pietersen's technique, but they were right not to be concerned by Marcus Trescothick's method.

———

[*The Sunday Telegraph* UK, 23 July 2005]

English cricket fans are a strange breed. They fret over Kevin Pietersen's technique whilst remaining blissfully unconcerned about Marcus Trescothick's flimsy defence against the game's premier new-ball bowler.

On the (one-day) evidence so far Pietersen has one of the better techniques in the England batting line-up and also the temperament to complement his counter-attacking outlook on batting. Pietersen will be fine: but as Glenn McGrath underlined at Lord's, it's some of the others they need to be concerned about.

However, the English batsmen weren't the only ones who had trouble coping with a pitch that assisted the seam bowlers. There were a few Australian batsmen who looked distinctly vulnerable following the opening onslaught from England's fast bowlers. This resulted in unmistakable signs in the second innings that Australia's policy of all-out aggression has already been binned. Nevertheless, all the batsmen have the basic foundation for long-term survival in a prolonged battle, and Michael Clarke showed that once they scent victory it'll be a case of: 'Don't leave any ammunition in the locker.'

Clarke's belligerent assault exposed a brief moment of weakness in Michael Vaughan's captaincy. It won't require many and England's chance will be lost.

Vaughan is a pleasantly proactive captain, but against a strong and bloody-minded side like Australia he can't afford to totally back off under fire. I learnt a lot about the most difficult task in captaincy – placing a field that balances the need for containment with the desire for wickets – from a wily Ray Illingworth, and Vaughan would do well to have a chat with a fellow captain from Yorkshire.

When Vaughan finally got the Australian innings back under control he wasn't helped by some butter-fingered fielding. It is basic mistakes like this that will quickly boost Australian confidence and have the England players thinking: 'Why do we save our worst for Ashes series?'

The crucial dropped chances were by Geraint Jones, who was always considered a risk worth taking because of his batting. However, if he loses confidence in his glove-work it will impact on his batting, and if he has to be omitted it will adversely affect the versatility of the England line-up. The other area with potential for a large Australian advantage to emerge is in spin bowling. Whereas Shane Warne had an immediate impact on the second-innings chase as he caused problems for the England openers, Ashley Giles was quickly reduced to the role of fieldsman and useful lower-order batsman.

These are not surprises: that McGrath is a dangerous pace-man, Warne is always a threat and Gilchrist is a far superior batsman-keeper. However, added intangibles in favour of Australia were amply displayed when Brett Lee took an athletic diving catch in his bare hands whilst Geraint Jones was unable to cling on to a similar offering earlier in the day despite wearing gloves.

In both cases the catch was desperately needed, but ironically the side that could most afford a lapse prospered. England was always going to have to play at their absolute best to beat this Australian side. The mistakes made at Lord's by England will only bolster the visitors' feeling that they are superior not just in skill but also in mental strength. It is this latter advantage where the gap will widen quickest.

There is no doubt England is a much-improved bowling side from recent Ashes series. However, they missed a glorious opportunity to gain an important psychological advantage when they failed to build up a substantial first-innings lead. In fact all England's first innings achieved was to allay the fans' fears about Pietersen.

The ease with which Australia completed the Lord's victory may well have contributed to Ricky Ponting's blunder at the Edgbaston toss. I'm not sure what to blame for my monumental error of judgement.

[*The Bulletin*, 25 July 2005]

The Ashes evolved from a burned bail and a memorial written in the London *Times* newspaper mourning the death of English cricket back in 1882.

I have another headstone offering that won't thrill English cricket fans: 'Here lie Glenn McGrath and Shane Warne, two Australian bowlers who never played in a losing Ashes series.'

There is no doubt the bowling of the current England team has improved dramatically from the lame trundling that often passed as their international attack from 1989 to the present. However, it is equally evident that the batting has gone in the reverse direction and the only England player who looked like mounting a threat at Lord's was Kevin Pietersen, the man whose technique most local fans maligned in the pre-match build-up.

Not only does Pietersen have the best technique in the England line-up, he also has the temperament to complement his counter-attacking outlook on batting. The rest of the batsmen at Lord's were cannon-fodder for McGrath in the first innings and then played like rabbits frozen in the headlights when Warne appeared at the crease in the second stanza.

McGrath's march to five hundred Test wickets and beyond was typical of the man. He nominates his prey and then goes out and mesmerises them with metronomic accuracy.

Warne may cause himself heartache off the field, but on it he is a constant headache to batsmen with leaden feet and minds dulled by the fear of the unknown. The unknown in England's case is what type of delivery Warne has unleashed.

England missed their chance in the series when they failed to capitalise on bowling Australia out cheaply in the first innings. Having failed to build a substantial lead on the first innings, England was sized up by their opponents and Australia then went for the kill.

The great strength of this Australian side is its mental toughness, which allows it to ruthlessly punish an opponent's mistake. That and two great bowlers who will ensure the Ashes always stay in Australian hands whilst they are playing.

A review of one of the truly great Ashes series.

[*Inside Cricket*, 30 August 2005]

After so many lopsided matches and series this was payback time for the patrons. Two evenly matched sides passing like ships in the night, England on the rise and Australia on the wane, producing entertainingly aggressive cricket and nail-biting finishes.

The only thing missing from the 2005 Ashes series was a tied match. Nevertheless, this has been the best series in my memory, surpassing the epic struggle in 1960–61 between Australia and the West Indies, which featured the first ever tie in Test cricket.

For an Australian side lulled into a false sense of security by feasting on weak opponents, this was a series destined to ruin reputations. In the case of the skipper, Ricky Ponting, he is one of the few Australians who enhanced his batting reputation, but his standing as a skipper took a bit of a battering.

Ponting made two crucial mistakes in the series: he inserted England at Edgbaston without the services of Glenn McGrath; and at Trent Bridge, once again deprived of the controlling attributes of the miserly metronome, he conceded ground when confronted by the bludgeoning bat of Andrew Flintoff. His first error of judgement probably stemmed from a feeling that after their second-innings debacle at Lord's 'this was the same old England'. By the time the fourth Test came round Ponting was painfully aware the opposition was anything but a cardboard replica of past England teams, and the 'fear of Flintoff' caused him to concentrate too much on containment when the situation cried out for bold captaincy.

When Ponting conceded easy runs to Flintoff and allowed him to steadily build a decisive liaison with Geraint Jones it was reminiscent of the first Ashes Test at the Gabba in 1986–87. On that occasion Allan Border showed way too much respect for Ian Botham, virtually gifting him his first fifty runs, and when Botham went on to complete a scorching century it set England firmly on the path to retaining the Ashes. Ponting's misjudgement at Trent Bridge resulted in England winning a thrilling encounter and gave them their best opportunity to get their hands on the urn for the first time since Border's blunder.

It's not as though attacking a feared opponent at a crucial stage of a match guarantees a captain success; it's just that taking the opposite route almost certainly ensures failure. This has been the most disappointing aspect of Ponting's captaincy: he has failed to take his gambling instincts onto the field. A bit more of the 'Punter' Ponting that emerged in the second-innings fightback and Australia may not have been forced to come from so far behind on the first innings.

To be fair, Ponting is a victim of circumstances. He took over from Steve Waugh, an extremely successful captain who employed similarly conservative methods on the rare occasions his team was challenged by the opposition. Ponting was then able to expand on Waugh's success without being challenged to the point where he had to be imaginative in order to subdue a pesky opposition. Prior to the 2005 Ashes, Ponting's team had displayed great resilience in fighting back on a number of occasions to win seemingly lost causes. However, this series was different in one crucial respect: this time Australia had to fight back against an opponent that suddenly they weren't certain they could overcome.

It's no coincidence that Ponting's two misjudgements came in games from which McGrath was missing. When the Australian captaincy passed from Steve Waugh to Ponting it was always going to be a poisoned chalice; it was just a matter of whether the administered drug was a small dose of strychnine or the fast-acting cyanide. At some stage Ponting was going to have to face life without McGrath and Shane Warne affording him the control that had been critical to the success of the two previous Australian captains. It's probably a safe bet that with a fully fit McGrath to complement the indomitable Warne at Edgbaston and Trent Bridge, Australia wouldn't have lost both matches. However, the art of captaincy is not what a skipper could do with great bowlers; it's what he does with the attack at his command.

Captaincy is like playing: if you learn from experience you become better at the task. Ponting was one of the few Australian batsmen who adjusted to playing against a strong bowling attack in an enthralling Ashes series, and his defiant knock at Old Trafford was a wonderful exhibition of leading by example. There can be no doubting his temperament or his heart for the fight.

Having participated in one of the great series of all time and contributed to its lustre, Ponting's captaincy will be defined by what he does in the aftermath. If he can build on the 'Punter' Ponting attributes he displayed in the second innings at Trent Bridge, then there will be less to fear when the day eventually arrives that McGrath and Warne aren't there to ensure Australia's domination.

A look at Shane Warne following his remarkable Ashes series.

[*The Bulletin*, 14 September 2005]

The greatest disappointment in my time of following Australian cricket is that Shane Warne will never captain the Test side.

I first saw Warne captain during a Super 8 series played in northern Australia in the winter of 1996. He skippered Victoria like his life depended on it: he adjusted field positions as though they were a delicate chess move, bowling changes were carried out decisively, and when he was cornered he attacked. Boy how he attacked.

Opposition needing four runs to win off the final over with two wickets in hand – no problem. Call up a front-line bowler, support him with a few catching men (even though he only had six fieldsmen plus the keeper) and victory would be assured. It was exciting, like watching the lotto draw when your numbers are still alive, and, importantly, his positive approach obtained results.

I was so excited I rang Richie Benaud in the UK: 'Benords, I've just seen a leg spinner captain a side with flair and initiative,' I blurted out. 'Australia could have another bowling captain like you.'

If the selectors and the ACB (as it was then) had been really brave they would have given Warne the captaincy following

Mark Taylor's successful reign. He would have been the right age and at his peak as a bowler. He would not only have made the cricket interesting for his players but also exciting for the crowds. None of this 'let's grind the opposition into the turf' for Warne: he is a captain who takes his gambling instincts onto the field, and the tighter the contest, the more he's likely to take a punt.

The only reason the recent Ashes series wasn't over as a contest long before The Oval was Warne. Strong man Charles Atlas was once depicted as carrying the world on his back, but Warne carried the country on his shoulders for four Tests. Then, in one of the cruel ironies that epitomises sport, the man who had done the most to keep his country in the contest will be remembered for dropping the vital offering from Kevin Pietersen that put victory out of Australia's reach. Sport has a way of crucifying its gods, but Warne will rise again. His brilliant bowling and razor-sharp cricket brain allied with his competitiveness and iron will kept Australia in the pulsating Ashes contest to the bitter end. He is the most strong-willed Australian cricketer since Dennis Lillee, and that is not the only thing they have in common.

At The Oval in 1972 with Australia trailing 1–2 in the series, Lillee took five wickets in the first innings. Following his fourth wicket in the second innings his team-mates gathered round to congratulate him, but he was having none of it. 'We can't let these bastards [England] get any further ahead,' he raged.

With that he stormed back to his mark, turned and charged in to clean bowl the obdurate Allan Knott, completing ten wickets for the match. It was Lillee's fifty-seventh over of the match at the end of a long, hard series and he didn't beat Knott with pace or movement, it was just sheer bloody-minded will-power. Warne employed exactly the same method to conjure up six wickets in the first innings at the same ground thirty-three years later.

On a good pitch, with England cruising at 0 for 82, only needing a draw to regain the Ashes after an interminable period, Warne somehow cajoled Marcus Trescothick into edging a delivery that had more thought behind it than spin. Matthew Hayden dived to complete the ambush: the door was ajar and Warne came barging through. A little over two hundred deliveries later, with an aching back and a creaking shoulder, Warne had stifled an England innings that could have ripped the enigmatic urn out of Australia's already shaky grasp. He'd done it with spin and thought, with smoke and mirrors, and good old-fashioned iron-willed determination: this was Lillee reincarnated as a leg spinner.

The difference between Warne in 2005 and Lillee in 1972, apart from the fact that thirty-three years ago Australia levelled the series, was that the leg spinner also played some valuable innings and got heavily involved in the team strategy. Warne's contribution to the on-field tactics increased exponentially the deeper Australia got in the mire after the loss at Edgbaston. His highly developed competitive spirit wouldn't allow him to just stand by and see all those years of success erased without a fight. And he put up one hell of a fight.

This was the nearest Australia will get to seeing what Warne would have been like as a Test captain. Not that a player can do much without the authority and the power.

Benaud says that Keith Miller was 'the best captain never to lead Australia'. Unfortunately, Warne will fall into a similar category as the colourful all-rounder. Miller frightened the hell out of cricket authorities in the Fifties the same way Warne did in the Nineties. That is not an unreasonable comparison if you understand there were no mobile phones when Keith was playing.

As a mate the hardest thing to cope with after one of Warne's indiscretions was when people came up and said: 'Your pal Warney is a dumb bastard.'

I would quickly correct them: 'He may have made dumb mistakes like the rest of us but don't ever think he is stupid.'

Like Miller, Warne doesn't see himself as a superstar. They are likeable larrikins with a carefree approach to life: Miller's brought on by fighting in a war and Warne's through enjoying a hassle-free youth. Because Warne sees himself as 'just an ordinary bloke who likes to have a good time' he has no inbuilt preservation mechanism. Consequently he's been vulnerable to exploitative English newspapers and his own approach to life. Only now is he starting to feel the consequences of having lived his life in a goldfish bowl for more than a decade. Whilst he was super-human on the field in the Ashes series, he admitted, 'Some of the nights are hard work.'

I have always found Warne to be a straightforward person who is not looking to be devious, unless he has a cricket ball in his hand. I've seen him not only sign autographs but also inquire about the person's well-being and actually take an interest in the answer. If he offers to help he'll go out of his way to live up to his promise, like sending his signed Australian shirt by courier from New Zealand to a junior cricket club in Sydney.

Most of his indiscretions have harmed himself. As a woman once wrote in a letter to the editor after a text-message story: 'If Mrs Warne can forgive him, why can't the ACB?'

Warne now has to live with the fact that Simone finally didn't forgive him. This means being apart from his children, which will hurt him more than losing the Ashes series, and we've just seen to what lengths he went to avoid that happening.

At a Test a few years ago I was waiting to interview the captains at the toss, when Shane came bounding up. 'Why are we doing these stupid forty-five-minute fielding drills?' he exploded.

'What I need is to bowl a few balls in the nets and then sit in the dressing room, have a smoke, a cuppa tea and think about the guys I have to bowl at today.'

'You should've played in our day,' I replied.

'I'd have loved to play with you guys,' he chuckled.

He would have been just perfect for our era. There were no mobile phones then and he would have taken a load off Lillee's shoulders at The Oval.

Brian Lara, a batsman of incredible feats.

[*Inside Cricket*, 14 September 2005]

Two players, Brian Lara and Sachin Tendulkar, have been the dominant stroke-makers in the last decade of international cricket. If you put a gun to my head and forced me to choose only one it would be Lara slightly ahead of Tendulkar, but with the proviso that Brian had his brain in gear.

There was a period early in the new millennium when Lara appeared disenchanted with the game, and his batting suffered. In 2000–01 against Australia Lara looked like a man fighting to maintain concentration and he was more prepared than usual to take the aerial route in search of easy runs. This was a far cry from the young Lara who impressed with a brilliant double century at the SCG, in 1992–93.

Two things stood out in that innings of 277: his impeccable placement and the fact that the greatest batsman I've seen, Sir Garfield Sobers, watched every shot of Lara's knock. Sobers was a great player but like a lot of cricketers not an avid watcher – however, he was so enthralled by what he saw from Lara that he didn't miss a ball. It wasn't surprising as Lara's placement was superb in threading the field and accumulating thirty-eight boundaries without clearing the pickets once. On this occasion he wasn't looking for easy runs but worked hard to beat the fieldsmen on a ground slowed by rain.

Twelve months prior to Lara's entertaining knock, eighteen-year-old Sachin Tendulkar had impressed everyone with a mature innings of 148 at the same ground. When Lara then upstaged Tendulkar it was obvious these two young men were destined to become the next great stroke-makers in world cricket.

However, from then until the end of the century Tendulkar shaded Lara with the exception of one monumental knock in 1994. The gifted left-hander broke Sobers' world-record score with a brilliant 375 against England in Antigua. Sobers was watching when his record was eclipsed and the two then embraced on the ground as Lara was acclaimed by the Caribbean faithful.

It was Sobers who first brought the name Lara to my notice. On Australia's tour of the Caribbean in 1991, Garry told me: 'There's a young left-hander named Lara who should be playing ahead of some of the joke batsmen they've got in the team now. He should have been in the team for the last eighteen months.'

When Lara scored the double century at the SCG, his graceful style, high wrist-cock and long follow-through reminded me of the incomparable Sobers playing through the on-side. On the many occasions he sent the ball flying through the off-side field square of the wicket, it was more like dashing former West Indies opener Roy Fredericks. However, Lara is no copy, no cheap imitation. Lara is the genuine article, a world-record holder twice over.

This is a great achievement by Lara: to claim the world record is a difficult enough feat but to reclaim it ten years later is quite remarkable. It takes a special batsman to maintain the hunger for big scores when he is in the twilight of his career, and in this regard Lara has aged better than Tendulkar.

When Lara became the first man to score four hundred in Test cricket (2004 against the same opposition and at the same venue as where he initially claimed the record), he copped some flack from a few Australian players. Ricky Ponting hinted at selfishness and claimed Lara put his own interests before those of the team. Ponting's claim failed to stand up to scrutiny, because as captain Lara left his team long enough to bowl out the opposition twice.

The average strike rate for Test bowlers in the last decade is a wicket every twelve overs. When England's first innings concluded in Antigua there was still a minimum of 137 overs remaining in the game, meaning the West Indies only had to take a wicket every thirteen overs to complete an astonishing turnaround victory. The fact the West Indies' bowlers weren't able to achieve this result might be blamed on Lara's captaincy or poor catching, but definitely not on his batting for too long.

Lara seems to attract criticism, especially for his captaincy, but I saw him lead the West Indies to the Champions Trophy in England in 2004 and his leadership was exemplary. He had the misfortune to take over the captaincy at a time when the once fast-bowling-rich West Indies were in the midst of a depression. In Sri Lanka in 2001 Lara scored 688 runs and the West Indies still lost all three Tests. With bowlers like that on his side, Lara could empathise with the Duke of Wellington's comment about his troops before the battle of Waterloo: 'I don't know what effect these men will have upon the enemy, but, by God, they frighten me.'

Four years on, Sri Lankan cricket aficionados still rave about Lara's play against Muttiah Muralitharan in that series. Nobody in the modern game plays spin as well as Lara: he's quick on his feet, reads the ball out of the bowler's hand, and when he has his mind on the job places the ball better than anyone. Former champion leg spinner Bill 'Tiger' O'Reilly once said: 'Leg spinners demand footwork, and expert footwork denotes top-class batting.'

By O'Reilly's definition Lara is the best of his generation. If you need further proof, two Test world records and being the only man to score four hundred in a Test match and five hundred in a first-class game is irrefutable evidence: it's like being caught with the smoking gun in hand.

A look at captaincy and the contrasting styles of Michael Vaughan and Ricky Ponting.

[*Clean Bowled* magazine, 16 September 2005]

Good captaincy is like a throw: it's hard to define but you know it when you see it.

During the recent Ashes series Michael Vaughan led with authority whilst Ricky Ponting appeared to captain by committee. Vaughan was always seen making decisive moves in the field: he knew where he wanted the fielders and after a few firm but unobtrusive hand signals it was on with the next delivery. Meanwhile, Ponting would often be seen in a long discussion with the bowler, and sometimes other players would wander up and join in with a suggestion before the captain would eventually move the fieldsmen and then trot back to his position.

Vaughan's method smacked of a man in charge; Ponting appeared to be unsure of himself at times, a man who could be swayed in his decision-making. It's fine to be all-inclusive as a captain as long as it doesn't manifest itself as a leader trying to please everybody.

A lot of good captaincy is about perception. Lyn Marks played for New South Wales under Richie Benaud and he once told me, 'Benaud would stand in the gully with his arms folded, always looking like he had the situation under control even if the score was 0 for 200. All of a sudden, he would change the bowler and move a couple of fieldsmen and the game altered dramatically.' Marks believed that half of Benaud's success as a captain resulted from the fact that he looked assured, and this gave the players confidence. When Benaud made a move they believed it was going to work, and consequently most of the time success would follow.

Vaughan looked assured, and many times in the Ashes series an Australian wicket quickly followed an English bowling change. Ponting, on the other hand, appeared at times to be unsure, and often that was the time there was a burst of scoring and the England batsmen took charge of the game.

Vaughan has shaped this England team and he is the man in charge. Ponting had the misfortune to inherit a very good side. Now that the Ashes have been lost Ponting may have the opportunity to mould his own team if the selectors make changes. However, he will only do that successfully if he takes charge and lets the players know he is the leader.

There is a simple reason why a cricket team must be led by the captain and not a coach. Crucial decisions have to be taken on the field, and if the message has to come from someone in the dressing room then the moment for action has already passed. If the right decisions aren't being made on the field, getting a new coach won't help: that means it's time to sack the captain and find one who can lead with authority.

Benaud says a good captain needs a slice of luck. The best fortune that can befall a captain is to have a couple of champion bowlers at his command. Nevertheless, a good captain will not lament any absence of great bowlers but instead work out how to best utilise the resources he has at his command. A good captain will get the best out of his team; after all, that is his job.

I don't judge captains purely on wins and losses but more on what they do with their team and how they react when they're in a tight contest. Mark Taylor inherited a good Australian side from Allan Border and then promptly improved it. He led them to victory in Pakistan and South Africa, two things Border wasn't able to achieve, and his crowning glory was winning in the Caribbean over the world-champion West Indies. Taylor took charge from the moment he was appointed: he assessed his assets (attacking batsmen) and then created an atmosphere where they could fully utilise their talents. With an improved scoring rate Taylor then had more time for his bowlers to capture the twenty wickets required to win the match: it's pretty simple really, but mighty effective.

Arjuna Ranatunga led an under-manned Sri Lankan side to Australia in 1989–90. By shrewdly exploiting his resources Ranatunga kept his team in the series for longer than expected against a strong Australian side. Sri Lanka eventually lost the series but Ranatunga's captaincy was first-class.

Under Mike Gatting England retained the Ashes in Australia in 1986–87, but his most daring ploy came in the only Test they lost. With his team in trouble at the SCG and opposition fieldsmen clustered around the bat, Gatting mounted a counter-attack that very nearly saved the game for England. Suddenly, Border was unsure whether England was actually chasing the target and he began to deploy fieldsmen to save runs, which made it easier to survive on a pitch that was encouraging spin. Gatting fell just four short of a century and Border claimed victory, but the England captain had forced his opposite number to dramatically change his tactics when Australia was clearly on top. This is a tactic rarely seen in Test cricket because very few captains have the nerve to attempt a counter-attack when they are staring down the barrel.

The most difficult moments for a captain are when the opposition scoring rate is mounting but the game is still there to be won. The art of hitting the right balance between attack and containment is one that not many captains get right. The modern trend of 'in/out fields' leads to way too many easy singles being presented to the opposition and is not a method to be encouraged.

The best captain I opposed was Ray Illingworth of England. He was able to let the opposition know he was still trying to dismiss them no matter how much they appeared to be on top. I learnt a lot about this most difficult art from Illingworth.

There is a rhyme and a reason to everything a good captain does on the field, and he always exudes firm but controlled authority. Don't expect me to adequately explain what constitutes good captaincy, but you'll recognise it the moment you see it.

REVIEW

Following the upset loss to an ultra-aggressive England in the 2005 Ashes series it appeared that Australian cricket's extended period of success, its fifth Golden Era, had come to an abrupt halt.

However, typical of a team that had shown enormous grit and determination (not to mention immense skill) throughout this remarkably successful run, Australia wasn't ready to just lie down and bask in the glory of past deeds. The team quickly bounced back with resounding series victories over the West Indies, South Africa (home and away) and then Bangladesh, having heralded these triumphs with a convincing win over a World XI that looked strong on paper but played like they'd arrived at a tourist destination.

The relentless Australian machine may have missed a beat whilst in England, but following a return to more familiar conditions it was firing on all cylinders. So what caused the machine to misfire, resulting in the surprise loss in the Ashes series?

In the lead-up to the Ashes, Australia had pulverised some moderate opposition by bullying the bowlers into submission. The same approach was adopted against a very good England pace attack and it quickly became obvious this method wasn't appropriate. However, the batsmen were slow to adjust and, to compound matters, the English bowlers skilfully utilised swing to confuse opponents hell-bent on stroke play. Throughout the history of the game even the best batsmen have been troubled by the ball that swings late.

Australia's tardiness in adapting to a potential threat could be marked down to over-confidence or arrogance – take your pick as the two are closely related. However, there was no doubt about Ricky Ponting's first major blunder of the series: winning the toss at Edgbaston and inserting the opposition.

When a team has two match-winning bowlers and one of them is injured the skipper should look for ways to assist the other one. Glenn McGrath trod on a ball half an hour before the toss, and consequently Australia should have favoured Shane Warne by batting first so he could bowl in the fourth innings.

I have little doubt that after the way England capitulated in the second innings at Lord's the Australians felt this was the same old England: they might look good for a while but put them under pressure and they'll fold like a deckchair. The weakness in this assessment was that McGrath was responsible for applying a lot of the pressure with nine wickets at Lord's, and he was missing at Edgbaston.

Had England lost at Edgbaston following the comprehensive defeat at Lord's they would have struggled to win a Test in the series. However, from the moment they bludgeoned 407 runs on the opening day of the second Test the series was thrown wide open. During that onslaught England were made aware of the magnanimous tendencies of all those Australian pace bowlers not named McGrath, and it convinced them the best way to win the series was by being aggressive.

This knowledge was to stand them in good stead when Ponting made his second major blunder. By virtue of an exceptional match-saving century in the third Test at Old Trafford, Ponting had single-handedly kept his side in the series. He then undid all his good work in the fourth Test, at Trent Bridge, by backing off when the highly explosive Andrew Flintoff was joined by an uncertain Geraint Jones at the fall of the fifth wicket.

The dangerous Kevin Pietersen had just been dismissed with the score at 241 and Australia had to push hard for another quick wicket. Instead, Ponting hesitantly waited for the opposition to make a mistake and a 177-run stand resulted. As with all hard-fought Tests there are critical points in the match and if a captain fails to grasp the first opportunity there often isn't a second chance.

On this occasion Ponting, thanks to the skill and determination of Warne, was given another chance in the second innings. He attacked sensibly this time and almost brought off a spectacular comeback victory, which only served to further highlight his first-innings dithering. If Ponting had adopted that same approach earlier in the match it probably would have negated the need for such desperate measures later in the game.

Before the series I did a chat-room session with Rod Marsh (then the head coach of the English academy) and I asked him if England would have the nerve to select Pietersen.

'They'd better,' he replied indignantly, 'or else they won't win.'

The implication was that England could only beat Australia by attacking, not by sitting back waiting for them to make mistakes. Marsh then made another telling observation when I asked him if the England players actually believed they could beat Australia.

'I know the young guys do,' he replied. 'I'm not so sure about the senior players.'

As it turned out England didn't retain many of the players who had been scarred by previous Ashes disasters. A number of the players who starred in the series (Flintoff, Pietersen, Simon Jones and Andrew Strauss) had trained under Marsh at the academy, and the former Australian keeper obviously knew his men: they definitely believed Australia could be beaten and they judiciously attacked their opponents at every opportunity.

When, at the end of our chat-room session, I asked Marsh which team he'd be barracking for he provided a very diplomatic answer. 'I'll be barracking for the guys who went to the academies,' he chuckled.

It was no surprise that the English players who trained under Marsh quickly realised the value of attacking cricket. Rodney always preaches the twin pillars of 'attacking cricket and entertainment'. The big surprise was that Ponting, who spent two of his development years under Marsh at the Australian academy, forgot the first part of this lesson when he needed to remember it most: at Trent Bridge.

What Australia's hiccup in England did was confirm that the day of reckoning for this highly successful team was always going to be when McGrath and Warne called it a career. It was no coincidence that the two Test losses during the Ashes series came when McGrath was incapacitated. If it wasn't for the superhuman feats of Warne, the Ashes defeats would have been heavier and there would have been more of them.

Since those two narrow losses Australia has bounced back strongly, and Ponting insists that the lessons of defeat in England have been learnt. I'm not so convinced. There have certainly been some gains since the Ashes but there are still some major concerns. The captain has proved himself to be a most adaptable and skilful batsman: he has made runs by grafting and then counter-attacking when his team is in trouble and by unmercifully carving up any bowler who displays signs of struggling to maintain line and length under fire. He is now the pre-eminent batsman in world cricket and stands well above his colleagues.

The addition of Michael Hussey since the Ashes defeat has been a good one but also prompts the question: why wasn't he selected as far back as the 2001 tour of England? Hussey didn't just suddenly become a good player; he was one of the more impressive batsmen at the academy in the Nineties.

After Ponting and Hussey the doubts start to creep in.

Will Justin Langer fully recover from another horrible blow to the head? Is Damien Martyn past his best against good quick bowling? Has Matthew Hayden reached the age when a batsman has other things on his mind that detract from the single-minded approach that was his great strength? Has doubt started to replace the absolute confidence that Adam Gilchrist requires to play nerveless, counter-attacking innings? And can Michael Clarke recover his stroke playing touch and assist Ponting and Hussey to keep the juggernaut rolling?

And that doesn't account for the questions about the bowling.

Can McGrath ever regain the urge to be a champion again with all his family concerns? Is Jason Gillespie fully rehabilitated as a fast bowler or is he now just a medium-fast all-rounder?

And then the big two.

Will the conservative side of Ponting's nature win out over the aggressive guy who wields the willow when the tough captaincy decisions have to be made? And how much longer can Warne keep plying his magic?

There is no doubt the questions surrounding the futures of both McGrath and Warne are the most crucial with regard to how much longer this highly successful period might last. This is difficult to tell, and the only thing we can be sure of is that Australia's fifth Golden Era began following the defeat of the West Indies in 1995 by Mark Taylor's team.

According to history the previous four Golden Eras were: the Warwick Armstrong side of 1920–21, Bradman's Invincibles of 1948, Richie Benaud's team of the late Fifties and early Sixties, and the side from the early Seventies. I suspect that a squad from the Victor Trumper era around the turn of the twentieth century and another from the period 1930 to 1934 are being short-changed in this summation. This is probably because neither era had much in the way of pace bowling, although the voluble Ernie Jones, who played with Trumper and once said: 'I could kick my hat faster than Larwood bowls' may have had something to say on that matter.

There is no doubt that Trumper's team had two very good bowlers in Monty Noble and Hugh Trumble, and Jones wasn't just a good talker – his record in that period is excellent. And whilst the Thirties squad didn't have any pacemen of note they did have two champion bowlers in Bill O'Reilly and Clarrie Grimmett, and they also had Bradman. In fact you could mount a strong argument that the batting line-up at The Oval in 1930 – Bill Ponsford, Bill Woodfull, Bradman, Stan McCabe, Allan Kippax and Archie Jackson – is the best Australian top six ever entered on a scorecard.

The one thing that is evident about the five nominated Golden Eras is that the sides had a few things in common. The first and most obvious is that they each had at least two champion bowlers: you can't consistently win Tests without taking twenty wickets for a reasonable cost.

In 1920–21 it was 'Jumping' Jack Gregory and Ted McDonald who provided the pace barrage, and Arthur Mailey was no slouch as a leg spinner. In 1948 Bradman had Ray Lindwall and Keith Miller as fast-bowling spearheads, but 'Big' Bill Johnston shouldn't be underestimated as a pace bowler. Johnston was quick and had a terrific record until a knee injury slowed him later in his career. It is also worth noting that there were two leg spinners, Colin McCool and Doug Ring, in the 1948 side, but a nonsensical playing condition whereby a new ball was allowed every fifty-five (six-ball) overs negated their value on that tour.

In Benaud's time he had himself and Alan Davidson as the two champion bowlers; no blistering pace but a deadly combination of swing and accurate leg spin. There was no shortage of pace in the Seventies with: 'Ashes to ashes, dust to dust, if Lillee don't get ya, then Thommo must'. There was also capable back-up with the swing and seam of Gary Gilmour and Max Walker, and Australia's greatest off spinner, Ashley Mallett. I've already spoken of the virtues of McGrath and Warne as a combination but they have been well supported by pace bowlers Gillespie and Brett Lee, whilst Stuart MacGill is a proven wicket-taking leg spinner.

The other similarity in these champion sides is that they all contained a stylish and smart wicket-keeper. In 1920–21 it was 'Dapper' Bertie Oldfield; in 1948, Don 'Deafy' Tallon; whilst under Benaud, Wally 'Grizz' Grout ruled supreme. In the team of the Seventies 'Bacchus' Marsh was a fine custodian and in the Nineties it was the admirable Ian 'Savlon' Healy.

In nominating a team of twelve from each period on page 434 I have done so more to familiarise fans with the incredible talent than to raise conjecture about which side was best.

The first two Golden Eras were defined periods so there is little argument about the teams as they are chosen from definitive squads. However, the next three teams are from eras and consequently there are more players available to choose from, and what I've done (with a little help from Messrs Benaud, Taylor and Healy) is pick the best twelve. This may mean that the names didn't actually appear on the one scorecard but it should be remembered that some players retired early because a cricket career didn't become lucrative until after 1977 and the latest Golden Era has been exceptionally long.

The team from the latest Golden Era is likely to cause the greatest argument so I'll add these observations.

One thing that is often overlooked when selecting a 'best of' side is that you must assume they are playing against the 'best of' another country. By making that assumption you are more likely to choose the best bowling and fielding combination to dismiss a very strong opposition batting line-up. That makes the ability to hold catches crucial.

On that basis I don't see how the bowling of McGrath and Gillespie would have been improved by having Adam Gilchrist, Warne, Ponting and Justin Langer behind the wicket compared with when they had Healy, Taylor, Mark Waugh and Warne (in that order) as the catching cordon. If you want to be the person who explains to McGrath and Warne that the guy who dropped a couple of catches off their bowling was selected because he could blaze centuries then you are welcome to go ahead, but don't come running to me complaining about your black eye. And I should also point out that Healy (with four Test centuries) was no mug with the bat.

I also don't believe Matthew Hayden and Justin Langer could be a better opening combination than Taylor and Slater when the current incumbents had to wait their turn because of the presence of the latter pair. The Wagga connection had to contend with some high-quality new-ball bowlers and Taylor did it with a sound defence and a watchful eye whilst Slater took them head-on and often won the battle by a knockout. Taylor is captain as he was clearly the best leader in this period, taking over a good side from Border and making it better.

It has been fascinating and entertaining to watch this latest Golden Era of Australian cricket unfold. It appeared that this period, which had arisen like smoke from a fire, might have been blown away by an English whirlwind in 2005. However, in the typically resilient style of Australian cricket some names have changed since the Ashes loss but the winning still continues.

Australia is about to face another challenge to their dominance, in the form of an England team holding the Ashes. It will be tough and exciting, and whilst the questions surrounding the Australian team are many, England is not without its problems.

Will they bowl as well under Australian conditions as they did under English ones in 2005? Will their sometimes fragile batting line-up implode occasionally on the bouncier Australian pitches? Can Simon Jones avoid injury and once again dominate with his fast swinging deliveries? Can England unearth a quality spinner? Will the dodgy glove work of Geraint Jones cost them dearly? And, most importantly, will the heavy demands on Flintoff, especially as a bowler, take a toll, on the harder Australian pitches?

I believe Australia will regain the Ashes and extend the Golden Era just a little longer. How long? At least until McGrath and Warne both leave the game.

THE GOLDEN ERAS

1920–21	1948	1958–61	1972–76	1995–2001
W Bardsley	A Morris	W Lawry	K Stackpole	M Taylor
H Collins	S Barnes	R Simpson	I Redpath	M Slater
C Macartney	D Bradman	N Harvey	I Chappell	R Ponting
C Kellaway	L Hassett	N O'Neill	G Chappell	M Waugh
W Armstrong	K Miller	P Burge	P Sheahan	S Waugh
J Ryder	N Harvey	K Mackay	D Walters	A Gilchrist
J Taylor	S Loxton	R Benaud	R Marsh	I Healy
J Gregory	C McCool	A Davidson	G Gilmour	S Warne
B Oldfield	D Tallon	W Grout	A Mallett	B Lee
E McDonald	R Lindwall	R Lindwall	D Lillee	J Gillespie
A Mailey	W Johnston	I Meckiff	J Thomson	G McGrath
C Pellew	D Ring	L Kline	M Walker	S MacGill

ACKNOWLEDGEMENTS

I would like to thank Eric Beecher, who, in 1973, encouraged me to contribute a column to *Australian Cricket*, when he was the boy-genius publisher of the magazine. Eric then introduced me to Graham Perkin, the editor of *The Age*. At the time Graham was the youngest ever editor at a major Australian newspaper but sadly he passed away at the age of 46. Graham was thoughtful enough not to insist on my using a ghost writer when I started filing my column with *The Age* in 1974, and ever since that day I have always written my own pieces.

There have been many other newspaper and magazine people since then who were not only helpful but also damn good company over a beer. I would like to thank them for both their assistance and their companionship over the years. I would especially like to thank Bill Casey and Ken Laws from the old *Sydney Sun* newspaper. Both of these incorrigible characters encouraged me not only to drink but also to not be afraid to experiment with my writing. From that encouragement evolved a mythical character called Everton Valentine. Occasionally writing to 'Dear Everton' provided me with the opportunity to say a few things in print that wouldn't have been so easily expressed in a normal column. I still treasure the words Laws sent in a telegram when I wrote my first Dear Everton column: 'Congratulations. Move over Neville Cardus.'

In more recent times I have had the pleasure of working with such helpful people as Garry Linnell of *The Bulletin*, and Jon Ryan and Peter Mitchell at *The Sunday Telegraph* in London, both of whom were kind enough to ignore a horrendous 2005 Ashes prediction and still print my columns. Clayton Murzello of Mumbai's *Mid-Day* newspaper has always been helpful and must be the most conscientious of all editors.

And finally I would like to thank Barbara-Ann, who has been my wife and mate for more than twenty years. Apart from being an exceptional animal behaviourist who has chosen brilliantly in bringing Rastas, Trinidad, Cassie, Cinnabar, Samantha, Bella, Kipling, Lucia and Tiger into the house to enrich our lives, she has also acted as my sub-editor throughout our time together. She has never failed to improve any column of mine she has read and was also responsible for the advice: 'If you want to be a good writer, read books written by good authors and at least that way you'll learn to recognise good writing.'

That advice has resulted in a large library of books in the house that has not only helped me to recognise good writing but also given me a lot of pleasure.